Minds on Music

PRAISE FOR *MINDS ON MUSIC*

"Kaschub and Smith address an issue of great importance in the development of a twenty-first-century music curriculum. They argue—most forcefully, thoroughly, and thoughtfully—that all children should be encouraged to compose music. Their work is truly pioneering and fills a need that has been present for quite some time. At every level of the preK–12 spectrum, *Minds on Music* provides valuable observations, insights into student psychology, introductory comments on notation, memory, musical form, instrumental timbre, and the like. The fascinating 'scenarios'—a sampling of creative assignments at each educational level—should go a long way toward dispelling fears, on the part of both student and teacher, about entering this uncharted territory. One hopes that *Minds on Music* will be read by many music education professors and school music teachers!"—**Elliott Schwartz**, composer and professor emeritus, Bowdoin College, Maine

"This excellent book is important for music educators, composers, and musicians dealing with composing in the class and in communities, but also for parents interested in the creativity of their children. *Minds on Music* focuses on two basic ideas: 'composition can be taught' and 'children learn to compose by composing.' The authors address important and diverse research fields and present models for teaching composition from early childhood to high school. I recommend this book to everyone who is focusing on composing with young people."—**Vít Zouhar**, professor of music education and composition, Palacky University, Olomouc, Czech Republic

"An excellent resource for drawing out the composer in every child as well as drawing out the child in all of us."—**Thomas Priest**, Weber State University, Utah

"I was hesitant to attempt composition in my band rehearsal, but *Minds on Music* encouraged me to try. While the product at the concert was amazing, the educational rewards in the classroom were far greater. Now my students are more invested in the program than ever before!" —**Benjamin M. Potvin**, Woodstock Union Middle and High School, Woodstock, Vermont

Minds on Music

Composition for Creative and Critical Thinking

Michele Kaschub and Janice Smith

Published in partnership with MENC:
MENC: The National Association for Music Education

ROWMAN & LITTLEFIELD EDUCATION
A division of
ROWMAN & LITTLEFIELD PUBLISHERS, INC.
Lanham • *New York* • *Toronto* • *Plymouth, UK*

Published in partnership with
MENC: The National Association for Music Education

Published in the United States of America
by Rowman & Littlefield Education
A Division of Rowman & Littlefield Publishers, Inc.
A wholly owned subsidary of The Rowman & Littlefield Publishing Group, Inc.
4501 Forbes Boulevard, Suite 200, Lanham, Maryland 20706
www.rowmaneducation.com

Estover Road
Plymouth PL6 7PY
United Kingdom

British Library Cataloguing in Publication Information Available

Library of Congress Cataloging-in-Publication Data
Kaschub, Michele, 1967–
  Minds on music: composition for creative and critical thinking / Michele
Kaschub and Janice Smith.
      p. cm.
  "Published in partnership with MENC: The National Association for Music
Education."
  Includes bibliographical references.
  ISBN 978-1-60709-193-6 (cloth : alk. paper) — ISBN 978-1-60709-194-3 (pbk. :
alk. paper) — ISBN 978-1-60709-195-0 (electronic)
  1. Composition (Music)—Instruction and study—Evaluation. I. Smith, Janice,
1952– II. MENC, the National Association for Music Education (U.S.) III. Title.
  MT40.K28 2009
  372.87'4—dc22   2009003905

∞™ The paper used in this publication meets the minimum requirements of
American National Standard for Information Sciences—Permanence of Paper
for Printed Library Materials, ANSI/NISO Z39.48-1992.

Thank you to all the wonderful people in our lives who have generously offered their encouragement, patience, and support:

Richard C. Sang
—JPS

Alan, David, Kathryn, and Daniel Kaschub,
and Mango (a.k.a., *Writing Support*)
—MK

Contents

List of Tables   ix

Foreword   xi
Bennett Reimer

Preface   xv

Part I   Rationale and Research

1   Learning and Teaching Music Composition   3

2   On Young Composers Composing: Characteristics,
    Creative Capacities, and Compositions   23

3   Supporting Roles: Tools, Tasks, and Teachers   49

Part II   Conceptualizing Compositional Pedagogy

4   Preparing for Composing   63

5   Assessment   89

6   Designing and Working in a Composing Community   101

Part III   Teaching and Learning Composition

7   Composing in Early Childhood   127

8   Composing in the Upper Elementary Grades   159

9 The Transition to Middle School: Composing in
   Grades Five and Six   185

10 Composing in Upper Middle School   205

11 Composing in High School   233

Part IV: The Future of Composition Education

12 The Composition Program   261

References   273

About the Authors   283

List of Tables

Table 2.1   Compositional Capacities   28

Table 4.1   Critical Components   64

Table 4.2   Sonic Snowstorm   73

Table 4.3   School Song for Our New School   87

Table 5.1   Assessment Rubric for a Small Group Compositional Etude   99

Table 7.1   Compositional Capacities in PreKindergarten through Second-Grade Students   140

Table 7.2   A Song for Our Teacher   151

Table 7.3   Tik Tik Tak   155

Table 8.1   Compositional Capacities in Upper Elementary Students   171

Table 8.2   Rondo for Invented/Found Sounds   179

Table 8.3   Rondo Checklist   180

Table 8.4   Creating Variations   181

Table 8.5   The House That Drac Built   182

Table 9.1   Compositional Capacities in Young Middle School Students   192

Table 9.2   My Piece   200

Table 9.3	Classroom Instrument Piece Based on "Russian Sailor's Dance" by Glière	201
Table 9.4	Soundscape for a Poem	202
Table 10.1	Trifold Reporting Form	213
Table 10.2	Compositional Capacities in Older Middle-School Students	215
Table 10.3	Personifying Colors	227
Table 10.4	Radio Jingles	229
Table 10.5	Quintet	230
Table 11.1	Compositional Capacities in High-School Students	240
Table 11.2	Art Song	251
Table 11.3	Tonic and Dominant Songs	256
Table 11.4	Film Scoring	257

Foreword

For many years I have advocated for more comprehensive offerings in our school music programs, building on the great success we have had with performance by modeling new opportunities on that impressive accomplishment. We engage students in performing starting in kindergarten and into the middle-school grades in general music instruction, in elective opportunities from upper elementary grades through high school, and—for those who choose to become music educators—throughout their music teacher education program for the bachelor's degree. By the time they are certified to teach in the schools, performance has become part and parcel of their lives, well equipping them to share their expertise with whomever will be their students.

This is impressive indeed, and worth learning from as we widen our perspectives to all the other ways to be musical that our culture provides. By doing so, we potentially will serve *all* students rather than the small minority that chooses the one musical path we now make available so effectively. As a result, our profession is likely to be strengthened dramatically as a basic offering in education.

Along with all the other new paths awaiting our exploration, composition has entered our consciousness as having striking potential for engaging many, if not most, youngsters in creative musical challenges and satisfactions. However, composers have been beset throughout history by the many difficulties entailed in creating music because they required performers to complete the musical experience by making the sounds they previously have imagined (I prefer "audagined"). In that historical model, composers had to notate their sound ideas, secure performers capable of translating the notations into sounds correctly and musically, make or be involved in all the arrangements for a performance to take place (all of this likely incurring significant costs in time and money), and, finally, presenting what is often a one-time-only event.

We now have alternatives available to that traditional situation for the composer that add to the model of composer-to-performer-to-audience. Technologies allowing direct composer-to-audience transmission of sounds have for the first time become easily and widely available. This is, in effect, a whole new ballgame for the art of music. Some who are drawn to composing continue (thank goodness) to be sufficiently driven to share their musical contrivances by going through the complex steps entailed in the traditional mode of getting their musical ideas to their intended end—that is, the listener. But for many who simply can't or won't follow that mode, we can now offer genuine compositional satisfactions in a more easily attainable way.

This constitutes a magnificent supplement to the still-viable composing tradition, because it expands the potentials of what music can attain beyond the sounds humans physically can bring into being. Exciting opportunities are here that can revivify and expand our profession's horizons. We need to act on them, and we need a lot of help to do so effectively, given our general lack of experience in teaching composition both in the traditional and newly developed ways.

Fortunately for us, we are beginning to benefit from courageous initiatives to supply us with the know-how that will enable us to meet the demands of this history-making turn of events in music and in music education. *Minds on Music: Composition for Creative and Critical Thinking*, by Michele Kaschub and Janice Smith, is a major contribution to our field, one that I have no doubt will be considered foundational for preparing teachers who are able to offer effective composition instruction in schools and other settings. As I read the manuscript, several words sprang to my mind, all centering on "wisdom." By that word I mean understanding that is broad, deep, and significant. All three of these characteristics are present in the book in abundance.

First, the breadth of their understanding is impressive. It embraces the act of composing itself in its many permutations and applications: the ways students at each of the school levels think musically, the specifics of strategies relevant at each level that encourage and nurture thinking through composing, the curriculum implications of developmental learning in composing from level to level, and the challenges for teachers to assist that development in ways that are appropriate both for each particular level and for each particular student.

The second term related to wisdom, *deep*, is evidenced by their probing insights into the compositional thinking capacities of youngsters at different stages and, accordingly, how teaching can best encourage learning in each of the many dimensions of the compositional act. Their knowledge base encompasses theoretical constructs on music, composing, and teaching, along with solid grounding in practical experience as composition teachers who have seen (or "heard") it all. Their book is neither a theoretical reflection on teaching composition to youngsters nor a "how to do it" manual. Instead, it weds the two dimensions—each necessary for success—in a synthesis in which the practical is securely based in theory and the theoretical foundation is brought to life in effective practice.

This combination of depth of understanding, both in theory and in practice, yields the pragmatic thoughtfulness—the significance—the book exemplifies: its wise guidance is found in knowing why composition is valuable, what composing and teaching composing require if they are to be successful, and the specificities of knowing how to provide that guidance successfully to real students in musically real ways that foster their creative musical growth over the school years.

Wisdom indeed. It was a joy for me to encounter it, revel in it, and learn from it as I perused their book. Their wise counsel extends beyond their clear explanations to the utility of the many charts, lesson examples, teaching scenarios, assessment approaches, grading challenges, portfolio-building suggestions, useful settings for composing in individual, small groupings, and large group contexts, how to situate composing within the dimensions of all the other musical roles, and on and on with broad, deep, and significant guidance.

It all makes so much sense, demystifying this seemingly mysterious musical role and demonstrating that this role is, in every way, playable successfully by students and teachers. Both will benefit significantly from this exemplary book, as will our profession as a whole from the wider contribution it enables us to make to our culture's musical fulfillments. The authors' wisdom takes us a big step forward toward ensuring the continuing viability of music education.

Bennett Reimer

Preface

We recognize good compositions when we hear them, but do we really know exactly what it is that makes a good composition or how to teach children to compose well? We'd like to suggest that we do and we can, with the proper tools and guidance. In the creation of this text we have assumed three things: children can compose, children want to compose, and children possess the knowledge, interests, and experiences to compose.

Without our help, young composers may never know that their beautiful songs—their sound effects, their hummings and whistlings, their joyfully clapped rhythmic soundfests—are all wonderfully significant indicators of their innate musicality and their emerging selves. Our challenge as educators is simply to help children develop and refine these abilities to the fullness of their potential.

This text is an invitation to consider the relationships between skill acquisition and creativity, the ways that relationship can be strengthened, and how teachers can support young composers throughout the growth and development of their compositional capacities. As Betty Anne Younker has noted, "There is little guidance for music educators—both in the field and in training—about how to devise, structure, and engage students in appropriate compositional activities, and to assess their outcomes in school-based music programs" (2000, p. 24). This book seeks to offer that guidance.

The first section of this text provides a foundation for practice by examining rationales and the research on teaching and learning composition. Chapter 1 suggests a rationale for teaching music composition as well as an approach that we have developed and found to be effective within our own classrooms. The research literature that serves to inform the practice of teaching composition is reviewed in chapters 2 and 3.

With a foundation for thinking about composition in place, part II conceptualizes the pedagogy we have used in our teaching. Chapter 4 outlines a planning process that teachers can use to tailor compositional learning engagements to fit the needs and interests of their own students. In partnership with creating and implementing composition activities, it is important to assess what students are learning and the effectiveness of instruction. Chapter 5 provides both rationale and tools for assessing student work. Part II concludes with advice addressing the establishment of composing communities within the larger context of school communities.

Part III directly addresses learning and teaching in specific kindergarten through twelfth-grade settings. Composition instruction for the elementary grades is the topic of chapters 7 and 8. They include ideas for full classes as well as small groups and individual students. Chapters 9 and 10 focus on the middle-school learner in classroom and performance settings. Part III concludes with high-school offerings addressed in chapter 11. It includes a broad range of music courses and activities. Each chapter in part III provides an overview of the characteristics of the composers, their general musical interests, the work they are likely to be drawn to, and the capacities that they may develop. Sample lessons are offered for novice, intermediate, and advanced composers in each chapter.

The final part of the book addresses possibility. While most schools do not offer full programs in the study of composition, it is certainly possible to do so. The final chapter describes what such a program might entail and offers guidance for teachers interested in establishing a composition program within their own schools.

I

RATIONALE AND RESEARCH

1

Learning and Teaching Music Composition

Listen carefully when children are near. Their songs fill parks, front yards, and playrooms. Some are quiet songs lulling dolls and teddy bears to sleep. Others are declaratively triumphant works underpinning flying machines and wizard duels. As these children grow, their desire to make their own music draws many of them to gather in garages and dens. With guitars, keyboards, drums, computers, and other instruments in hand, they work alone or with their friends to compose music that charges the air.

From lullabies to love songs, children's music takes many forms and unfolds through diverse practices. It serves as a unique and special way of experiencing and sharing what it is to be alive. Although children have always invented their own music, formalized American music education historically has focused more on the expansion of outstanding performance programs than on engaging children in the development of their innate compositional abilities. However, providing opportunities for students to engage in the generation of original works of music is equally important in the development of musically educated people.

Composition requires the interweaving of *knowledge about* and *know-how*. When combined synergistically, composers are able to create pieces that represent their *knowing within* and *of* music. Despite these highly valuable attributes, music composition still constitutes either a new or expanded opportunity to learn in many music programs. Its somewhat novel presence in music education requires educators to identify how students benefit from its study.

A RATIONALE FOR COMPOSITION IN MUSIC EDUCATION

Rationales supporting the inclusion of composition within school music curricula must have integrity within the domains of education and music as well as sufficient explanatory strength to inform and inspire learning and teaching. The rationales adopted by the teachers are significant because they underpin future curricular and pedagogical decisions directly impacting how children engage in composition. Additionally, teachers must bear in mind that students whose musical experiences offer perspectives from the roles of performance, listening, composition, improvisation, and movement are best prepared to fully engage with the world of music.

The unveiling of the National Standards for Arts Education in 1994 served to highlight the breadth of the domain of music as it can be presented in educational settings. It also focused attention on underdeveloped areas of music study within school-based music programs. In the decade and a half that has transpired, numerous researchers and music education specialists have provided rationales for teaching composition. Nearly all fit into one of five thematic clusters: (1) promoting music cognition, (2) strengthening understandings of music theory and practice, (3) training beginning composers, (4) increasing appreciation for contemporary music and its techniques, and (5) providing access to creative experiences (Barrett, 2003).

Though each of these themes represents a possible educational end, the study of composition should lead to more than the creation of adept theorists, appreciative listeners, or students who have dabbled in composition activities. Beyond the development of skills, attitudes, and preferences, the study of music composition allows children to explore their innate emotional and intellectual capacities within and through an artistic frame. This is a critical element in any rationale for having children study composition.

This text is based on the rationale offered below. It guides this approach to learning and teaching composition across school-based, PreK–12 music settings.

Every child should have the opportunity to study composition because the act of composing:

1. challenges children to consider their understanding of the world in new ways;
2. allows children to exercise their generative potential in music;
3. develops a way of knowing that complements understandings gained through other direct experiences of music;
4. invites the child to draw together the full breadth of his or her musical knowledge;

5. is a process that allows the child to grow, discover, and create himself or herself through artistic and meaningful engagement with sounds.

This five-point rationale honors children's natural curiosities and ways of making sense of the world and their existence in it through means uniquely offered by music. Each point, however, contributes significantly to the overall development of the child composer in a different way.

The act of composing challenges children to consider their understanding of the world in new ways. A variety of materials, each with its own set of intrigues and rules, are used in composition. When children imagine music, they actively control sounds in their heads. In this process they may encounter a few challenges. Can they remember their whole song? Can they produce it or is it too complex in some way? These wonderments lead to singing. In singing, the child's voice is activated and its vibrations can be felt. This results in one type of knowing in the body. The child may further discover that the voice has range and dynamics and that it can produce a variety of timbres.

The use of nonhuman sound sources requires experimentation. Children are compelled to discover what sounds can be made by the instruments that are available. They want to know how each instrument can be played. Once this is known, there is still the problem of selection, not to mention performance. In each of these problem identification and solution scenarios, children's present and future thinking is shaped through interactions with materials from the world around them.

Composers are also interested in inspirations. Very young composers often enact their compositions by singing melodies or motifs that enhance their play. They may not be consciously aware of their sources of inspiration. Older children, however, may actively seek inspiration. Some add music to storybooks or create elaborate songs to reflect their feelings. Others create music in ways that conceal their sources of inspiration. As children continue to develop their compositional abilities, inspirations may be found in increasingly complex situations. This reflects their developing understandings of the larger world.

Composers focus significant attention on relationships. While the dynamics of any relationship can be informative, composers are particularly interested in the way that people react to sounds. Loud noises met with "shhh" become intoxicatingly attractive to some creators, while others are more easily socialized into sounds acceptable in their current contexts. In either case, the composer has learned something of the reactions that loud sounds draw, and they can use that knowledge in immediate or future work to invite responses from listeners. Relational studies help composers understand the balance of forces among objects, people, and events that they use in shaping balances of sound within their own works. Indeed, every interaction with others, objects, sounds, and environs challenges children to consider their understandings of the world in new ways.

The act of composing allows children to exercise their generative potential in music. Creating music where none previously existed is a powerful act of self, but one that children naturally exercise. Just as children who hear others tell stories usually begin to create stories of their own, children who hear music are eager to create their own songs.

The sounds that children experience in the world around them are imbued with meanings as they are experienced. While the exact meanings may be explicit or held subconsciously, children come to understand the value of music as a human practice. Their appreciation and understanding of this practice grows as they invent, structure, and produce their own music. Deciding what sounds to use, what meanings to shape, and whether or not to share the finished product requires both musical and personal autonomy to be exercised. In this way, children exercise their generative potential and their ability to make meaning through the artistry of music.

The act of composing develops a way of knowing that complements understandings gained through other direct experiences of music. Each experience a child has with music is informative in some way. Singing, playing, composing, improvising, listening, and moving to music are all ways of directly interacting with sound. Through these six different types of engagement, children learn how music works as well as how to work with music. In addition to gaining personal knowledge of music through varied exposure, young composers are learning how others may interact with their own compositions.

Composers who work collaboratively or who interact with performers in preparing their compositions for performance often need to model their musical ideas in a variety of ways. Notation, although a helpful tool in communicating musical intention, is not always the most expressive vehicle for indicating how a piece of music is shaped or feels. Composers may model musical gestures physically to portray how a sound moves or is shaped. Physically enacting sound, which is a natural mode of composition used by children, allows the composer to acquire and represent physical or bodily-based understanding of musical gestures and intents.

Some composers find that singing and playing instruments while composing allows them to think through and experience musical ideas in expanded or additional ways. It can be argued that singing and playing instruments also provide composers with insights into the realm of performance. While it is unlikely that composers will become proficient performers on all instruments, the challenges faced when attempting to play one instrument or sing with technical proficiency and artistry allow composers to appreciate the challenges that performers encounter.

Perhaps the most critical contributory experience is found in musical activities that involve listening. Listening to music fills several critical roles. First, it allows children to develop their personal definitions of music. Through exposure to music children discover universal, cultural, and individual ways of thinking about and within music. Secondly, developing analytical and critical listening skills is an important component of self-assessment. Young composers need to be able to objectively evaluate their own compositions. And finally, it is through listening that young composers develop their aural palettes—the bank of sounds and sound gestures that are available for manipulation within their own work. Every direct engagement with music fosters another way of knowing and understanding music that can inform compositional practice.

The act of composing invites the child to draw together the full breadth of his or her musical knowledge. Composition allows students to examine human experiences through imagined, enacted, and even carefully crafted sound gestures that correspond to the qualities of human life. It is an interactive and creative process that explores myriad relationships. It seeks to identify and establish balances that provide unique insights into how experiences feel.

No activity within the domain of music requires a more varied palette of experiences and understandings than does composition. Composers work at the vast frontier of music—a place where knowledge and possibility are always twisting and turning in elaborate dance. In the act of creating music, the composer draws upon all prior musical learning to construct works that uniquely represent perspectives on and in music. Some composers follow previously identified trails as they pursue personal artistic frontiers. Others blaze new trails and forever alter the conceptual map of music. Regardless of the pathway pursued, any generative interaction with musical materials is likely to challenge the composer to draw upon previous experiences to inform compositional work.

The act of composing is a process that allows the child to grow, discover, and create him- or herself through artistic and meaningful engagement with sounds. Composers create by identifying and addressing conceptual and perceptual problems or challenges. Depending upon the issues addressed, the music evolves to reveal new concepts and percepts while the composer evolves to possess new levels of insight and understanding. In this way, the process of composition shapes both the musical product and the composer.

The continual interchange between concepts and percepts, problems and responses, and insights and understandings invites the use of prior knowledge and new ways of thinking. As composers explore their own experiences, what they understand of the perspectives of others, and how these two viewpoints can be expressed artistically, they develop a perspicacious capacity for discovering and shaping new meanings and understandings.

ADDITIONAL BELIEFS ABOUT
TEACHING MUSIC COMPOSITION

Normally functioning children, as well as many children with unique and special needs, have the capacity to compose music. The ability to structure sound and use sound to express conditions of experience is observable from birth. Babies quickly find ways of expressing their needs. As they grow and mature, their communication skills quickly expand to include not only language, but also music. Communication through speech is a routine form of human interaction, but one that has proven incomplete in its province for meaning making. Music, therefore, has evolved as another way in which human beings structure sound. Through its complex and refined structures, music can be used to construct and share meanings that surpass the limitations of verbal communication.

Composition can be taught. Just as children learn to structure their verbal communications, they also may learn to organize sounds to convey their knowledge of the world and themselves in music. Young composers simply require support. Providing young composers opportunities to learn through the careful design and implementation of composition lessons and activities can support the development of new skills and strategies. Further, teachers who compose alongside their students serve as models as they develop their own compositional skills and interests.

Teachers can help students become better composers. Research indicates (see chapter 3) that teachers play a crucial role in the development of young composers. Teachers who provide opportunity, inspiration, guidance, feedback, and support through all stages of the process allow children to develop and exercise their musical autonomy. This is a powerful gift. Given the highly influential role of the teacher, it is critically important that instructional theories and research addressing all areas of composition teaching and learning be studied. Teachers must be able to translate their personal knowledge into practices that benefit their students. This ability represents a lifelong learning process but one that is highly rewarding when pursued enthusiastically.

Children learn to compose by composing. Music classes are filled with information about music. Students learn to identify and name and classify multiple components of music. However, no number of class discussions about music, analyses of listening examples, or exercises in applying rules extracted from historical or cultural practices will, in and of themselves, teach children to compose. Young musicians learn to compose by composing. The more composition experience they have, the more they will learn.

Moreover, the more children compose, the easier it becomes to compose and the more motivated they are to do it, as long as they own their process. Composers learn from every composition. The decisions they make, the problems they encounter, and the solutions they find build their overall compositional and musical knowledge base to support increasingly complex artistic endeavors. Put another way, composers are built in the process of composing.

Children require high-quality compositional experiences in order to grow and develop. Teachers need to develop instructional strategies that allow them to focus on what children are actually composing rather than trying to teach one concept to all children at the same time. Time must be devoted to conferring with individual composers. However, composers also need time with one another to benefit from the social interactions that support their individual work. Classroom environments need to be "safe zones" in which children feel free to explore, make mistakes, and re-envision their work. Finally, teachers must find ways to assess and provide feedback within the flow of composition so that hands-on time is maximized in every way.

Composition is process. It is unfortunate that we have but one word in music, composition, to describe both the process and the product of the act of originating music. People often think of compositions as written works. Composers, while certainly working toward a final product, are long involved with the process of composing. They invest considerable time in thinking about sound, thinking in sound, exploring sound, generating ideas, testing ideas, and selecting ideas. They may create dozens of musical gestures or idea fragments and then discard them all. However, these efforts are not without value. It is often within these processes that the composer finds new perspective, discovers a particular technique, or finds a solution to the problem currently at hand or perhaps just on the horizon.

Since composition is a learning process, teachers and young composers must attend to both the process used to produce music and the criteria for evaluating finished work. Familiarity with compositional techniques, strategies for identifying and solving musical challenges, and an overall awareness of the process from initial product intention to performance reviews help young composers frame their work. Most importantly, composition instruction must help young composers discover the processes, approaches, and strategies that serve them best as they progress from one compositional challenge to the next.

Composition is a tool for developing musical thinking. Composition develops the musician's intellectual and intuitive flexibility by intertwining the impossible with the probable, the imagined with reality, and the practical with the inspired. When composers create music they think of things and discover new things that they were previously unaware of before they began to interact with sounds. The process of composing helps composers generate new ideas. Since the process of composing ignites different patterns of thinking, composition can be used to identify issues, solve problems, question practices, re-envision traditions, or unabashedly pursue innovation. Understanding that composition is not about having all the ideas in mind and simply writing them out (the fabled practice of Mozart) supports the importance of drafting and revising as opportunities to learn more about the musical ideas and meanings shaped within each musical work.

Because some of the compositions that children create are for others and some are only for themselves, children need opportunities to explore a wide array of compositional assignments. Simple exercises may be suitable for developing new techniques as they are broached or surface within compositions. At other times young composers benefit from self-defining their processes and products. Logs, reflective journals, notebooks, sketchbooks, blogs, podcasts, or websites featuring collections of compositions completed and in process are all tools that can be used to encourage children to think about their own compositions as well as compositions they would like to attempt in the future.

Composition is a form of research leading to the generation of new knowledge. From its very beginning, creating a musical work is a research project. The process involves defining a problem, testing hypotheses, formulating an original response, and sharing the results. The outcome of the effort is the construction of knowledge, understanding, feelings, and experiences that surpasses the limitations of words. As a medium for intellectual inquiry, composition provides a means for exploring historical and cultural practices within new contexts and from new perspectives. Composition affords composer, performer, and audience an opportunity to chart explorations of the inner, subjective facets of human experience in order to make sense of the world.

Composition may arise from many motivations. Composers create music for many reasons. Some composers are hired to write music for special events or particular ensembles. Other composers write music to forge social bonds, connect with a peer group, or offer commentary on social injustices. The type of composition a composer pursues is directly related to the specific motivations for the work. As such, the different forms and purposes allow the composer to create a range of relationships with the music they create and its future audience.

Young composers benefit from engagements with multiple types of writing. They need to work alone and with others. They need opportunities to explore a range of compositional sound sources and tools. They need to write songs, string quartets, choral works, percussion pieces, as well as pieces for every possible performance configuration that they can imagine. They need to discover that there exists a wide range of purposes for composing and that specific types of composition are often suited to particular settings or events. As young composers engage in this wide-ranging exploration, they have the opportunity to discover and develop their own compositional voices.

Composition exists within a web of relationships. A wild array of lines and arrows could be drawn to model the relationships among composer, composition, performer, conductor, audience, peers, friends, teachers, family members, and so on. However, of most immediate importance to many young composers is the intertwined relationship between the sounds of the composition and the audiences hearing them. The influence of the audience is paramount in their work. For schoolchildren, this is often a peer audience. The need for social acceptance can be overwhelming for some children and yet motivational to others. As young composers work, it is important that the teacher be aware of the balance of relationship between the composer's actual intention and the intention as it is influenced by outside sources. Helping young composers recognize the difference between the two allows them to develop a stronger artistic perspective.

Composition employs a range of technologies. The evolution of compositional practices mirrors in some ways the advances of technologies that promote information transmission and preservation. Just as hand signs yielded to single-line and multi-line staves and printing presses replaced quill and parchment, computers make skipping traditional notations possible and even desirable in certain circumstances. The computer, still viewed by some with a certain amount of suspicion, will eventually be replaced by yet another technological evolution.

For young composers, this means that experimentation in every realm of transmission and preservation is desirable. Composition evolves to reflect what is available and to push for new technologies that match artistic visions. Students who write for acoustic instruments and computers, who work with live performers and recording technology, and who seek to understand an array of transmission and preservation tools are prepared for the next musical evolution.

Assessment of composition requires both objective and subjective perspectives. The assessment of any work of art requires more than checking off a list of criteria as fulfilled or unmet. Music is apprehended both conceptually and perceptually. While criteria can be developed to assess craftsmanship and technique, expressivity is often situated in music by the perceiver. What is important for young composers to grasp is that they can create the potential for expressivity and affective response. While each assessor may react differently to the expressive qualities of a work, well-trained assessors can also identify expressive intentions and potentials.

BODILY BASES OF MUSICAL
EXPERIENCE AND UNDERSTANDING

> We should not pretend to understand the world only by intellect; we apprehend it just as much by feeling.
>
> —Carl G. Jung

> We know more than we can tell.
>
> —Michael Polyani

Though it is easy to identify the process, products, and potential benefits of composing, there still exists the foundational question of what enables people to create music. The observations of Jung and Polyani provide a partial answer because they call into question an emphasis on intellect as the only way of knowing. While the composer's ability to describe and explain techniques, styles, and practices is certainly of great importance, equally influential is the ability to comprehend through feeling. But what is it that provides the bases for these feelings?

Implicit and Explicit Learning

Every experience that a human being has contributes to a multilayered complex of understandings. As people interact with others or their surroundings—or even rethink previous experiences—the brain engages in an elaborate process of collecting, sorting, and storing related information into two broad categories. These categories are commonly referred to as explicit and implicit learnings. Aspects of an experience that people can describe and explain are characterized as explicit knowledge. These elements are often things that received conscious attention during the experience itself. Because this learning is accessible, it receives significant attention in education.

In contrast to explicit learning, implicit learning occurs subconsciously as the brain gathers, processes, and stores a body of subjective experiences. Reber (1993) describes this action as a fundamental process of the brain that "takes place largely independently of conscious attempts to learn and largely in the absence of explicit knowledge about what was acquired" (p. 5). The feelingful components of every experience that humans have are collected, sorted, and stored even when those feelings are not within a conscious focus of attention. This information tends to be undervalued because it is more difficult to assess.

The processes of the brain that involve continuous data collection in both conscious and subconscious realms are critical because they explain the two manners of "thinking" that appear in compositional work. First, there is the knowledge that people use to describe, explain, and report their experiences. This knowledge, as Jung and Polyani note, is highly valued. However, a second type of knowledge is also present: the knowledge of subjective experience. This tacit knowledge underpins our conscious understanding of events and experiences and provides a context for our impressions. This is also the knowledge that is drawn upon when people say things such as, "I have a hunch," or "I just feel that we should go the other way." This is intuition. It plays a critical role in connecting composer's knowledge of techniques and craftsmanship to the realm of feelingful capacities.

Intuition's Specialized Role

Intuition represents a feeling-based way of knowing. It occurs when there is an embodied match (a feeling that matches a previously experienced feeling) between implicit learning from a previous situation and the feelings that are being experienced in the current situation. Composers know that a decision or solution is right because they have experienced a similar instance or situation before, even though the experience may have been processed subconsciously. Because the same feeling sensation is being triggered, the brain seeks comparable experiences in memory. In this case, the memory is not of an explicit nature, but implicit. It is built of information gathered while the composer's attention was focused on something else. Dewey (1925) explains that

> These "feelings" have an efficiency of operation which it is impossible for thought to match. Even our most highly intellectualized operations depend upon them as a "fringe" by which to guide our inferential movements. They give us our sense of rightness and wrongness, of what to select and emphasize and follow up, and what to drop, slur over and ignore among the multitude of inchoate meanings that are presenting themselves. (p. 244)

Just as the feelingful components of an experience may exist subconsciously as implicit learning takes place, so may the resulting knowledge continue to function subconsciously as it informs future experiences. The composer employs intuition—the knowledge gained in the subjective experience of implicit learning—to inform explicit artistic decision making. Therefore, as composers make musical decisions in the process of composing there exists a balance between intuition (feeling based/knowledge within) and intellect (conscious awareness/knowledge about). This balance, in constant flux from decision to decision, represents the knowledge base for compositional decision making.

Connections: Body, Brain, and Mind

The idea that the brain stores information beyond that which is the apparent focus of attention suggests a more detailed consideration of the connections between the body as a mediator of experiences and the brain as a meaning maker. Music is often discussed in terms of values, intentions, and experiences. Yet people come to know music through physical energy as it is encoded and decoded by the brain. This physical energy is absorbed throughout the body, but most acutely attended to by the auditory system. The brain measures frequency, duration, and the timing of events to discover patterns. The anterior frontal lobe draws on previous experiences to predict whether or not expected patterns emerge. Finally the medial temporal lobe busily connects sounds to previous experiences.

The workings of these three sections of the brain contribute significantly to our understanding of the musical mind. The mind does not think about music because it is directly engaged in constructing a conception of music from the energy patterns it collects, recognizes, and categorizes. In this process, the body functions as the mediator of physical energy. Consciousness of music arises after the brain has processed the information it receives from the body. This order of operations suggests that the body plays a significant but underappreciated role in the construction of musical knowing.

Writings about music often emphasize what humans think about music and its structural components after the body-to-brain-to-mind transactions have occurred. However, focusing attention on the physical correlates of sound energy—those aspects of musical experiences that the brain collects, categorizes, and stores in its quest for knowledge—may present new insights into the processes underlying composition. In gaining access to the sensory side of the musical equation, humans may be able to make explicit the ways of knowing that are often sidelined when focus is placed on naming, identifying, and describing the theoretical constructs of music. As Meyer (1956) noted, "Once it is recognized that affective experience is just as dependent upon intelligent cognition as conscious intellection, that both involve perception, taking account of, envisaging, and so forth, then thinking and feeling need not be viewed as polar opposites but as different manifestations of a single psychological process" (p. 39).

Attention to feeling as both literal sensation and the emotional percept that follows is what enables composers to parallel the feeling of human *being* as sound. The feelings of being alive, implicit or explicitly present, are analogous to the qualities found within musical gestures. In order for sound, feelingful sensation, and knowing to intertwine in the workings of the subconscious and conscious in the process of composition, a foundation of musical experiences must exist.

MUSICAL PRINCIPLES DRAWN FROM BODILY CORRELATES

Researchers from the fields of psychology and music theory have placed great emphasis on the cognitive dimensions underpinning musical experience. However, new research is revealing a connection between music and body that allows us to draw experience, perceptions, and conceptions into reframed relationships. The musical mind exists as the result of the brain's sorting out of information gathered through the body as it encounters sound energy. Therefore, it is logical to seek some correspondence between the experiences of the body and the manner in which the brain organizes sound energy to be recognized as music. In both form and practice, music and the body draw upon five foundational correlates: sound/silence, motion/stasis, unity/variety, tension/release, and stability/instability.

Sound and Silence

Sound and silence constitute the very nature of musical being. Without sound, either internally imagined or externally audible, music does not exist. Human beings with normal hearing function are constantly aware of the sounds around them. While the presence or absence of sound can imply either safety or danger, sudden changes in the surrounding sounds spark increased attention. These same features are found within the ways that sound and silence are used in music.

Sound and silence can be balanced within pieces to create expressive impact. Sound and silence can occur as absolutes: sound is either present or absent. Sound and silence may also be considered in terms of structural entities. An "A" section has been heard, but it is now silent while the "B" section sounds. On a smaller scale, one set of instruments might be heard as another is silent. Still smaller, rhythms are constructed of patterns of sounds and silences. These are just a few examples of the ways that sound and silence through presence, absence, and presentation can impact both human and music.

Motion and Stasis

In many cultures, music and the movement of the body are deeply intertwined (Blacking, 1973) in all aspects of musical interaction. Motion and stasis are experienced as perceptions of horizontal and/or vertical pitch structures as well as in temporal constructs and the changes that occur within them. Complete pieces, sections, phrases, rhythms, even the initiation-sound-stop of an individual tone reflect the passage of time. Works may be experienced as moving quickly or slowly in relation to external conceptions of time, such as a clock. Indeed, creating illusions of time is one way that composers play with motion and stasis.

Connections between musical and bodily motion have received considerable research attention. Highlighting a direct correlation between experiences of the moving body and music, Kronman and Sundberg (1987) found that the experience of time in music holds both physical and mental analogs with locomotion. Similarly, Carroll-Phelan and Hampson (1996) affirmed the connection between cognition and body motion in music perception and production by demonstrating that rhythmic components of music cannot be activated without recruiting neural systems known to be involved in motor activity. Other research has suggested the beat perception is literally an imagined motion engaging the sensorimotor loop of the brain while musical phrases correspond to a mobilization of motor schemata based on an internal sense of motion (Todd, 1992).

In writing that "the listener does not merely hear the sound of a galloping horse or bowing violinist; rather, the listener hears a horse galloping and a violinist bowing," Shove and Repp (1995, p. 59) suggest that musical motion is primarily audible physical motion. This ecological perspective on perception acknowledges that listeners apprehend environmental objects giving rise to sound (Gibson, 1979). Musical perception, then, would necessarily involve an understanding of body-based motion and call upon the listener to engage in a type of empathetic embodied cognition when experiencing music.

Unity and Variety

Unity and variety invite and pique interest. Unity is achieved when composers use a particular set of sounds to establish commonality within a work or even across multiple works, songs, or movements. This commonality provides a foundation for expectation. People engaging with the work expect to play or hear a certain musical gesture repeatedly. Such gestures might take the shape of repetitive chordal passages, the consistent use of a grouping of instruments, a set rhythmic pattern or metrical grouping, or any other device that has a sense of constancy. Once the brain figures out the pattern, it loses interest. The inclusion of new sounds, little twists or major shifts, adjustments, and changes that catch the ear serve to re-engage the brain. However, because it is also pleasing to the brain to recognize patterns that it has previously identified, composers often bring back the main unifier after new material or other substantial changes have occurred.

Lehrer (2007) explains that the corticofugal system of the brain is delighted to encounter constancy and unity. The brain literally becomes better at hearing "those sounds that we have heard before" (p. 142). Lehrer continues to suggest that artists constantly battle this looping feature of the brain and they do so "by paying attention to art" and purposefully generating ideas that are new. They introduce variety. The variety enacted by composers invokes "a network of neurons that respond *only* to surprising sounds" (p. 141), and the brain responds by releasing dopamine, the chemical responsible for intense emotion. Dopamine has the job of reorganizing the auditory complex to make the unfamiliar familiar. In this way, unity and variety keep the brain busy.

Zeki (2001) echoes Lehrer's position and explains that the brain works on two laws: constancy and abstraction. Constancy serves to provide frame of reference against which variety can be appreciated. Zeki explains that art is one expression of the variability of the brain. It reflects the brain's ability to change and adapt to new information. He also posits that artists are neurologists in their own right, working with the materials of their craft to understand the brain (1999).

Tension and Release

The brain is constantly seeking patterns as it processes and stores information. It can signal tension when a pattern cannot be identified or when a pattern it perceives does not conclude. The buildup of tension and its subsequent release is tied to the biological need to survive. Tension is danger. When the brain cannot resolve a pattern, the resulting feeling is called tension. It signals a need to change situations or to escape, which causes the brain to seek release.

Sloboda (1991) studied the impact of musical structures, primarily melodic and harmonic gestures, and discovered that subjects reported physical reactions (shivers, laughter, tears, lump in throat, etc.) when their musical expectations were either fulfilled or frustrated. While early studies relied on subject-provided data, more recent studies have measured electrodermal activity or heart rate and used electroencephalogram in addition to subject response to gain both subjective and physiological data. Steinbeis and others (2006) discovered that frustrating harmonic expectations resulted in increasingly strong physiological reactions. Further, they noted that people with musical training reacted more strongly and sooner than did nonmusicians.

Huron (2006), building on the work of Meyer (1956), suggested that the musical mind engages in rounds of imagination, tension, prediction, reaction, and appraisal as it sorts out incoming auditory information. The feelings that occur prior to an expected or unexpected musical event relate to imagination and tension (anticipation), while prediction, reaction, and appraisal occur after a musical event has been encountered. The brain is constantly engaged in prediction and evaluation, seemingly asking, "What is going to happen?" and "Did it happen as expected?" in its attempt to stabilize experience and assign meaning.

The patterns that the brain works to identify and resolve extend beyond simple rhythmic patterns such as *ta ta ti–ti ta* or *do–re–mi–re, do–re–mi–re*. The brain searches for all kinds of patterns. These may be built of slowing and increasing tempos, steadily decreasing dynamics, entrances and exits of instruments, repetition of harmonic patterns or melodic fragments, and hundreds of other prominent and subtle facets of music. All of these things are tools composers use to tease our biological mechanisms.

Stability and Instability

Stability and instability are tied to the biological foundations of the human body (Damasio, 1999). The body executes a set of ongoing operations to observe and control biological stasis. A portion of the brain is devoted to monitoring these operations and reporting, "Everything's the same," over and over. However, things change. Humans can detect these changes because they occur against the biostatic backdrop that remains stable.

Musically, this stable background may be comprised of nearly anything. It can be a repeating rhythmic pattern or a set of chords. Indeed, Schenker, a German music theorist, thought that the musical background within the works of German composers of the classical and romantic periods could be reduced to a single and constant I–V–I progression (Schenker, 1935, 1979). Although his focus was rather narrow, the overall idea that music has a background is important. The background that exists in both human function and music allows people to notice changes that occur in other places. Any change in the status quo signals instability and snaps the brain to attention, inviting it to identify what is going on.

On a larger scale, every major composer has introduced some instability to the world of music. In fact, the ability to introduce instability contributed to the very notion that they were a "major" composer. Here are a few stories to consider:

Haydn. What a wild and crazy guy. The orchestra was playing along nicely as people were enjoying cocktails and predinner conversation, and then, out of nowhere, this loud blurt out of the musicians' horns. The conversation probably sounded like this: "What was that? I nearly spilled my drink. Oh! He did it again! Who writes music like that?" Haydn understood stability and instability. He was thinking, "Got your attention, didn't it? Surprise!"

Beethoven. More subtle in his approach than dear Haydn, but still challenging expectation on a large scale, Beethoven added voices to the final movement of his Ninth Symphony, undoubtedly causing more than one listener to ask, "Singers? In a symphony? Can he do that?" Instability.

And then there was Cage. Walking out onstage, sitting at a piano for a full four minutes and thirty-three seconds, playing not a note, and then walking offstage. It is easy to imagine that those conversations echoed for days. "What? A piece of music with no music? Where was the music? Was there music?" Ah ha! Instability can be found in the very definition of music. Brilliant.

Music's wealth lies in the fact that its power to sooth, challenge, and arouse varies among individuals. However, in order for individual variance to occur, there must be some stability against which variance can be observed and experienced. Therefore, music's evolution is marked by the presence of principles that are universally present, employed through cultural definition and individually interpreted and experienced.

MASTERING COMPOSITION THROUGH PRINCIPLES-BASED LEARNING AND TEACHING

Educators who teach from the belief that composition provides a unique means for children to engage their developing understanding of themselves and the world around them allow young composers to exercise their own thoughts, feelings, and intuitions as they create music. By acknowledging that learning begins with the experiences of the child, teaching composition becomes a process of drawing out what the composer already knows while providing challenges that invite growth. This approach requires teachers to embrace an "evolutionary planning" process in which overarching goals are achieved through a focus on the development of the individual child. In this way each child is empowered in the act of learning as he creates his own music.

Traditional Practices and Approaches

Teachers accustomed to leading performance ensembles may be tempted to place primary focus on the creation of performable products. This approach leads to studies that place form and technique before idea generation and meaning making. In turn, the skills of artistic craftsmanship become artificially isolated and disconnected from their potential use as meaning makers. The teacher's need to see evidence of products that tightly adhere to preconceived notions of right and wrong often prompts the imposition of strict production guidelines. Concomitant with this practice, the teacher makes many of the major compositional decisions for students. This reduces student autonomy and, eventually, student motivation. Certainly this approach may produce successful products, but successful by what definition?

Teaching composition within an approach that places primary value on principle relationships differs from approaches that focus on identifying and replicating the use of the elements of music. One of the dangers of planning instruction related to the elements is that it is easy to neglect what becomes the second, yet more vital stage in which students make the connections between the overarching meaningful gestures of music and the elements as components of those structures. By focusing on the processes used to create music and the products that emerge from those processes, teachers and students create space for creativity and expressiveness to emerge.

Principles-Based Composition Learning and Teaching

The word *educere* means "drawing out." To teach composition, teachers have to help children learn how to draw out what they already know, both intellectually and feelingly, in music. Student composers need to be immersed in learning experiences that respect their intuitions, that value and encourage their individuality, and that emphasize innovation and creative freedom as inseparable from expression (Lapidaki, 2007). Children recognize sound and silence, feel how music moves and rests, are assured by familiarity, and are invigorated by novelty and change. They have experienced all of these things as auditory correlates of their physical selves: they are our human points of reference.

The music that children make is simply a part of their existence. It is deeply connected to who they are and what they do. As children become increasingly self-aware, they are more able to think about music as an entity apart from themselves. This developmental step paves the way for the objective distance needed to make analytical and artistic decisions about music as the child's musical world continues to grow and expand. It also provides points of entry where teachers can invite students to consider music in new ways.

Children must be asked to do more than identify musical events. They need to consider how composers craft music and why sounds and structures have been used in particular ways. How did the composer create the feeling of motion and rest that we experienced when we heard this piece? How did the performers capitalize on familiar and unfamiliar ideas as crafted in this piece? Or, perhaps, how did the composer use note durations to change the feeling of time in the piece? Questions of this nature frame the elements as components of principle relationships that exist to allow composers, performers, and listeners to construct meaning in the sounds they experience.

Educators responsible for leading children to discover and study the musics of the world are then challenged to create learning activities where thinking *about* music contributes to thinking *in* music. Imbalance toward the side of thinking *about* is evident when products are described as "flat" or "formulaic." Such works are termed "uninspired" or "lacking heart" because technique has overbalanced intuition. Similarly, pieces described as "failing to develop" occur when intuition has not been partnered with the technical skills necessary to capture music's full meaningful potential.

The composition teacher's challenge is to help children find the balance between thinking *in* music (the naturalistic finding and making of meaning in sounds) and thinking *about* music (using knowledge of tools and techniques to enhance the artistic craftsmanship that can shape sounds into meaningful organization). It is a worthy instructional goal to assist children in exercising their understanding of musical meaning through the process of original creation. Moreover, it is a goal that is compatible with music education's overarching mission to engage every child in exploring music through multiple perspectives and activities so that they might become adept contributors and partakers of the art of music.

2

On Young Composers Composing

Characteristics, Creative Capacities, and Compositions

There is still room in the art of music for countless gifted composers!

—Heinrich Schenker

Teachers considering how to guide and assist child composers can gain valuable insights from the world of research. Although composition research comprises a relative new branch of inquiry within music education, existing studies have much to offer. Over the past forty years, researchers have worked to identify the multiple facets of the composer, the process of composing, and the compositional product. Careful attention has been given to the roles of the child composer and to music as an influential mediator in the creative process. Researchers have also considered how data is framed and interpreted as well as how practitioners implement and lead composition activities in a variety of settings.

Composition research has forged a dramatic trajectory, quickly moving from a simple analysis of "what is" to a much more complex set of questions addressing "what can be." Educators can capitalize on this growing body of knowledge as they consider how and why children create music, what activities appeal to them, and what engagements foster the greatest learning. These perspectives serve to frame and define composition's potential as a tool for teaching and learning in music education.

This chapter examines what research reveals about young composers and their development, working contexts, and processes and products. Each of these factors plays a crucial role in shaping and implementing composition engagements with children. Four key perspectives will serve as guides for thinking about the research findings offered and interpreted in this chapter:

1. What does the compositional process tell us about the child-composer?
2. What does the composition tell us about the composer's developing understanding of music?
3. What does our interpretation of the compositional process and/or product tell us about ourselves as interpreters?
4. What does all of the above tell us about the role of music in our lives?

FORGING MUSICAL FOUNDATIONS

The desire to create meaningful sounds begins at a very young age and continues throughout childhood. Every step a child takes toward making music leads to another that builds the knowledge necessary to compose. Over their first five years, most children will

- imitate sounds, tunes, rhythms, and inflections that others use in talking and singing;
- dance and move to music;
- listen to music accompanying audio books, cartoons, and movies;
- discover that music is heard from start to finish and has a beginning and ending;
- recognize that pieces of music often begin with introductions and are built of multiple sections;
- identify and learn cultural songs (national anthems, lullabies, songs of celebration);
- learn that people use different types of music for different occasions;
- develop a fondness for a particular song (which may change several times as the child grows);
- predict musical events within familiar systems (e.g., filling in the musical blanks when a line of a song has been only partially recalled);
- sing songs sung to them or frequently heard;
- combine bits and pieces of several songs into personal songs;
- invent original songs and music to accompany play or as a primary activity;
- share personal songs or other invented music with family members or friends.

Each of these accomplishments heralds the potential for generative music making. Future musical growth of this type, however, is most likely to continue only if it is nurtured as formal education begins. Therefore, it is important to consider what we know about school-age children and their interests and abilities in creating original music.

COMPOSER CHARACTERISTICS

In thinking about young composers, it is important to consider why children compose, how age and experience shape student work, and whether stages of compositional development exist. These questions seek answers that help teachers consider another set of questions: children should compose, what activities are appropriate at different times, and is there a natural structure for curricular design?

The Purpose of Composition

Children compose music to make sense of their feelings and experiences. The creation of music by children is a natural act needing no prompting from adults. Just as children "story" the events of their day to make sense of their experiences, so do they "music" to make sense of the feelings that arise from their many interactions with people and their environment (Burton, 2002). The songs that they create, whether alone or with peers, are sound-based representations of their understandings of their world. Whether using music to control their own perceptions of time (Zur, 2007) or to influence others (Adachi & Trehub, 1998), the understandings revealed in their music are not literal, but experiential, personal, and powerful.

Children invent music to make ordinary experiences special. Dissanayake (1988) suggests that people create art to reorder reality in ways that reframe or juxtapose the ordinary in new ways. People "make special" things that have particular meaning to them. The musical pieces created by children, be they full compositions or even fragments of musical ideas, are for them highly valued objects (Kaschub, 1997). Their creations represent an intrinsic form of deep personal understanding brought to existence through a specialized artistic effort. The music that children create becomes an extension of their personal agency (Ruthmann, 2005) uniquely manifest with their conceptions and perceptions (Reimer, 2003).

Children compose music to define who they are. In defining the role that music plays in the development of personal knowledge and understanding, children's musical engagements contribute to the identity formation (Barrett, 2003; Davis, 2005). Beyond contributing to the overall definition of "who I am," children who compose music consider themselves "composers" when the role is familiar to them and acknowledged by others (Stauffer, 2003). Further, several studies have noted that composers develop preferences for musical gestures that eventually become the audible signatures of the composer—a moniker in sound. The composition of music, then, plays a crucial role in the growth of both musician and person. It contributes to the development of self in unique and varied ways.

The Roles of Age and Experience

Questions addressing the influence of age and experience on children's composition are heavily confounded. As children grow older they are likely to engage in experiences that may influence their compositions (Kratus, 1994). Similarly, children provided with additional opportunities to compose are likely to refine or adapt their processes and produce an array of ever-evolving products (Swanwick & Tillman, 1986). They will, however, also mature as they take advantage of these opportunities. Given the complexity of the landscape, many researchers simply acknowledge that age and experience are highly individualized influences (Barrett, 1996; Davies, 1992).

The combined effects of age and experience are most noticeable in the areas of musical training, audiation, and direct compositional experience. Exposure to music and musical training significantly shapes children's future interests as well as their ability to imagine a variety of musical products to compose. Prior training does not limit children's natural curiosities or their desire to test musical boundaries (Blacking, 1967; Glover, 2000; Marsh, 1995) but defines the baseline for composition as well as the children's working attitude and pace of process (Freed-Carlin, 1998; Seddon & O'Neill, 2003). Experience also allows for the process of enculturation that leads children to expand their definitions of musical products and, in turn, broadens the range of musical works that children produce (Wilson & Wales, 1995; Barrett, 1996). Recent work has shown one enculturating endeavor—playing an instrument—to be highly influential (Folkestad et al., 1998; Swanwick & Franca, 1999), while instrument choice plays a significant role in shaping composition (Ainsworth, 1970; Burnard, 1995). Exposure, in conjunction with emerging abilities, may also contribute to the shift of thinking that unfolds between the ages of five and fifteen, when children's compositions typically expand from horizontal to vertical sonic structures.

The ability to imagine the sounds of music internally, or audiation, develops over time (age) and with practice (experience). Skilled audiation directly impacts the amount of time children devote to different tasks within the compositional process (Kratus, 1989, 1994). Children able to audiate are more likely to evenly divide time between exploration, development, and repetition, rather than just searching for an initial idea. The ability to hold a musical thought in mind and manipulate it allows composers to develop and refine their ideas. Further, it has been suggested that the ability to imagine musical wholes also develops with experience (Wilson & Wales, 1995; Wiggins, 1994, 1995; Stauffer, 2001).

Stages of Compositional Development

What is currently known about children's compositional development stems from a large body of single-event or cross-sectional research studies. Such snapshots of young composers and their work provide valuable insights to compositional development but cannot track changes or trends across the lifespan as longitudinal studies might. It is possible, however, to infer from the available literature that composition is likely to unfold along a continuum similar to those found in other areas of human learning and behavior.

The absence of an "ages and stages" theory of compositional development from longitudinal studies provides opportunity for a different type of grounded theory to emerge (Glaser, 1992). Composition researchers with innumerable intentions have employed a variety of data collection methods to a wide-ranging subject pool engaged in diverse tasks with equally diverse tools. The resultant data, apart from addressing study-bound questions, also constitutes material suitable for analysis and categorization leading to conceptual themes.

Meta-analysis of composition research studies reveals three such themes—intention, expressivity, and artistic craftsmanship—to be widely reported as present in children's work. These themes, here termed *compositional capacities*, appear to varying degrees at all ages and skill levels represented in the extant literature. Across nearly all discussions of children's work researchers highlight the role that one or multiple capacities play as composers make and execute hundreds of greater and lesser decisions in the creation of music. Further, data analysis suggests that each capacity can be developed with instruction and experience.

COMPOSITIONAL CAPACITIES

Regardless of particular entry points, children must engage all three capacities—intention, expressivity, and artistic craftsmanship—to develop basic compositional skills and abilities. As compositional capacities appear to unfold in stages tied to experience and tempered by age, they are best considered in general terms. Young composers with little or no previous experience are *novices*, while students who have some compositional experience and have created a few pieces are described as *intermediates*. *Advanced* composers, perhaps fewer in number in many current school music programs, will possess a substantial set of experiences. Each stage of development—*novice, intermediate,* and *advanced*—is marked by general tendencies related to intention, expressivity, and artistic craftsmanship.

Table 2.1 Compositional Capacities

Compositional Capacities	Novice	Intermediate	Advanced
Intention—May be based upon a feeling, a memory of a feeling, a projection of a feeling, the context of a feeling, a feeling being experienced at the moment, or even an extramusical connection or connotation. It is this idea that the composer wishes to sonify.	Composers experience the feeling of their compositions as they create them. The composer may not have a "musical intention" at the outset, but in the course of other activities (play, hobbies, recreation, social interactions) creates music. This compositional process is "enactive" in that children create sounds that are parallel to, or partner with, what they are experiencing or have experienced as part of their activities. Most pieces are *storied*, or *about* something.	Composers develop an awareness of their own feelingful response to music and use this knowledge to predict how others might experience music. Careful consideration is given to the feelingful character of compositions. Composers' catalogs continue to include but also expand to include pieces that are *about* something but also expand to include pieces that are expressive *of* something.	Composers set out to achieve a particular feeling or affect in their compositions. Composers decide to create works that are *programmatic* or *absolute* music.
Expressivity—An awareness of the relationship between sound and feeling that grows into the ability to imagine how a feeling might be experienced as sound. This ability draws upon an understanding of how principle relationships within a piece of music can invite human response.	Composers begin to acquire the tools of expression by noticing the feelingful impact of sounds as they enact (or possibly imagine) music.	Composers consider the impact of musical sounds and begin to use sounds to purposefully invoke feelingful response.	Composers carefully consider how sounds can be used, connected, organized, and presented to achieve greater affective response.

| Artistic craftsmanship—The ability to use the elements and control principle relationships to achieve affect. This ability can be used within a particular stylistic system or used to break the rules of a particular system meaningfully. | Composers may accidentally create sounds that are musically satisfying—*fortuitous accidents*—but most often engage in experimentation or trial and error until satisfying musical ideas are created. Composers adopt and maintain a personal sound vocabulary of musical ideas. | Composers learn about and adopt an initial array of conventional tools and forms. Most composers create music that fits preconceived norms. Composers begin to transition from reacting to external sounds to imagining sounds internally while composing. | Strong familiarity with the tools and forms of convention are exemplified in compositions. Composers may seek innovation by using conventional ideas, tools, or forms in unconventional ways. Composers have developed the capacity to imagine the impact of compositional choices in the absence of external sound. |

Intention

Musical intention may be based upon a feeling, a memory of a feeling, a projection of a feeling, the context of a feeling, a feeling being experienced at the moment, or even an extramusical connection or connotation (Kaschub & Smith, 2007). It is this idea that the composer wishes to compose or, in the case of younger composers, enacts. Intention may be shaped by available materials, context, presence of a text or story, the composer's personal desire to create, or the composer's prediction of a potential audience reaction. Subconscious or not, intention is the seed of composer action.

Novice composers experience the feeling of their compositions as they create them. The composer may not have a preconceived "musical intention" at the outset, but in the course of other activities (play, hobbies, recreation, social interactions) creates music. This compositional process is "enactive" in that children draw upon embodied knowledge to create sounds (Burnard, 1999) that partner what they are or have experienced as part of their activities. Most pieces are *storied*, *about* something, or *of the action* in which they are presently engaged (Burton, 2002; Barrett, 2001; Marsh, 1995; Davis, 2005).

Intermediate composers first develop an awareness of their own "feelingful" response to music and then begin to use this knowledge to predict how others might experience music. These composers grow to give careful consideration to the feeling character of their compositions. The composer's catalog continues to include pieces that are *about* things but also expands to include pieces that are expressive *of* something (Hall, 2007; Hamilton, 1999). This transition marks a key development point.

Composers of advanced intentional capacity set out to achieve a particular feeling or effect in their compositions. They may decide to create works that are *programmatic* or *absolute* but will do so with an ever-increasing awareness of listeners' sound-effect relationship. Advanced composers are fully cognizant of, and capitalize on, the predicted impact of their creative choices on future audiences (Jaffurs, 2004; Davis, 2005).

Novice, intermediate, and advanced composers experience intention in different ways. Novice composers may simply act without an awareness of particular intent but can often describe post-composition what inspired their work. Composers in the intermediate stage are transitioning between enacting their work and using an awareness of music's potential impact to guide their compositional choices. Advanced composers capitalize on their awareness of listeners and make choices that predict and even shape audience reaction to their work. This progression from "all about me" to "about the listener" characterizes growth in intentional capacity.

Expressivity

Expressivity is found in an awareness of the relationship between sound and feeling. Early awareness of this relationship may be evidenced in the way children adopt and apply cultural norms that define musical structures. Expressive capacity develops when children begin to imagine how a feeling might be felt if it were experienced as sound within these structural frames. As children develop the ability to recognize and control how sounds connect to human response, they begin to experiment with conveying their feelingful intentions.

The foundation for expressive capacity begins when novice composers notice the feelingful impact of sound as they enact (or possibly imagine) music. While children may have experienced feeling music many times themselves, personal awareness of this experience may not occur until children notice someone else reacting to a piece of music. Recognizing that music is related to feeling opens the door for an exploration of the broad parameters of cultural norms (Barrett, 1996).

Now able to more fully consider the impact of musical sounds on themselves and others, the intermediate composer begins to use sounds to purposefully invoke response. The transition from reacting to external sounds to imagining sounds internally while composing is one of the key indicators of compositional development in intermediate-stage composers. Composers who can audiate music are able to consider the feelingful impact of many different sounds and to select the musical gestures that most accurately match their intentions (Stauffer, 2001).

Advanced composers are adept facilitators of sound-feeling relationships. They carefully consider how sounds can be used, connected, organized, and presented to achieve the greatest potential affective response. Advanced composers have developed the capacity to imagine the impact of compositional choices in the complete absence of external sound.

Unfolding along a developmental continuum, expressivity ranges from the unconscious employment of feeling-sound relationships to a full-throttled exploration of potential sound-inspired affect. Growth of expressive capacity is evident in the way composers draw on personal experiences of music's sound-feel as a source of information. This awareness establishes the foundation for considering and advancing relationships between sound and feeling.

Artistic Craftsmanship

To employ artistic craftsmanship is to release from the imagination the sounds of feeling in a manner that requires the guidance of intention and the forces of expressive awareness. Compositional actions are based on an understanding of musical styles and conventions. Artistic decisions are then made in adherence to particular style systems or to meaningfully break the rules of such systems.

Children with little prior experience in composition most often engage in experimentation and rounds of trial and error (Kratus, 1989). They may unintentionally create sounds that are musically satisfying through fortuitous accidents, but much of their work stems from direct and immediate experience rather than precognition. Initial technical skills may emerge from discovered gestures and techniques. These fledgling gestures are often immediately satisfying to the composer who chooses to use them repeatedly within the current project or in closely following future projects.

Composers adopting and using conventional tools and forms are in the intermediary stage of artistic craftsmanship. These composers tend to place great emphasis on creating music that fits preconceived norms (Hall, 2007; Kratus, 2001). Security and certainty within existing forms is very appealing to intermediary composers, though they may attempt minor innovations within familiar organizations.

Advanced composers possess strong familiarity with tools and forms of convention exemplified in compositions. They may seek innovation by using conventional ideas, tools, or forms in unconventional ways. Likewise, they may use traditional sounds and gestures in unfamiliar ways. Regardless of approach, advanced composers possess technical skills that allow them to fluidly facilitate sharing their musical thoughts.

Acquisition and growth of technical skill is perhaps the most easily observed development within the three compositional capacities. Novice composers begin with only a rudimentary ability to assemble multiple sounds and often limit their work to horizontal structures. With time and experience, intermediate composers begin to expand the boundaries of the sound structures they use and grow to advanced composers who easily design and assemble multiple layers of sound.

COMPOSING CONTEXTS

People often imagine music composition as a single-person activity. Children regaled with stories of "great" composers form a mental image that features the lone composer sitting with an instrument and notating music (Glover, 2000). This vision, however, represents but one model of composition, common in one style of music and perhaps tied to a particular period of time. Many other configurations exist and are beneficial to the development of young composers.

Many Contexts to Explore

Different composing processes belong to different cultures and are evidenced in the countless musical styles that exist throughout the world. Presenting composition as a solitary role places excessive value on that particular experience and the music that results from that practice. It simultaneously diminishes the value of other practiced forms of creating and the music that arises from those traditions. Such teaching may send a message to students that the music of their own culture and preference is of less importance and is less developed, less sophisticated, less desirable, and even less musical. Presentation of multiple contexts, then, is both pedagogical and political (Abrahams, 2005).

The composer's working context is of vital importance as presence or absence of peers or other collaborators may influence the creative process. Composers working outside of school settings are most likely to compose music with a small group of friends (Jaffurs, 2004), though they may also choose to partner with a single friend, sibling, or even parent. Espeland (2003) notes that even when young people compose alone, they are acting within a context in which their previous experiences with culture, tools, and other people are omnipresent in their music making.

Whether contexts are entered in home-based or school-based settings, if and how working groups are formed is of significance. Composers working alone may do so by necessity or by choice, but both the need and the choice are often their own. As teachers establish working groups in school-based composition, it is important to consider which context is most appropriate to the task. Students should be given ample opportunity to work with advanced composers, with peers, or alone, as each context presents a unique set of benefits and challenges.

Unique Features of Single-Composer Contexts

Composers working alone in the creation of a composition are simultaneously free to do as they wish and bound to rely on the limitations of their own capacities. In these contexts, some young composers may hesitate to begin while others will enthusiastically start. In either case, individual composers will benefit from access to a mentor who can offer strategies to balance personal working styles.

Solitary composers require ample resources to accomplish their artistic visions. Individuals may create pieces that are beyond their performance capacity. In these situations they will need tools or performers to perform their pieces both during and at the conclusion of the composing process. This is particularly important for composers who are just beginning to

develop audiation skills as they need to constantly hear their pieces externally in order to compose.

Composers working individually may also desire to interact with people
who can listen to and provide feedback on drafts of their work. While working alone grants a degree of freedom from compromising with peers, it also
means that the objective distance that co-composers bring to the analysis
of individual ideas or emerging products is absent.

Unique Features of Multicomposer Contexts

Composition in school-based settings occurs in ensembles, large groups,
small groups, partnerships, or even solitary contexts. The social parameters
of composing in school settings ranges from students donning earphones
and working alone at computer stations to students spread far and wide
across floors and through hallways while surrounded by instruments,
markers, and paper. Although both individual and multicomposer contexts
provide valuable learning opportunities, community-based classrooms in
which all composers may interact most consistently align with tenets of
popular learning theories (Papert, 1993; Piaget, 1976; Vygotsky, 1978).

The exact nature of within-group composer interactions is critically important and influences both group function and musical learning. Composers
partnered with friends tend to engage in more interactive verbal and musical communications (MacDonald et al., 2002). They report higher levels of
personal achievement and task enjoyment (Burland & Davidson, 2001). The
musical works produced in these groups also draw high evaluative scores
(Miell & MacDonald, 2000).

The level of shared understanding of the compositional problem, possible
solutions, resolution strategies, and the music itself form the glue that holds
groups together in their compositional vision (Kruger, 1993; Wiggins, 1998).
As children draw on their personal knowledge and the knowledge possessed
by their peers, they initiate a cognitive collective that allows groups to create
pieces that frequently exceed what any individual child might create independently (Bakhtin, 1981; Beals, 1998). Within the collective, students learn
to evaluate musical ideas and negotiate the proper placement of those ideas
within the group's work (McGillen & McMillan, 2005; Ruthmann, 2005).
This process strengthens their evaluative artistic capacities.

Several researchers have closely examined within-group working styles
(Burland & Davidson, 2001; Hamilton, 1999; Kaschub, 1999; Wiggins,
1994). As teachers observe groups working, insights gained from identifying common working styles can be used to guide group action in ways that
maximize student learning and improve the experience of each group mem-

ber. Common interaction styles may be categorized as having concurrent, collaborative, and executive tendencies (Kaschub, 2007).

Concurrent style: Composers working concurrently engage in side-by-side composition and then assemble their individual pieces into one larger work. Compositions created in this manner vary in quality in relation to the level and caliber of the planning process. The products produced in concurrent working style often lack musical unification, and composers tend to report personal satisfaction with both process and product as low.

Collaborative style: Composers who employ a collaborative working style engage in high levels of verbal and musical discourse. Decisions are made through modeling and discussion that may include idea amendments or refinements before an idea is incorporated into the larger musical work. Composers working in this format rarely can reconstruct the composition process to identify "who did what." They simply report contributions to be equal among all members of the group. Collaborative composers generally report being very pleased with their process and the resultant products.

Executive style: Executive working style is marked by the appearance of a dominating group member. This composer holds an impenetrable vision of product intent. The executive may appear willing to listen to ideas from other group members, but rarely will these ideas surface in the final product unless substantial adaptations have been made to suit the executive's vision. The remaining members of the group are often "tools" of the executive and are used to execute another's plan. High levels of frustration may be observable, but there also exists the possibility that supporting members will be content to let another steer the process and do the work. Composers from executive groups report differing perceptions of product directly related to their sense of personal agency. Composers believing they had made significant contributions to the product were generally pleased with the outcome, while composers feeling marginalized tended to be harsher critics.

Since group size also impacts interactions and shapes learning within multicomposer contexts, the formation of groups must be approached with careful forethought. It is important that composers form, or be placed in, groups that can successfully interact. Larger groups face bigger challenges in the areas of inclusive participation and personal agency, but these can be overcome. Careful attention should be given to what roles composers might adopt within their groups and to the methods used to collect and test musical ideas. This approach ensures that every child will have the opportunity to contribute in meaningful ways.

PROCESS OF COMPOSITION

The process of composing involves ordering sounds into forms with expressive potential. Composers and researchers describe this process as comprising a variety of steps, including impulse and inspiration, planning, exploration, selection of tools and materials, idea generation, testing, and selection, preservation, product assembly, verification, development and extension, re-envisioning, editing, sharing, seeking feedback, performance, evaluation, and receiving and processing criticism (Berkley, 2001; Bunting, 1987; Christensen, 1992; Cohen, 1980; Daignault, 1996; Fautley, 2003; Freed-Carlin, 1998; Freed-Garrod, 1999; Hickey, 1995; Kaschub, 1999; Kratus, 1989; Levi, 1991; Smith, 2004; Wiggins, 1992; Younker, 2000).

Confounding understanding of the process is the fact that similar steps are reported across multiple studies yet appear in diverse orders and receive varying degrees of attention. Only one generalization is abundantly clear: the process of composition has a starting point, a midpoint characterized by great activity, and an end point marked by the presence of a "piece."

It is surprisingly difficult to predict exactly what will be observed as children compose. Within the composition process, a generative dialogue (Wertsch, 1991) evolves between the composer(s) and the materials of music (Reimer, 1989). This artistic exchange may unfold verbally or in musical sounds. It is likely to be mediated by a variety of notational and tactile tools. It also may be outwardly observable or transpire before a solitary witness in the mind of the composer. Regardless of the components of the process, each exchange impacts future decisions and choices in ways that influence the composer's steps toward a final product.

The dialogical nature of the creative process indicates innumerable possible pathways for composers to select. As an influential partner in the process of composition, the emerging piece itself makes some steps more necessary than others. Composers may employ a set of actions that vary between pieces. Some steps will become part of the composer's personal working preferences, and others will be enacted as a creative necessity. Regardless of its place in the unfolding process, each step plays an important role in composition and in the development of creative and critical thinking.

Impulse and Inspiration

People live in a body-stable mode of operation that serves as the backdrop against which changes in themselves and their surroundings can be observed (Damasio, 1999). As motion (change) is noticed, impulse occurs. Conscious awareness of such change causes people to act differently, to respond, or to make sense of what they have experienced. In this way, people are moved to act.

The motivation to create begins as an impulse but is often described as *inspiration* because it is connected to something physically or mentally tangible. Anchoring impulse, inspiration may be credited to ideas, feelings, or sound fragments. Works of art, literature, and theater have motivated some composers, while others have sought inspiration in relationships between people or in the ways in which animals move within their habitats. The roots of inspiration may run deep or shallow, but they play a significant role in shaping the processes and products of composition.

Uninhibited impulse and inspiration can be easily observed in the song and music making of preschool children (Adachi & Trehub, 1998; Barrett, 2001). They regularly and spontaneously create songs and compositions to partner, support, and enhance their daily activities and play (Burton, 2002). As composers grow older, societal expectations of appropriate behavior and other factors may inhibit the production of in-the-moment composition, but the desire to create should then simply be matched with a window of opportunity.

Bunting (1987) suggests that the musical aspect of the compositional process begins with an initial impulse reflective of melodic, rhythmic, or harmonic materials. These sound inspirations comprise the opening lines of the compositional dialogue that transpires between composer and materials. They frame key decisions made within the planning process. The transition from impulse and inspiration to some form of planning generally occurs when the composer or composers accept a task given to them or recognize their own general product intention. Deciding how to tackle the task, redefining the task in comfortable and familiar terms, and developing a belief in the project (Van Ernst, 1993) comprise the rest of the transition.

Planning

Planning is the "orchestration of diverse and interdependent cognitive and motivational processes that are influenced by context and that are brought together in the service of reaching a goal" (Friedman & Scholnick, 1997, p. xi). In the absence of an impulse, planning may provide impetus for actions. This is often the case when composers working in school-based settings are assigned tasks designed by teachers and then required to complete these tasks within the time frame of the music class period. Planning also may occur strictly as a necessity when impulse does not originate within one person so that multiple composers need to experience a change together.

Within composition research, planning has been described as a precompositional activity in which a composer or composers conceive of a piece in its entirety before working out its constituent parts (Allsup, 2002; Bamberger, 1991; Berkley, 2001; Folkestad, Hargreaves, & Lindstrom, 1998;

Kaschub, 1999; Wiggins, 1994). Other views suggest that planning reveals itself during the generative steps of the compositional process as composers and materials interact (Hickey, 1995; Kaschub, 1997; Younker, 2000). Regardless of when planning occurs, it fulfills both managerial and musical needs.

Composers working independently or with others need to determine how work time will be used, what resources and materials are required to achieve the intended product, and perhaps how the performers or computer will bring their work to audience ears. Composers filling the role of performer-composers (equivalent of singer-songwriters) often evolve plans based on a "who-plays-what-when" set of decisions. Managerial choices must also advance musical concerns. A clear vision of what the piece will be, an overview of the entire project, and a unifying group vision for those working in multicomposer contexts (DeLorenzo, 1989; Wiggins, 1998) are all necessary for success.

Selection of Supporting Tools and Materials

Materials that support composition include those designed to make as well as preserve sound. Good tools can fulfill multiple purposes and possess aesthetic qualities sufficient to encourage a composer's future growth (Upitis, 1989). The materials found to be most appealing are those that are immediately accessible or those promising the greatest potential determined personally achievable by the composer. Regardless of selection criteria, choice of materials is perhaps the most influential factor in the conception of music (Ainsworth, 1970; Burnard, 1995; Kratus, 2001).

Novice composers are more highly influenced by tools than by musical ideas in their earliest work (Wilson & Wales, 1995). Stauffer (2001) describes one young composer who limited her compositions to the visual space defined by her computer screen. As composers gain experience and familiarity with supporting materials, their choice of timbre, musical gestures, and desired products evolves (Ruthmann, 2008; Stauffer, 2001). Material choices become increasingly deliberate as students gain experience and expand their compositional palettes and portfolios.

Exploration

To the casual observer, the exploratory step often appears no more than "fooling around" or "off-task" behavior. Yet it fulfills a vital role. Exploration provides an opportunity for composers to familiarize themselves with the tools and materials available to them for the purposes of composition (Kratus, 1989). It reveals the sounds that can be drawn from chosen instruments or the capabilities of software programs. These engagements with tools and materials define the sound palette immediately available to the composer. Beyond serving these functions, playing with tools and materials can produce musical ideas that later are incorporated into the composition product. Indeed, the process of exploration may offer the spark that inspires an entire work.

Idea Generation

Composers engage in idea generation as they encounter and identify compositional challenges or problems. As students often note, "It's hard for me to come up with ideas when that's what I'm *supposed* to do. It's so much easier to get them when I'm supposed to doing something else!" While it is certainly possible to create only one solution to a problem, composers with more experience tend to consider multiple ideas and attempt to find the best possible solution. Creativity researchers characterize thinking that leads to multiple possible solutions as divergent, while convergent thinking allows the composer to choose from among a number of options (Webster, 2003).

The ability to brainstorm multiple ideas is important as subjective adherence to a single idea can limit or even halt the compositional process. Several researchers have noted the value that students place on the ideas they contribute to a musical work (Davidson, 1990; DeLorenzo, 1989; Ruthmann, 2005). Individual ownership of ideas begins as ideas are generated and may carry throughout the remainder of the process. This sense of personal agency can prove motivational or can bring the process to a grinding halt if students working in groups find the ideas they value being discarded by others in the group (Kaschub, 1999).

Once a number of ideas have been generated, composers begin the process of determining how appropriate the ideas are in the context of their work. Some ideas may be quickly discarded while others are manipulated and refined. Students often go back and forth between idea generation and testing. Portions of this step may strongly resemble either exploration or editing as composers search for the sounds that they feel are just right.

Idea Testing and Selection

Determining which ideas to incorporate and which to discard is a complex test. Composers must be able to make aural comparisons, either internally or externally, so that they can make artistic discriminations. This process often occurs in two modes: the first involves composers comparing ideas one against another, while the second requires situating the winning ideas within the musical whole being produced. In both cases, repetition

(Kratus, 1989) is likely to be observed. Because they need to be in the presence of external sound in order to do their work, novice composers use repetition to keep ideas within hearing (Christensen, 1992). Repetition also allows more advanced composers to temporarily adopt the role of audience so that they can measure the musical cogency of their ideas.

Music composition research has yet to address how repetition impacts preference for ideas. Recent research from the field of neuroscience notes that functions of the corticofugal system of the brain allow us to become "better able to hear those sounds that we have heard before" (Lehrer, 2007, p. 142). New sounds and unfamiliar sounds "release unpleasant amounts of dopamine" that make us uncomfortable and uncertain. Thus, as composers repeat the music they have created, either to keep it in memory or perhaps finding some already familiar aspect making it desirable, it becomes increasingly appealing. This may explain why composers who repeat their musical creations in attempts to remember their work (prenotational) are most subjectively attached to their own ideas and find it difficult to gain objective footing.

Composers working in groups face the challenge of introducing their ideas to their peers and the additional challenge of marketing their ideas as worthy of inclusion in the joint project. Group work may be punctuated by argument, debate, justification (Kruger, 1993), and even episodes of voting (Kaschub, 1997, 1999) as composers attempt to select ideas. Voting belongs solely to group work, but even individual composers who can position themselves objectively wrestle with inner judges in determining which ideas are expressive and which should be set aside.

Preservation

At some point in the process of creating ideas, composers must decide whether they trust their work to memory, need to write things down, or will make use of computers or other recording devices to keep track of their work. Composers who rely on memory often engage in repetition (Fautley, 2003; Kratus, 1989; Smith, 2004) or use the division of performance responsibilities to have individuals within the group memorize musical chunks. In this way, the performer-composers form a memory-collective for their work.

The decision to notate work, in either invented or standardized systems, usually occurs when composers realize that they cannot hold all of their ideas in memory. This may be due to the creation of longer pieces that are difficult to hold in memory or may also occur with shorter pieces that are being created across multiple composing sessions. Researchers have noted that the process of developing notational systems can both reflect and alter composition thinking (Auh & Walker, 1999; Barrett, 1997, 2001; Upitis, 1992).

Access to computers and software for either composing or recording, or other recording devices, offers composers yet another mode of preservation (Emmons, 1998, Folkestad et al., 1998). Although composers usually turn to recording for completed pieces, they may also record works that are evolving over several composing sessions to preserve ideas that have not been notated. Composers may also use this type of recording to provide additional details when only rough notations have been sketched.

Product Assembly

Children often generate ideas in "musical blocks." These blocks, often referred to as the "drum thing" or the "flute riff," are pitches and rhythms that exist as a unit in the composer's thinking. Once assembled, these building blocks will form the musical composition that exists in the mind of the composer and that likely will evolve through the processes of composing.

Individual composers and composers working in a truly collaborative style (Kaschub, 2007) tend to assemble their pieces as each new idea is generated, tested, and selected (Bunting, 1987; Glover, 2000). In these contexts assembly and rehearsal are often interlinked activities as creators fill both composer and performer roles (Davis, 2005; Jaffurs, 2004).

Group composers working in division-of-labor contexts usually assemble their compositions at the point when each group member has finished his or her individual task. This process can meet with varying degrees of success dependent upon the strength of the group's initial vision (Wiggins, 1999/2000) of the product. Additionally, assembly can sometimes pose considerable challenges for composers with less-developed skills in the capacity of artistic craftsmanship. They may find it difficult to align and synchronize the parts to achieve a product that matches their initial intentions.

Product Verification

Researchers have asked students to offer descriptive evaluations of their completed pieces (Christensen, 1992; Freed-Garrod, 1999; Kaschub, 1999; McCoy, 1999; Smith, 2004), but less is known about how composers determine the efficacy of newly emerging products in the moment of their origination. Reimer (1989) describes consideration of the evolving product as one of the fundamental actions undertaken by artists as they work. This happens innumerable times during the composition process.

Product verification begins when two musical gestures are unified. The individual ideas, verified during idea testing and selection, become a potential product as they are joined. Although this process is present in both individual and group work, it is most easily observed within the context of group composition. Composers frequently generate musical ideas or sound blocks apart from the group, but verbal or musical actions external to the composer are needed to share the product with compositional peers.

Another point of product verification is found each time a composer successfully imbeds a new idea into an evolving work. With each musical gesture added, reshaped, adjusted, or tweaked, the composer is likely to imagine, listen to, or play the piece again. Each hearing is evaluative—the piece is either working or not (Barrett, 1996; Campbell, 1995; Davis, 2005). It has been suggested that with each hearing the composer measures the unfolding piece against an internal model of the completed piece (Wiggins, 1992). Composers make changes and alterations until the external hearing and the internal model match. While this is one possible strategy, others may exist. Composers may hold a much more open conception of the final product. This would allow for the creation of specific music gestures shaped in the dialogue between materials and composer (Reimer, 1989) or multiple composers (Kaschub, 1997).

The final point of verification occurs when the composer initiates a self-evaluation of the entirety of the work. The composer may encounter similar process moments as smaller formal sections are completed. However, the next section is always waiting for attention. Final verification is the point at which the composer determines the process of creating to be complete. This decision point is a complex one and may be influenced by work time, task structures or other decisions imposed by the teacher, the composer's assessment of his or her compositional or performance skills (Kratus, 1989; Smith, 2004), or interpeer actions (Davis, 2005; Jaffurs, 2004; Miell & MacDonald, 2000).

Development and Extension

Folkestad (1996) defines development as involving the expansion of existing musical ideas in either horizontal or vertical fashion, while extension requires the addition of new musical ideas to an existing work. Researchers have noted varying degrees of these processes across novice, intermediate, and advanced levels of composing. However, aside from identification and definition, the processes of development and extension have been marginalized in research addressing children's composition. Studies designed to specifically examine how each process is carried out have yet to be undertaken (Webster, 2003).

Observations drawn from studies of the broader processes of composition suggest that novice composers, who are those most widely cast as the subjects of composition research, are likely to spend more time engaged in finding ideas than in developing and extending those ideas (Kratus, 1989). Even when experiences from other topic areas support idea development and extension, novice composers may lack the musical skills necessary to fully enact those strategies. Development and extension, then, may be more easily observed in the work of intermediate or advanced composers (Stauffer, 2001). These composers have acquired many of the skills of basic craftsmanship and are naturally drawn to the creation of longer and multilayered pieces similar to those regularly found within their own sound environments.

Revision

The revision process begins when the composer considers whether or not the finished product satisfactorily matches the intentions it was created to fulfill. This process is very short if the question is met with a definitive "yes." Any other answer, however, indicates that the piece should be subjected to additional scrutiny.

Composers often execute their intentions to the best of their abilities throughout the composition process. The process, though, is one of discovery that leads to growth of new skills and new understandings. Composers may discover valuable ideas and knowledge as they work through a compositional challenge. This means that composers view their final work from a new perspective rather than the one they held at the outset of the project.

Smith (2007) suggests that revision may involve the total reinventing of a piece. For some composers, this may mean discarding all of their work. More commonly, composers will preserve major ideas or structures. These components of the work will resume their status as musical ideas or gestures and be considered again for inclusion in the new musical product.

This revision process often begins with composers critically and objectively listening to their work. They may revisit how decisions were made, what arguments of support were offered for various ideas or idea pairings, and even whether the original intention was sufficient. This process can be revitalizing or terrorizing. Some composers will find the promise of new possibilities exciting. They will be eager to begin and jump quickly into "what-if" scenarios as new plans begin to take shape. Other composers, however, may look at a finished work, even one that is a bit disappointing, and see completion—a release from a project.

Composition is a physical, emotional, and intellectual investment. The choice to reopen a project once thought finished is not easy for some composers. Revision takes an investment of both time and faith. Composers may want assurances that their earlier work was of value and will not be lost. Most importantly, composers want to be assured that their additional efforts will lead to a more successful product.

Editing

Composers edit their work to address either musical or mechanical issues (Carlin, 1997). Musical editing enhances the clarity, coherency, voice, and style of a composition through minor refinements. Composers may adjust rhythmic motives to create a stronger relationship between two main ideas or consider altering an instrumental timbre to better match an internal model or even facilitate performance. Mechanical issues also arise as compositions near completion. Score preparation often involves fixing minor details, adding notations, tinkering with musical ideas, and adding interpretive performance instructions. Musical and mechanical changes do not significantly alter the character of the work, but bring refinement to its details (Levi, 1991).

Editing may occur toward the end of the composing process, or it may take place throughout the creation of a work. Pieces created on computers and to be performed by computers generally require little work in this phase. The introduction of live performers, however, may motivate composers to be more attentive to the final details of score preparation in an attempt to ensure an accurate performance of their work.

When the composer is also to be the performer, other editing practices may emerge. Performer-composers often make changes in their compositions as they rehearse (Christensen, 1992; Wiggins, 1992). Simultaneously experiencing music from multiple perspectives often encourages the performing composer to enact on-the-spot edits. Some of these edits are incorporated into the final work, while others appear to be brief explorations or tests to confirm that the composition is truly right.

Sharing and Seeking Feedback

Interaction with others contributes significantly to the process of learning to compose. Although composers may choose to create pieces that are just for themselves, most of the time they will want others to hear and respond to their work (Hamilton, 1999). This often occurs informally as composers work together or in close physical proximity. Teachers are often able to follow an idea as it hops from group to group within a classroom (Kaschub, 1999).

The motivation to share compositions comes from many sources. Sharing can be a form of celebration. When a composition pulls together easily or a challenge has been met, composers will want to share their success. Musically satisfied composers are content to observe the reaction of others, but they may not request constructive criticism (Upitis, 1992). At other times, composers share because they are hungry for feedback. Peers are often more than willing to oblige. Several researchers have noted that, within group composition, peers immediately evaluate ideas. They voice their opinions (Freed-Carlin, 1998; Marsh, 1995; Wiggins, 1999/2000) and determine whether ideas should be accepted or rejected.

When informal sharing time is absent from the compositional process, students benefit from the creation of opportunities for discourse with other composers (Kratus, 2008). These interactions can take the form of works-in-progress performances. This allows composers to ask for very specific feedback from the listeners. In settings where time is short, composers can sit in pairs and quickly share their goals, their work, and their questions in order to benefit from one another's perspectives.

Performance

Composers often remark that premiere performances constitute the most exciting step in the composition process. Although some composers may prefer to keep the occasional work private, most will desire to share their finished products. Preparation for performance requires careful planning to ensure that important details are not overlooked.

The addition of performers, whether they are people or computers, brings new challenges to the composition process. If the composer is to perform his or her own work, only brief rehearsal may be necessary. In this situation the performer already understands the vision of the composer. Performers who did not contribute to the conception of the work benefit from time to learn their parts, interaction with the composer, and time to interact with other performers. Finally, compositions being performed by computers may be ready to go on the computer, but additional time may be needed to check and verify sound systems used to deliver the work to a larger audience.

Evaluation

Evaluation of final products is found in many research studies. This process usually takes place after compositions have been performed in class, ensemble, or even concert settings. It is often formalized by teachers or researchers. However, what is important to consider is that the composer has probably engaged in a process of evaluation long before the "official" evaluation has begun.

The first evaluation that composers complete is a mental checklist confirming that intentions have been fulfilled. The completion of this evaluation leads the composer to declare his or her piece ready for performance. The composer most likely internalizes many more evaluations as performers bring the music from plan to sound in rehearsal. The actual performance of the work is also evaluated. These thoughts may even be revisited as the composer replays the performance in his or her own mind, deciding what really worked and what did not happen as planned.

By the time composers are handed a formal evaluation form, they have invested a considerable amount of time in considering the pros and cons of their work. Composers who are pleased with their work generally note that they had strong ideas or worked well together in group settings. Dissatisfaction is generally attributed to inability to match external sounds with internal models (Wiggins, 1999/2000), displeasure with assigned task, group dysfunction, problems with assembly or performance, and insufficient work time (Freed-Garrod, 1999; Kaschub, 1999; Van Ernst, 1993).

Receiving Criticism

As children's compositions rarely receive significant public attention (Glover, 2000), young composers seldom experience formal criticism. Yet the ability to weather the comments of critics is part of being a creative artist. Further, young audiences, often comprising classmates, engage in quiet criticism with or without invitation. It is more beneficial to engage this natural tendency than to try to stifle it.

Criticism of product is different from feedback in process. Feedback can be formative. It allows the composer to learn while still in the process of shaping and molding materials. Criticism of product occurs after the composer has reached a point of satisfaction. The work has been called to a close. The piece is finished. At this point, the composer owns, or is responsible for, the decisions made and the product as it will be presented to performers and audience. This means that criticism, especially negative criticism, can be taken very personally (Atlas et al., 2004).

Engaging in music criticism is one way for young composers to learn how outsiders come to understand a piece of music. Eisner (2002) writes that effective engagements within the arts involve identifying, describing, analyzing, and making judgments. Critics identify the musical ideas presented by the composer and describe what the composer did with the ideas. They may identify relationships that are interesting to the listener. Good critics will also analyze how the composer achieved the sound relationships presented to the listener. Value judgments about the effectiveness of the piece may be offered as the composer's work is compared to the works of others. As composers learn how to apply these thinking processes to the works of others, they will also develop a frame for understanding the comments they receive in response to their own compositions.

COMPOSITIONAL PRODUCTS

The processes and products of composition are inextricably intertwined as children compose (Daignault, 1996; Freed-Carlin, 1998), but many attempts have been made to unravel their individual mysteries. While the process of composition is marked with numerous steps and multiple pathways, the products of composition are fixed and more easily identified.

Much of what is known about compositional products is drawn from two sources: outside evaluators and the composers themselves. Many of the earliest research studies examining children's composition focused on elemental structures or overall quality of musical products (Davies, 1992; Kratus, 1985, 1994; Swanwick & Tilman, 1986; Wilson & Wales, 1995). These studies revealed increases in predictable patterning, rhythmic complexity, and harmonic structures as children age (Henry, 1995; Kratus, 1985). Rhythmic complexity and the ability to hold musical ideas in memory was also found to increase with age (Kratus, 1994). Researchers also determined that quality of work was directly proportional to quantity of time invested in the process (Daiagnault, 1996; Hickey, 1995; Kratus, 1994), but Smith (2004) noted that was not true for all students.

More recent studies have sought to discover what composers think of their final products (Carlin, 1997; McCoy, 1999). Listening to the composer's perspective allowed researchers to reframe some of the earlier product findings. As young composers described their processes and products, it became increasingly evident that adult and child conception varied. Young composers were able to elaborate on how instruments shaped their work. They also explained that performance considerations such as insuring that "everyone in the group getting a turn to play" impacted their product visions (Kaschub, 1999). The use of computers also changed products. Performer-composers tended to string ideas in succession, while computer-using composers found stacking ideas very appealing (Hickey & Reese, 2002).

The products of children's composition tell us many things about their development, but the products cannot fully reveal the wealth of critical and creative thinking and learning involved in the full process of composition. It is possible that "a picture is worth a thousand words" because there exist a thousand explanations for what that picture offers. Similarly, the voices of young composers hold thousands of incredible explanations for the thinking and the actions that contribute to their musical knowledge and their music making.

3

Supporting Roles

Tools, Tasks, and Teachers

In addition to composer characteristics, their developing capacities, the context where they work, and the processes they use, additional factors shape students' compositional work. The availability of tools, accessibility of task requirements, and facility to draw on prior knowledge and experiences all contribute to the development of young composers. Teachers play an important role in providing resources, guiding work, and creating opportunities for composers to develop skills. While each of these factors is present in the experience of composing, careful planning and consideration must be given to how tools, tasks, prior learning, and teachers impact compositional activities to ensure that the contributions made are positive ones.

COMPOSITIONAL TOOLS

The interactions between composers and their music can be described as an exchange that is both mediated and influenced by materials (Reimer, 2003). Aptly referred to as thinking tools (Wertsch, 1991), items external to and manipulated by the composer to enhance the process of thinking in sound serve to facilitate creative action (Bruner, 1990; Erkunt, 1998; Rogoff, 1990; Vygotsky, 1978). Whether selected by the composer or provided to the composer by others, tools such as keyboards, classroom instruments, computers, blank or manuscript paper, other preservers of sound, voices, and other sound makers may fundamentally shape the composer's interaction with the musical product as it evolves. Therefore, the process used to select tools and the use that composers make of tools can provide some insight into the ways in which composers conceive of their compositions.

Tools for Thinking in Sound

The tools that composers use can be categorized into sound makers and sound preservers. The four primary sound makers include the mind, voices, instruments, and computers. Each is a tool that composers think with during the composition process.

Of these tools, the mind is the most challenging. Its complexity lies not only in its operations, but also in our inability to observe its processes and products. It may be employed solely, but it is also required in the operation of every other tool that a composer may choose to explore or employ. The ability to imagine and manipulate music in mind, without the need for external tools, is often considered the highest achievement in the process of composition.

While the mind holds a special category as both sound maker and sound processor, the sounds made by voices, instruments, and computers are musically equivalent to a painter's brushes and paints. The first instrument that children explore is located within the body. The voice is a powerful tool that allows children to make deep connections between the sounds that they can produce and their experiences and feelings as ways of knowing the world. Children begin their explorations of the voice shortly after birth by signaling their needs and mimicking others, and eventually transition to speech and song. Many composers working with instruments draw on their own singing to actualize and verify the musical ideas and gestures that they hear internally.

Similar to early vocal forays, children often begin the exploration of instruments within themselves through body percussion. These early rhythmic actions are often relocated to the kitchen pots and pans before more formalized instruments are added to the young composer's palette. By helping the brain organize time and event sequences, playing instruments is critical to the development of the concepts and percepts that parallel movement in music.

Instrument availability plays an important role in the development of young composers. As Cutietta (2004) has noted, the nature and role of instruments is not only a pedagogical issue, but also a musicological issue. Composers seeking to work within particular stylistic or cultural norms need to have access to instruments authentic to those practices. Students who have listened to and studied blues recordings before being asked to create blues pieces on classroom instruments are immediately presented with an aural disconnect: the aural models they possess do not match the tools they have been provided to use in the task. This requires a transfer of knowledge that some students may be able to make quickly but that may disrupt and stall the work of others.

Composers have been creating music with and for computers since the 1950s, but only recently have computers gained the characteristics that allow them to be classified as folk instruments. First, laptops have become relatively affordable and easy to obtain. Most importantly, they have become highly portable. The programs designed for making music range from very accessible to challenging.

As tools for assisting in the composition process, computers have many positive attributes. Airy and Parr (2001) have noted that computers can give a musical voice to students who are uncomfortable with singing or playing instruments. Computers can also serve to bridge the gap between what children can physically play and what they can imagine (Hickey, 1997; Upitis, 1989). In this way, computers can be musically freeing (Landányi, 1995) in that children may be able to find ways to more accurately present in sound what they hold in their minds as intended musical products.

However, computer users face many of the same challenges that performers experience as they seek to gain artistic and technical mastery of their instruments/tools. The use of a computer requires a period of time for learning to manipulate and navigate hardware and software. This can be just as frustrating to the eager composer as trying to figure out a fingering pattern on a clarinet or how to perform a passage with rhythmic accuracy. Further, working with computers can be isolating unless efforts are made to connect with other musicians (Landányi, 1995). The interactions that occur as performer-composers work with other performers and composers often spark important changes in thinking that may be substantively different from the thinking that develops when interacting only with computers (Ruthmann, 2005).

Beyond using computers to "think with," computers can also fill the role of performer when the specific sound palette of the computer and its software are found desirable by the composer. This situation comes with both advantages and disadvantages. For composers who desire complete control over their pieces, it is possible to "perfectly program" a composition. There is no need to worry about possible performer misinterpretation. However, the decision to always have computers serve as performers also denies the composer knowledge that might have been gained through working with performers or hearing the interpretations that performers lend to a composer's work.

Because it is important for students to experience a wide range of thinking tools as they learn to compose, several criteria should be applied in deciding which tools are most appropriate for a given task: (1) Does the available tool enhance the student's ability to meaningfully connect with a world of sound? (2) Are the sound options offered by the tool sounds with which the composer has a personal connection? (3) Are the sound options authentic to the task the composer has adopted? (4) Can the composer make meaning with the tool? Tool choices that fulfill all four of these criteria are the options that will offer the composer the greatest potential success.

Preservation Tools

Items that are used to preserve sound make up the second category of compositional tools. Preservation is necessary both during the process of composition and once pieces are complete. Regardless of when tools of preservation are used, the ultimate goal remains to represent the composer's musical ideas and prevent them from being lost. Memory, notations, recording devices, and computers may all be used to preserve music, but each as its own set of advantages and disadvantages.

The first preservation tool that most composers employ is that of memory. It is a readily available tool, seemingly always present, but it varies in degrees of efficiency. Additionally, its strength must be developed. As a preservation device, it presents several problems. Composers often begin by creating short pieces that can be held in memory. However, as skills develop and pieces expand, memory capacity can be quickly outgrown. Composers working in groups often adapt by co-opting others to remember certain features of the piece they are jointly creating. This is usually observable as group composers discuss "who plays what when." Each composer remembers a general order of events and then the specific content of what they play. Nonetheless, at some point even this organization can fail. When composers discover that co-opted memory is no longer sufficient, they begin to create a new tool: notation.

Invented notations may take many forms but are designed to be memory boosters for the performer-composer. As such, invented notations are difficult to use when music is passed from the composer to a new performer. Composers who have experienced a misinterpretation of their invented notations become eager to learn a more codified system. Yet traditional notation presents a special challenge of its own in that people who are used to working with it tend to think that it is an essential part of the process of composing rather than one possible tool for preserving and transmitting musical ideas. It is important to remember that notations, either invented or codified, are representations of music—not actual music. Notation functions as a blueprint to guide performers in producing sounds as conceived by the composer. Therefore, once composers begin to use notation and understand its potential for ensuring a more accurate performance, a steady progression of increasing detail is often observable in their scores.

Notational skills are *not* a prerequisite to compositional activity. They are an outgrowth of generative musical thinking met with the challenge of limited memory. As children invent their own notational systems, they build in increasing levels of detail and carefully reflect on how their notational system serves their needs (Bamberger, 1991, 1994; Barrett, 1997; Davidson & Scripp, 1988; Gromko, 1994; Upitis, 1992). Most importantly, in order for notation to be meaningful, the need to notate must originate with the composer (Upitis, 1992).

Research on the cognitive development of children suggests that what children think about as they engage in particular tasks and create products is highly influenced by, and even dependent upon, the meaning that the child assigns to the task (Rogoff, 1990). Thus, when teachers instruct children to "Write whatever will help you remember your music," the children may still be notating to satisfy the idea that the teacher wants notation. They may believe that the task is about notating their music. This assignment of meaning to the task, by both teacher and child, creates an artificial need for notation—a need that might not be present in absence of the teacher's prompt.

Studies of children's notation have generally supported the idea that notational skills develop with time and experience. Children gather notational symbols from a wide range of sources. Letters, numbers, and pictures as well as traditional musical symbols are common features of evolving systems of notation. Barrett (2001) suggests that children "move back and forth between a range of notational strategies rather than progressively through hierarchically distinct stages" (pp. 34–35). Despite the mix of symbols and the evolutionary nature of their employ, young composers tend to use only one system of notation at a time (Barrett, 2000).

Researchers have noted that the type of notation used by composers can impact the products of their work. Composers using invented notations tend to generate works judged to be more creative than pieces produced using traditional notations (Auh & Walker, 1999; Hamilton, 1999; Upitis, 1990). Just like invented notation, traditional notation can have limiting factors. Traditional notation is a symbol system with rather rigid confinements in terms of the divisions of pitch and time, the relationships between horizontal and vertical structures, and even the overall organization of scores. Each of these factors can be found overwhelming and limiting in certain contexts.

It is also important to remember that notating is part of a compositional process within a particular cultural heritage. It is not, however, a part of every culture's musical practices. Further, in every culture that notates, the system of notation is evolutionary: it changes over time to reflect the needs of its users. In this way, children inventing notational systems are experiencing, and perhaps even contributing to, a living practice within the world of music.

The third tool of preservation, recording devices, can be used to preserve compositions in both their formative (in process) and summative (final product) stages. Recordings are helpful to students who are composing by playing instruments. These students often report forgetting or losing track of their best ideas. This may be because they were so busy thinking in the music that they forgot to write it down, or worked for so long that they forgot the finer details of their ideas. In these instances, recordings can serve as memory boosters or as artifacts that can be transcribed. Recordings are also useful for younger students when composition activities span across multiple class periods. When young students are not notating or are just beginning to use invented notations, recordings can serve as reminders of what they were doing in their previous work session.

Being able to hear a musical idea several times through the use of recordings is somewhat like time travel. Revisiting recordings of compositional ideas, excerpts, and even whole pieces enables students to develop a degree of self-autonomy and self-efficacy through repeated opportunities for reflection (Lebler, 2007).

While recording devices are quick ways of preserving musical ideas, they also present a few challenges. Recordings used to capture musical ideas before they are lost require composers to be able to recreate the idea based on what they hear and can transcribe. Composers who use recordings to extend memory from work session to work session need to remember how they were making the sounds on the recording. Finally, the most obvious challenge in working with recordings is that it can be difficult to pass music along to other performers without notation unless those performers have highly developed aural perception and imitation skills.

The music created by young composers can provide incredible insight into who they are, how they think of the world around them, and how they present their understandings musically. The scores that children create and the performances that they present are only part of the story of their musical thinking. Perhaps the fullest insight into the young composer's processes requires the triangulation of a notated score, a verbal explanation, and a musical performance. From these sources, insights into the composer's goals, expressive intentions, challenges of craftsmanship, dramatic shifts in musical thinking, and other significant insights to compositional development may be gained. These glimpses into the development of the composer provide a foundation for guiding future learning.

TASK STRUCTURES

Task design is at the intersection of knowledge about the student, music, and learning potentials. Finding a way to keep the compositional capacities in proper balance within tasks is a significant challenge. Historically, intention has been owned and determined by the teacher. However, without ownership of the task, students may become disinterested and disengaged. Expressivity, often only tacitly acknowledged in current teaching practice, needs substantial attention. It is the very basis of music's power but is often dismissed as impossible to assess. Overbalanced in this equation is artistic craftsmanship. As the tools of artistic craftsmanship share many features with typical music theory studies required in music degree programs, teachers are very comfortable with approaches focusing on theory-based tasks. Well-designed tasks allow for the coadunation of intention, expressivity, and artistic craftsmanship.

Whether or not children are successful in executing tasks is often determined by the presence or absence of sufficient groundwork on the part of the teacher. Identification of students' prior knowledge, experience, interests, musical skills, and motivations is critical. Students must sense that the task is something that they can do successfully, and they must believe that the task is real and worthy of their time. Task structures are scaffolding devices most appropriately used when students are acquiring new techniques. Leaps from theoretical constructs to active practice can be difficult—even overwhelming—to young composers. Task structures serve as a safe path between theory and practice.

Well-designed tasks involve the skills and knowledge applied by musicians of all types as they create new music (Savage, 2003). These tasks allow students to discover the important connections between musical ideas and experiences that allow for the meaning making in music. Rarely do composition tasks progress in a linear fashion or move from simple to complex ideas. Creative processes are not that tidy. Tasks that place excessive emphasis on technical skills limit expressive concerns and hamper artistic thinking. Most importantly, regardless of the specifics of task design, there is no one-size-fits-all method of composition. Every composer eventually will find his or her own pathway.

Freedoms and Constraints

Composition has been described as a dialogic process of meaning making comprising both freedoms and constraints (Barrett, 2003). This begs the question: Who determines which freedoms and constraints? Teachers are responsible for designing manageable tasks, but composers also desire a degree of autonomy. This is reflected in Stravinsky's statement, "My freedom consists in my moving about within the narrow frame that I have designed myself . . . the more constraints one imposes, the more one frees one's self of the chains that shackle the spirit" (1947, p. 68). The first part raises the issue of the composer designing task parameters for himself, while the second part suggests that as decisions are made, the composer becomes increasingly free to imagine new possibilities. However, the important part is that the composer is imposing the constraints, making the choices, narrowing the options to see/think/hear more clearly the dialogue between himself or herself and the musical work. Indeed, Van Ernst (1993) has noted that the most popular tasks are those that students set for themselves.

Views on the roles of freedom and constraint within task design remain split. Kratus (1989) has suggested that limiting tools and material usage can make tasks more approachable, while Paynter (1992) suggests that the same will hamper artistic freedom. The difference of opinion undoubtedly lies in the possibility that each student experiences freedoms and constraints differently within the context of their work (Kaschub, 1999; Smith, 2004). Students encountering new compositional challenges may find tighter task structures to serve as a useful guide. However, composers who are engaged in projects similar to those they have already experienced often seek additional freedoms to make a familiar project artistically challenging.

Wiggins (1999) has cautioned that the restrictions placed on tasks by teachers in attempts to scaffold learning or ensure successful products sometimes unintentionally focus students on the "game-like parameters of the assignment instead of the quality of the product or what it will express" (p. 31). Further, too many rules can force children into being self-absorbed by what they are doing wrong to the point that they cannot figure out what they are doing correctly. Finding the appropriate balance of freedoms and constraints for each composer is important since it will allow task structures to fulfill their role in supporting compositional growth.

Creating Definable Tasks

Composers must define their own problems and challenges even within tasks that are designed and assigned by teachers. Framing the compositional process involves discovering relationships "between creativity and problem-solving, and the extent of involvement in problem-solving, -setting, or -seeking which influences how students compose" (Burnard & Younker, 2004, p. 71). Therefore, the tasks that teachers set for students must be structured in ways that allow students to identify and define the compositional problem in their own terms.

The process of task definition can be influenced by a variety of factors. Composers begin evaluating tasks by considering what skills, knowledge, and prior experiences they can call upon. Performer-composers tend to view tasks in light of their personal performance abilities. They interpret tasks in ways that are compatible with their performance skills (Burnard, 1995). Similarly, composers working in groups extend this personal reflection to analysis of their peers. Each member of the composing group has skills to offer, but collectively the group must also develop a shared understanding of the problem before group work can smoothly progress (Morgan et al., 1997).

Within every task, students should engage in analytical, creative, and judicial thinking. Composition tasks comprise many smaller tasks that require students to analyze problems, generate possible solutions, and judge possible answers as appropriate or not. It is important that this thinking process not be delineated by the teacher and provided to the composer. The composer should discover the thought process through interaction with music materials. Close attention must be given to the progress that students make in self-defining projects, as well as the tasks that are provided by teachers. Students should define and undertake progressively more challenging tasks as their experiential base develops.

Influences of Time

Time is also an influential factor in framing task structures. When feeling the pinch of the all-too-short class period, teachers sometimes provide task structures designed to quickly lead to successful products. Attempts to speed up the process may lead to the exclusion of steps that students need to experience. While satisfactory products are certainly a goal, they are also part of a larger equation that must balance process and product to allow for the greatest range of musical learning to take place.

Time constraints can also alter students' work. Composers forced to complete products within a given time frame may abridge or abandon natural processes to bring work completion. While studies designed to highlight particular skills or devices are often employed with time limitations, true composition projects should have more flexible time parameters to allow students to fully and satisfactorily engage in the process.

THE TEACHER'S ROLE IN IMPLEMENTING INSTRUCTION

Many of the tasks that teachers undertake as students study composition fall into the category of "assumed." Curriculum development, materials preparation, staging spaces, arranging groups, providing resources, communicating with composers and performers, and working with performance space managers are simply par for the course. Though very important, all of these activities serve to provide a framework for the most important aspect of teaching composition: teacher and student interactions. As Berkley

(2001) has noted, "Teaching composition is more than delivering compositional technique. The teacher directs and guides students toward successful goals, enabling them to decide for themselves what works most effectively in the particular musical situation" (p. 127).

Very few research studies have directly examined the role of the teacher in implementing instruction as children learn to compose. Literature broadly addressing composition typically features teachers who have become researchers and returned to the classroom or rehearsal hall to gather data. Research conducted from this perspective is naturally somewhat biased. Because it is difficult for the researcher-self to objectively monitor the teacher-self, the teacher's role was often assumed rather than scrutinized. A second bias area is that teachers (now researchers) who are accustomed to monitoring student learning processes and products usually sought to formally document those processes and products. This also drew attention away from the work of the teacher.

It is clear from descriptions of music teaching in a variety of settings that teaching composition presents challenges that differ from those experienced in other areas of music instruction. Composition teaching is different from ensemble-based teaching in that representations of the intended product are not present at the outset of the planning and implementation process. The activities of singing, playing, moving, and listening all require the presence of music—either auditory or in print—at the outset of the activity. Generative activity, however, begins anew. Before the teacher can begin to guide a student in the development of intention, expressivity, or artistic craftsmanship, the student must present something that she has made. It is from this presentation of the student's work that the teacher begins to ask the questions that enable a drawing out of what the student already knows. Composition pedagogy, therefore, evolves in parallel with the composition process itself.

Teachers can best assist young composers by listening to their music as well as their comments before providing feedback. As Wiggins (1999/2000) has noted, "Engagement in creative processes makes tacit knowledge overt" (p. 65). Listening to children's products, however, yields very different information about learning than does listening to children's descriptions of processes. It is important to remember that teachers hear through adult ears that have been subjected to very specific sociocultural training. Children may listen very differently (Nawrot, 2003). Children's explanations of their intentions, frustrations, and successes will serve to more broadly educate the teacher about the students' musical thinking.

The feedback that teachers provide to students must spring from a discussion of the student work that begins in a place that the students find meaningful (Allsup, 2002; Webster, 2003; Wiggins, 1994; Younker, 2003). From this starting point, teachers can simply ask questions and listen.

As composers attempt to explain their work to an "outsider," their own perceptions are strengthened and refined. This process of questioning and listening often coaxes a solution to the current challenge with very little teacher intervention at all.

Barrett (2006) noted twelve strategies used during the interactions between a teacher and student to propel student thinking. The strategies included the following: extending thinking by providing possibilities; referencing works to and beyond tradition; setting parameters for composer identity; provoking students to describe and explain; questioning purpose and intention; shifting between macro and micro levels; providing multiple alternative analysis of the students' work; prompting the student to engage in self-analysis; encouraging goal setting and task identification; sharing problem finding and solving; providing reassurance; and giving the student permission to change course (pp. 201–2). Many of these same strategies are found in the "implications for practice/teaching" at the conclusion of other research studies (Kaschub, 2007; Ruthmann, 2005; Wiggins, 1999/2000).

Unfortunately, teachers may unknowingly hinder student growth. As Ruthmann (2005) has noted, personal agency is a highly influential factor in teacher-student interactions. For any given project, students and teachers each possess mental images of what products will emerge. When the teacher attempts to guide students toward conceptions of what is musically correct, the voice of the student composer can be lost. Telling students how to alter pieces to fit conventions does not advance the student's compositional palette and may well discourage future efforts by dulling motivation and interest.

Providing students sufficient freedom to express their understandings and make meaning through composing occurs when teachers allow for personal artistic understandings to be used. Barrett (2003) mindfully cautions that composing is a powerful personal experience. As such, the potential for negative feedback to be harmful is high. This is especially true in classroom settings where both group and individual composition may occur. Honoring personal voice, musical agency, and creative intentions of every student (Allsup, 2002; Ruthmann, 2005; Stauffer, 2003) is paramount in the learning process. Students can learn about their own work as they are guided to see the implications and consequences of the musical choices they have made and that have been made by others.

As teachers of composition, it is important to be mindful of the fact that aural images are very difficult to share. Teachers cannot access *all* that the children can imagine in sound. Observing children in the process of composition provides access to their "music think." It is the most direct way teachers have of capturing how the students work with music. Their thinking is revealed in musical sounds, verbalizations about sound, and the gestural choices their physical motions may reveal. The musicianship that they employ as they make compositional decisions reveals their aesthetic values. In this way, young composers are like books waiting to be read. Each holds a unique story, even when the theme is familiar.

Teaching music composition is exciting. So much of music teaching features lessons designed to guide children to a predetermined end. Ensembles prepare to perform music where the intention of the composer has been captured, to a certain degree, in the score. The processes of composition offer no such pre-set conclusion. The number of variables in any composition lesson is at least minimally equivalent to the nature and needs of every individual child that enters the room. The possibilities are quite literally endless.

II

CONCEPTUALIZING COMPOSITIONAL PEDAGOGY

4

Preparing for Composing

The late afternoon sunlight streamed across the floor and onto the empty risers. Ms. Jones sat at her desk and stared thoughtfully into her empty classroom. She had just returned from a meeting with her principal, Ms. Clement. Ms. Clement wanted to hold a competition to create a school song. The school was a new one and she felt a school song would help build a spirit of unity among the students. Ms. Jones was new to the school as well, but she had been teaching for several years before arriving at this school in September. It was now October and she had conducted several assessments to allow her to get to know her students and their levels of musical skill and understanding. While some of the students played piano or other instruments, most indicated on her surveys that they had never made up music of their own. Ms. Jones was surprised to find this because composing was included in district curriculum guides as well as state and national standards for music education. She had done a few group composition projects in her previous school, but none had included songwriting. She wondered where to begin this schoolwide activity and how to plan for student success so that there would be a variety of good songs from which the school song could be selected.

There are many things to consider when planning for composition projects with students. Chapter 2 discussed one of those in some detail: compositional context. That is revisited briefly in this chapter in the context of composer characteristics. Similarly, the compositional principles introduced in chapter 1 are referred to here. This chapter also considers the tools of creation and preservation that students have available to use. When thinking about planning composition projects, prerequisites and task guidelines are the focus. Finally, there are some suggestions regarding the assessment of students' compositions and the connections that can be made to other areas of music instruction as well as other curricula. Readers may find it useful to follow along using the composition-planning chart below as a guide while reading this chapter. It represents a summary of the chapter content.

CRITICAL COMPONENTS

Unit: Project: Level: Overview:	
Planning Elements	*Thinking Guides*
Composer Characteristics	Grade level: Skill level: Setting: Time:
Focus and Supporting Principles	Motion/stasis Unity/variety Stability/instability Tension/release Sound/silence
Compositional Capacities (When?)	Intention Expressivity Artistic craftsmanship
Compositional Context	Ensemble Large group Small group Partnered Individual
Tools	Instruments: Classroom, band, orchestra, keyboards, guitars, recorders, voices, computers Preservations: Invented or traditional notation, recordings
Prerequisites	Concepts: Musical skills: Intuitive understandings:
Co-compositional Activities (When?)	Singing Playing Improvisation Listening Moving
Task Guidelines	Product: Length: Specs: Time: Preservation: Performance:
Assessments	What? How? Why?
Connections	To past or future music lessons: To other disciplines:

COMPOSER CHARACTERISTICS

Grade and Skill Levels

One of the first considerations in planning for composition experiences is the age of the students. Planning compositional activities for a class of five- and six-year-olds is quite different from planning for a group of seventh graders. Children's natural abilities and interests vary significantly by age and contribute to their success as composers.

Similarly, it is important to consider their skill level both as performers and as composers. Students who have had some successful composing experiences may approach a new composing task quite differently from those who are composing for the first time. Those with several years of private instrumental instruction may also approach a composition task differently from students who have never studied an instrument. This is particularly true of pianists and guitarists who have experience in working with more than one line of sound at a time. Knowing about the background of the students can help teachers plan more appropriate instruction.

Teachers in public schools also need to plan for children with exceptional needs in their classes. They must consider any modifications that may be required by the child's individual education plans. These children, too, need to experience the joy of creation and can experience success if the lessons are created to take advantage of their specific abilities.

Setting and Time

The next thing to consider is where the children compose. Will they work on their pieces only at school? If so, will that work be done only during music class time?

Certainly, working only in school during class time might be appropriate for compositional études that teachers assign to highlight a particular technique. Yet even with group compositions, it might be possible for the work to continue outside of school. For some types of music ensembles, a location outside of school might be the preferred setting for a group composition. Individuals also may work better outside of the school in a familiar place. Their pieces then may be brought to school and performed for their peers and teachers.

The setting may also impact what resources the student has at his or her command. The resources of a computer lab differ from those of a private clarinet studio. The resources available at home in the student's bedroom are not the same as those of a rehearsal hall. Where composing takes place has always had a direct influence on the works created and the processes that composers use. Composition can take place anywhere the composer chooses to compose. Part III of this book includes examples from rehearsal halls, computer labs, private studios, classrooms, and home. Some of the examples require extensive materials and equipment. Most can be done with less elaborate materials.

Similarly, consider how long the student has to create the composition. It is quite different to have to summon all of one's resources in a thirty-minute class and create a product than it is to have a couple of months to create, extend, revise, and edit a composition. Often teachers allow too little time for the product to emerge. This may be especially true for group composition, where the creators need time to collaborate as well as to create. While the needs of a classroom curriculum may necessitate that there be a time limit of some sort, that limit should be as generous as possible to allow time for creative solutions to surface.

The first solution a student discovers is not always the best one, and it takes time for other ideas to occur to the student. Teachers need to encourage students to seek a variety of solutions to compositional problems and then to choose among them. This often requires more than one class period or lesson. Still, when making a plan, teachers need to estimate how long it will take the student to complete the piece. They then can decide how much time to allocate to the project. Composers often work under some kind of deadline as to when the composition must be completed. Students need a sense of closure as well. While it is important not to have closure too soon, it is also important not to allow the process to continue indefinitely. There are other pieces and projects to create.

FOCUS AND SUPPORTING PRINCIPLES

The principles of sound and silence, motion and stasis, unity and variety, tension and release, and stability and instability have been introduced and discussed in previous chapters. Focusing on principles helps students create more expressive pieces. In lesson planning, the teacher must guide students to consider the relationship between the principles that they are selecting and the responses they expect people to experience when they hear the composition. Connecting principle relationships to human experience is a fundamental compositional skill.

Beginning students tend to create pieces that reflect the continuum extremes of the principles. They may create pieces that are either highly stable (and quite repetitious) or highly unstable in that they lack any sense of cohesion (no repetition). Students benefit from creating compositional études (a composing exercise to teach a particular technique or concept) to explore how repetition can be used to balance stability and instability and draw the listener into a work.

Even though stability and instability served as the focus of the previous example, the principles rarely operate in isolation. While a lesson may have a specific emphasis on one of the principles, the others undoubtedly are included as well. Teachers should choose a principle for étudinal focus; but then include the others as appropriate. Each of the principles can be applied to many musical tasks. As teachers plan instruction, they should think about the many ways that principles can impact task design. They can then decide which seems the most logical for what they wish to accomplish and make it explicit to the students at some point in their instruction.

When planning compositional études that focus students' attention on principle relationships, teachers may wish to focus on particular musical elements or techniques. As they consider the ways they might teach such things as rondo form or motivic repetition, they can consider which of the principles might effectively enhance the musicality of the pieces, or which exemplify the specific concept or technique. Certainly, both rondo and motivic repetition emphasize unity and variety, although to differing degrees of emphasis and structure. Similarly, explorations of tone color and dynamics both emphasize sound quality and are related to sound and silence. The emphasis here is that the principles should be kept in mind so that musicality and expressivity are encouraged, even in creations that the students may well regard as exercises rather than compositions.

The elements of music are the tools a composer uses to express the musical principles. These elements can be grouped into three loose groups: elements of time (form, meter, rhythm, tempo); elements of pitch (tonality, melody, harmony); and elements of expression (dynamics, texture, tone color, articulation). Excellent lessons on any one element can fail to produce expressive compositions. Combining the principles with an emphasis on one or more of the elements usually results in something more musical. Principles are expressed in elements combined with compositional techniques. Conscious structuring of all three can lead to more expressive musical creations.

COMPOSITIONAL CAPACITIES

Compositional capacities are the capabilities of the students to make choices regarding feelingful intentions and product intentions, expressive qualities and artistic craftsmanship. These have been extensively discussed in chapter 2. However, two questions should be considered while planning composition experiences: (1) how to include all three in the compositional process and (2) when to discuss each of these with students.

Intention

Intention is included on the planning template to remind teachers to plan for when they discuss compositional intention with the composers. They must establish who is determining the intention to compose and to what degree. Intention might seem to be an either-or proposition. Either the intention is dictated by the teacher or left to the students. However, even when the teacher determines the composing activity, there is often space for students to add their own intentionality to the task if they are encouraged to do so.

For example, a teacher might create a task where the students are asked to create a scary-sounding piece. Students might on their own decide to use the assignment to tell a sonic story or to create a soundtrack for a story they already know. At some point a question about intention would need to be asked in order for that feelingful intention to be made explicit. Often this occurs just before or after the piece is performed.

Asking questions can also make explicit the composers' intentions even when they have composed a work on their own. Such questions as, "What is this piece about?" or "What feeling were you trying to evoke?" lead to discussions of composer intention and its expressive success. These questions can come at the end of the process, but often can also facilitate action if the young composer seems to be experiencing some difficulty during the process.

Expressivity

Teachers should discuss expressivity with the composers. Questions about expressivity may be necessary in order for children's expressive capabilities to expand. Sometimes this occurs as they listen to one another's compositions; at other times, it can occur while listening as part of a co-compositional activity. The point is that expressivity should be a focus in each composition project at some point. Teachers should plan when questions about it might occur. Expressivity is the foundational relationship between sound and feeling. Those relationships should be made explicit whenever possible to help young composers discover the skills of artistic craftsmanship.

Artistic Craftsmanship

Artistic craftsmanship is often the easiest of the compositional capacities for teachers to include in their plans. The difficult thing is to not let craftsmanship dominate the composing task. While teachers should certainly encourage growth in compositional artistry, it must be predicated on a growth in expressive intent. Otherwise, the techniques will be meaningless to the composers and the resulting pieces often less than satisfactory to all concerned. Craftsmanship should spring from a need to express something which the composer feels but lacks the skills to express.

Teaching the skills of composition works best when the lesson is prompted by a question from the composer. When a student asks how to do something, the teacher can ask leading questions, demonstrate, and provide examples. This is also the best time to create compositional études to practice these newer skills that have interested the young composers. These études are deliberately intended to be exercises and often not regarded as compositions by their creators since they are quite teacher directed. However, the techniques made explicit by the études often appear in subsequent works, and some students use the structure of the étude to create intentionally expressive examples of the technique.

Finally, artistic craftsmanship is evident in varying degrees in the works young composers create. This provides an opportunity for discussing with the composer why a particular technique or skill was used and how it impacted compositional choices. Teacher-facilitated discussions in group contexts are enlightening, not only for the composer of the piece under discussion, but for others in the group as well.

COMPOSITIONAL CONTEXT

Students create music within the compositional contexts that take place in a physical setting. The compositional context refers to the social aspects of that setting, while the physical location may be a rehearsal room, a classroom, or other space. Are students composing as part of an entire ensemble, such as, for example, a high-school choir? They might do this in conjunction with a guest composer who creates a work with them that they subsequently perform.

Similarly, is it an entire class composing a piece together for some purpose? In the primary grades chapter in part III, the "Song for Our Teacher" lesson does this. Is this a group compositional activity where a small group or a small ensemble work together to create a piece? Examples of this can be found in the middle-school sections of part III. Having partners compose together works especially well with novice composers and students at about the ages of seven and eight. Of course, individuals of all ages can also create pieces on their own. From the songs that preschoolers make up to accompany their play to adult singer-songwriters, individuals create music to express their own feelings.

Choosing a context for composing is often at least in part determined by the setting. Group compositions are not usually possible in private lessons. Finding time for individual composing in an elementary general music setting can be daunting. Still, creative teachers find ways to help their student musicians compose in a variety of contexts regardless of the setting. In a class setting, students can compose a single piece together, break into small groups and create group pieces, work in pairs, or work individually.

Students' work preferences should be considered when determining appropriate compositional contexts. Some students prefer to work with partners, while others want to work in small groups or even by themselves. As students gain compositional experience, they are likely to develop a preferred working style. At least at the early stages, it may be wise to see that students experience working in a variety of contexts so that one context does not dominate simply from lack of exposure to the others.

Students who create only in small groups may not appreciate the value of working with only one partner or by themselves. Some students find the whole class approach very limiting and are eager to work in a small group. Student guitarists often enjoy working with a student drummer or bassist as they create new pieces. Throughout their schooling, students should have the opportunity to experience composing in a variety of contexts. This usually requires deliberate planning on their teachers' part.

TOOLS FOR COMPOSING

The setting may partly determine the tools of sound production and of preservation that are available for composing. If the setting is a computer lab, composers have access to the myriad sounds on the computer and the Internet. However, many programs allow for sound input, and the students can play or sing in tracks that they create on acoustic instruments.

Still, there are some limitations to be kept in mind before beginning compositions on computers. A computer screen limits the literal vision of the piece. It reduces to just a few measures what can be in sight at a time regardless of whether students are using notation, graphics, or looping programs. This can allow the wholeness of a work to become blurred or lost, especially with young or inexperienced composers. Some composers who work at computers surround themselves with visual reminders of their musical sketch or plan to compensate for this.

Computers also allow for a different kind of composing—composing in the absence of sound. It is possible to create a work visually by various means without listening to it until the student feels it is finished. It is up to the skillful teacher to keep the emphasis on thinking and creating in sound. Visuals should be an aid to composing, not a replacement for hearing what is being created. The goal is to think in sound and not just create a picture or graphic that one then listens to once the visual aspects are complete.

In a general music classroom it may be necessary to provide some means of sharing instruments. The teacher needs to decide whether the children will choose the instruments from all those available, whether groups will have matching sets of instruments, or whether each group will have different sets of sounds. If the students work at home on their pieces, they may need sounds to use. Usually an instrument that they can play or a computer is the best source for those sounds, but students sometimes find other sounds to use as well.

It is important to remember that the voice is a source of many sounds. Even if this is the only tool available, composition can still take place. Some people compose by using only their voices, and some composers find it necessary to sing to themselves as they work. The human voice is not limited to singing and may create an extensive array of both pitched and percussive sounds.

Found sounds—such as those of keys rattling or metal wastebaskets being tapped with pens, rulers, or shoes—can become sound sources for composing. Even a sheet of newspaper can be used to create a variety of sounds that can then be combined in interesting ways (see Schafer, 1967). Students can be quite inventive when it comes to creating their own musical instruments. This also gives them a chance to explore the ways sounds are made and changed. It can be extended even further if these invented instruments then become the basis of a composition.

Similarly, composition should be a part of instrumental music lessons almost from the very beginning. This applies to piano, recorder, guitar, wind, and percussion instruments and beginning strings classes. Progress in playing technique and understanding notation goes much faster when students are trying to figure out ways to create their own music and preserve it to share with others. Creating a piece based on the first few notes beginners master pretty much guarantees that students will spend a good amount of time playing those notes. This is particularly true if teachers focus some attention on the musical principles used in the pieces in the students' method books and suggest that the students create pieces to share in their next lesson. One of the quickest ways to teach musical tension and release and the effect of dissonance is to have instrumental students create duets. The subsequent discussions with the students about what was intended and how things sounded can be very educational.

Over the course of students' musical education, they should have the opportunity to explore and create with a variety of tools. People do not expect students to learn to use pencils, crayons, paint, and computers all at once, but rather at different times and for different purposes. Similarly, teachers should guide students' exposure to the available tools used for musical creation and help them to select the most appropriate tools for their work.

THE TOOLS OF PRESERVATION

Once students begin to create pieces, they need a means of preserving their work. Initially this should be in some format that does not require students to know standard music notation. One of the quickest ways to discourage budding composers is to insist that they notate their music or to limit their compositions to only what they know how to write in standard notation. There are other means of preserving the work of beginning composers.

Just as beginning writers often use invented spelling and pictures to tell their first stories, beginning composers can invent graphic notations or other symbol systems to help them remember what they create. Pieces may also be recorded on computers or other recording devices. Later a teacher or other knowledgeable musician can transcribe the recordings to create traditional scores. Student work and transcriptions can be kept in the composers' paper sketchbooks or on their computers. Computer-based sketchbooks can easily house songs composers have sung into it, parts of incomplete pieces, and ideas for future pieces.

Always ask whether notation is necessary for the students. Does invented notation solve a memory issue? Does it allow students to work on a project across multiple class periods? Is it setting up the need for a more formalized system of notation? Is it simply creating a record of a project? Notation for the sake of notation is not a musical goal. Indeed, taking time to create notation because the teacher has required it may decrease the amount of time the students spend thinking critically and artistically about their compositions.

Finally, pieces can sometimes be preserved in standard musical notation. While not all creative works lend themselves to this format, it is one that has served musicians long and well and should eventually be a part of compositional training. However, it should not be used with young, beginning composers but postponed until they have some experience creating in sound. It has been our experience that children learn notation fastest when they have something they want to write down. There is no faster way to teach them standard notation than to have them attempt to write down something they have created and then to help them improve its accuracy. More will be said about this in chapter 8.

PREREQUSITES

With beginners of all ages and very young students, it is usually best to begin with as few prerequisites as possible, and that usually means with almost none. The "Sonic Snowstorm" lesson that follows is an example of a composing lesson that has very few prerequisites. The students need to know what a snowstorm is like, but even that can easily be taught through discussion. They have additional intuitive knowledge about how music works, such as that it has a beginning, middle, and end. They need the ability to follow directions in a group setting. Beyond that, they need little additional knowledge or skill to participate successfully in the composition.

SONIC SNOWSTORM

Unit: Wintry Music
Project: Sonic Snowstorm
Level: Novice
Overview: Prepare a collection of instruments that make metallic sounds (small suspended cymbals with mallets, triangles, jingle bells, finger cymbals, tambourines shaken, etc.) and have one for each child in class. Ask how a snowstorm begins. After taking several responses, direct attention to the fact that snowstorms often begin with just a few flakes and that gradually more and more snowflakes fall. Discuss that the snow becomes very thick and that the wind may blow off and on or steadily. Guide the conversation and help the class decide that snowstorms often end with a gradual diminishment of snow and the sun coming out. Review cuing and cutoffs and dynamics for conducting or teach it. Give these directions: "When I point to you, begin playing your instrument quietly. When everyone is playing, watch me for the signal to play louder or quieter. After a bit, I will look at you and give you a cutoff. You will stop playing one at a time." After several practice attempts, record the children's efforts and play it back to them. Invite various children to be the conductor and have the class create snowstorms that are recorded and discussed similarly.

Planning Elements	Thinking Guides
Composer Characteristics	Grade level: K Skill level: Novice Setting: Classroom Time allocation: Three lessons
Focus and Supporting Principles	Principle: Repetition/contrast in the creation of a beginning/middle/end form Principle: Unity/variety to produce the sounds of a snowstorm through texture and timbre
Compositional Capacities	Intention: Teacher established; capture the feeling of a snowstorm Expressivity: Beginning and during; how do we sonify a snowstorm? Artistic craftsmanship: Enacted through performance
Compositional Context	Whole class, group activity
Tools	Many metallic percussion instruments in a variety of pitch ranges
Prerequisites	Familiarity with snowstorms
Co-compositional Activities	Discussion of what happens during a snowstorm: beginning, middle, end Listening map and experience based on "Snow Is Dancing" by Debussy

Planning Elements	Thinking Guides
Task Guidelines	Product: Percussion sound pieces Length: Thirty seconds to three minutes Spec: Create a sonic snowstorm that has a clear beginning, middle, and end. Start and end with only a few sounds. Get louder and quieter during the piece. Teacher and students take turns acting as the conductor/composer. Time: Twenty minutes Preservation: Recording of class Performance: Group for classmates
Assessment	Are students able to use repetition/contrast to create a beginning/middle/end form? Are students able to use texture to create unity/variety to differentiate between formal sections? Are students able to select and employ timbres effectively to create unity/variety within the snowstorm?
Connections	Similar activity with rainstorms (other natural events) using a wider selection of percussion instruments Other pieces, poems, etc., about snow

However, as students progress beyond the beginner stages of composer development, they begin to seek ways to make their pieces more individually expressive and to have their ideas accepted in a group context. It is then that the prerequisites for compositional projects become more important for the teacher to consider. These prerequisites can be grouped into three categories: (1) conceptual knowledge, (2) musical skills, and (3) intuitive knowledge.

Conceptual Knowledge

In the "Sonic Snowstorms" lesson presented above, the knowledge of what a snowstorm is like is an example of conceptual knowledge. In the school song unit mentioned in the vignette at the start of the chapter, a knowledge of what a school song usually is like and what children of all ages and backgrounds agreed was true of their school would be examples of conceptual knowledge. Conceptual knowledge is knowledge about something. Musical knowledge can also be conceptual knowledge. Examples include knowing the difference between "around a line" and "in a space," the typical sections in rondo form, or how to write notation for viola in the C clef. This type of prerequisite is what the children need to know about something in order to complete the task successfully.

Musical Skills

Musical prerequisites include the musical performance skills, the perceptual skills, and the expressive capacities to create in sound. In order to create a duet using a computer program, the student needs to know how to use the computer to open the program, enter information, create, organize, record, and play back the sounds. To write a duet for two recorders it is usually helpful to have the ability to play the recorder. Anything that is related to producing the sounds and preserving them could be considered a technical skill.

Skills related to identifying and understanding sounds are perceptual skills. Tone color recognition is perceptual skill. Distinguishing sounds that move upward, move downward, or stay the same is another. Almost any musical similarities and differences that students need to identify from sound are perceptual skills.

Notice that notation skill is not a musical skill, but rather a conceptual understanding. Remember that it is not necessary that students understand notation in order to create with sound. Notation is a tool for composers to use, not a prerequisite to composing. Musicians without traditional notation skill have created many fine compositions.

The final kind of prerequisite musical skill is that of expressive skills. This is related to the ability to organize sounds with expressive intention. Beginners may not have the technical or perceptual skills to be able to create what they hear in their heads. However, as their skills develop and they become more accustomed to working with the principles of musical expression, they need to be encouraged to expand their abilities to evoke feeling in their pieces. For example, at an intermediate level of compositional skill, a prerequisite to creating music for a scary film clip would be a knowledge of what makes music sound scary to the intended audience. Similarly, creating a march for a solemn occasion such as a graduation or "moving up" ceremony requires a knowledge of what makes music sound solemn. These prerequisites are those of expressive skill.

Intuitive Knowledge

Students enter formal school with many kinds of intuitive knowledge about how music works. They often have a good sense of what constitutes a "song." Many have an intuitive sense of beat and phrasing. They have heard many hours of music on television and through other media. Some have even had formal music experience through early childhood music programs or instrumental lessons with teachers trained in the Suzuki method. Depending on their cultural background, they may have experienced music in many social or religious settings.

During all of this they are absorbing unconsciously an understanding of what music is and how it works. However, that understanding can be quite specifically culturally based. Teachers cannot assume that all students have the necessary intuitive understandings and may need to determine that before beginning. In the vignette at the start of the chapter, the students need to have an intuitive understanding of what a song is and possibly some sort of understanding of the types of purposes a school song might need to fulfill.

Intuitive knowledge can be difficult to assess and often is hard for teachers to predict in the planning process. However, assumptions about intuitive knowledge will quickly be tested when the project begins. Teachers need to think as deeply about these prerequisites as the knowledge of their students allows.

CO-COMPOSITIONAL ACTIVITIES

Whenever possible, teachers should make connections between composing and the other musical behaviors: listening, singing, playing instruments, improvising, and moving. Co-compositional activities are musical engagements that allow children to experience music in multifaceted ways. These are called co-compositional activities because they can go along with composing. Sometimes an activity may precede actual work on a composition, sometimes it may occur during a break in the composing work, and sometimes it may occur after composing is completed to point out how other composers have solved similar compositional problems. These may occur naturally during the course of a project. The teaching context often determines when to use a co-compositional activity.

There are many ways to use co-compositional activities to enhance composition study. In the "Sonic Snowstorm" lesson presented above, the co-compositional listening activity using Debussy's "Snow Is Dancing" could occur before the composing activity, in between conductors during the activity, or after doing the activity.

The co-compositional activity uses a listening map, but the youngest students also enjoy doing a movement activity where they all begin curled on the floor and rise to move like floating snowflakes when tapped gently on the head by the "snow fairy" (teacher). During the B section they run as if blown by the wind (no bumping allowed) and, as the music becomes less energetic, they drift to the ground until the sun comes out (the end). This movement activity helps build an intuitive sense of motion and stasis that perhaps must be predicated on movement of their bodies. It could be used as a precompositional activity. The listening map could be used following the creation of the snow pieces or a simple listening exercise where the children listen for how a piano can be a snowstorm (a la Debussy) and talk about how it is similar and different from the pieces they created.

Listening as a Co-compositional Activity

In many ways, listening to music is one of the most important co-compositional activities. Philosopher Bennett Reimer (2003) states, "Composing absent a broad repertoire of listening experiences is composing in a vacuum and therefore, in a real sense, composing in ignorance" (p. 260). Listening provides music models before or after composing. This can maximize student understanding of compositional techniques and their means of expression.

Creative decisions are often ruled by stylistic conventions that the students have adopted. To broaden students' options, they must encounter a variety of styles and learn to understand the conventions of each style. Because the music played for students comprises a foundation upon which future composition experiences draw, every effort must be made to ensure that only the music that exhibits the highest degrees of excellence is used. Music of this caliber exists in every genre, but so does music of lesser quality. If students are to discover how the musical principles are used, it should be music that is rich with both expressive gestures and craftsmanship.

Selecting music that works well with students requires careful planning and analysis. As teachers listen to pieces of music, they might consider the following questions:

1. Is this music exemplary of the craftsmanship and quality found within this genre or style?
2. What do my students already know about music?
3. What can my students easily identify in this selection?
4. What can my students be led to hear in this selection? What is its pedagogical value?
5. Is this selection of an appropriate length for my students? Can it be excerpted effectively and musically?
6. What type of activity could my students do to demonstrate their ability to perceive the elements that I wish them to focus on and identify in this selection?

The first time students listen to a piece of music serves to familiarize them with the overall content and character of a piece or logical excerpt. The first question asked of students should be one that they can all answer correctly to ensure feelings of success. As students hear the piece a second time, their attention should be drawn to a particular feature that becomes the focus of the lesson. The question asked this time should lead them to identify the feature.

For the listening experience, ask students to discuss what is happening in specific detail. For example, students might indicate that the flute and trumpet are having a conversation and sharing the melody or taking turns playing, or that the orchestra echoes their parts. The more detail elicited here, the better. It is during this step that teachers should model visually, through mapping or moving or some other representative way, what is happening in the music.

At this point teachers can ask the students to create their own representations (move, draw, write, etc.). If the majority of students seem secure with the skill, it is time to move on with the lesson to another activity. If many students are unable to represent individually the new knowledge, teachers should go back to the point where the attention was drawn to the principle, concept, or element of focus, and clarify it further. Repetition is usually a good thing in listening lessons. It takes time for students' ears to hear in meaningful ways.

Finally, listen simply to enjoy the selection. This final listening puts the music back together holistically. If students are listening to an excerpt, consider hearing it this time within the context of a larger section. The students select their own listening focus during this listening.

Singing as a Co-compositional Activity

The school song unit in the opening vignette might begin with learning to sing some songs of other schools and discussing their various strengths and weaknesses from the point of view of the students who will be composing the new ones. These discussions might also include a technical analysis of what works and does not work musically, particularly with reference to the range of the song and the form it takes (ABA? Verse and chorus? Thirty-two-bar song? Simple four-phrase song?). Discussions of the various ways the musical principles are applied would also be helpful.

Many young composers sing to themselves as they work on their pieces. As one might naturally expect, this seems to be especially true when students are setting texts. Trying to make the music fit the words or the words fit the music may be best tried out by singing them. Students also sing to get the feel of melodic lines, to try out a musical thought, and to test the phrasing of their musical ideas. This is singing to compose, rather than singing for performance or to demonstrate a compositional device or technique.

However, singing performances can also be used to help students understand how composers have used principle relationships, elements, and compositional devices. Teachers can ask leading questions about the music the children are learning to perform. The focus should be on emphasizing the principles, elements, and compositional techniques that were employed by the composer.

Students who are comfortable with their singing voices naturally sing to compose. Even toddlers sing to accompany their play and make up their own tunes as they do. So often children are silenced in school as they work. How wonderful it is to provide them with a space where humming and singing to oneself is expected and accepted.

Playing Instruments and Improvising as Co-compositional Activities

Playing instruments often takes the form of exploring new sound sources and experimenting with the sounds a composer has available. When confronted with a new sound source, most people intuitively begin to play with it to see what it can do. This is exploring the sound possibilities of the sound source. Teachers should allow time for this to happen and encourage finding nontraditional ways to produce sounds on instruments as long as it does not alter the instrument irreversibly.

Experimenting is very much like improvising, except that it is not intended as part of a performance "in the moment" but rather is a search for sounds that might be useful in the work being created. It is using a familiar sound source to search for a musical idea. Even in groups, individual students often experiment with an instrument until they find a beat or a melodic fragment they like, at which point they may share it with the other members of their group. Composers working alone sometimes work out a section of a piece only to reject it and start over when the experimenting does not seem to lead anywhere, or when they decide they do not like the fragment with which they have been working. Novice composers most often find instruments a useful tool to create, modify, and extend their ideas.

Improvisation is creating a performance without the opportunity to revise except in a subsequent performance. The opportunity to reflect on musical creations and to revise them is what distinguishes composition from improvisation. There is a continuum that begins with exploring and experimenting, continues with purely improvisatory performance pieces, and extends at the other end to composed pieces that have benefited from reflection and re-envisioning. In between are many overlapping areas of musical creation. All make use of the principles of music and the compositional capacities to varying degrees. There is probably no useful purpose served by deciding where improvisation ends and composition begins. This is particularly true for works created by novice composers and very young students.

Arranging as a Co-compositional Etude

Creating arrangements for the available instruments to play along with recordings is another way to approach compositional activities. Classroom groups often enjoy creating their own arrangements to accompany the same recording and then analyzing the products each group created. This can lead to further understanding of the musical principles and compositional capacities as they compare and contrast their differing solutions to the same problem. This form of arranging can be a step toward arranging more complicated scores for their compositions or as a way of approaching more complicated arranging tasks. It also helps clarify the differences between what arrangers do and what composers do.

Using Movement to Develop Musical Knowledge and Understanding

Movement and music are synonymous in many cultures. Humans are moving beings, and this natural tendency can be observed among young composers. Consequently, moving to music can be a particularly effective way of acquiring musical understanding. This can be as simple as using hand gestures to trace some aspect of the music in the air or as complicated as designing an interpretive dance to accompany a composition. Movement can often readily convey the musical principles and is especially effective for motion and stasis.

Since some students quite literally need to move in order to learn, movement as a co-compositional activity should be used to demonstrate the music principles and as many compositional techniques as practical. Very young children also often benefit from being able to move to demonstrate their understanding of musical principles and elements. They frequently can demonstrate a bodily understanding of musical feeling long before they can articulate these concepts verbally. Some very young composers need to be able to move to work out their expressive intentions as they make up their own music. They need to enact what it is they are creating.

Teachers can use co-compositional activities as a way to start a unit or to start a lesson within the unit. They can also conclude a lesson or occur in the middle. These directed learning engagements allow students to connect other aspects of musical experience to their composing and allow the teacher to incorporate easily additional conceptual or perceptual learning or further practice using newly acquired skills. Additional examples of co-compositional activities are in each suggested lesson included in the chapters in part III of this book.

TASK GUIDELINES

This book is dedicated to helping teachers teach composition, which implies that in some way they assist the process of learning to compose. However, the range of assistance that teachers provide can vary widely. Not all composing that children do is done in school or at the direction of the teacher. Sometimes they create only for themselves. At other times they may create works they share only with friends or family. Skillful teachers encourage students to share their pieces with them and, at times, with classmates and larger audiences. Composing occurs on a continuum from highly structured composition études designed for some instructional purpose at one end of the spectrum to compositions that students create purely because they have chosen to do so at the other end. Somewhere in the middle is where much composition in schools takes place.

Task guidelines in the planning template (table 4.1) refer to the parameters of the task specified in the directions. It also defines how much of the task the students can decide for themselves. As noted in chapter 3, too much task structure may stifle creativity and result in compositional exercises instead of expressive music. On the other hand, too little task structure can cause novice composers to have difficulty beginning their pieces or organizing them. Task guidelines are efficient and expeditious ways of proceeding pedagogically. However, educators need to consider carefully what impact their directions and procedures have on students.

Typically teachers think of creating more scaffolding of the task for beginners and less for more advanced students, but this is not necessarily true. Much depends on the task and its purpose. Etudes are much more highly structured and carefully scaffolded than are compositions or parts of compositions that children create by themselves and bring to the teacher for feedback and commentary.

According to Reimer (2003), "Students should be asked to identify and solve compositional problems" (p. 111). The authors agree, but with a note of caution: while students need to be engaged in problem finding, teachers must be aware of the size of the problem that students are allowed to create for themselves. It is best to prevent found problems from taking on inhibiting proportions. Young composers should be encouraged to extend the boundaries of their learning, but teachers must at the same time guide students toward a path that allows for the completion of a satisfactory creative work. So some tempering of enthusiasm may be advisable when students select their own compositional projects.

Teachers must also have ideas about what they want children to learn from a composition project. This includes not only the intended product—the piece the student creates—but also what experiences in compositional thinking the student will have while working on the project. It is natural to focus on the eventual product that will be created, but the process may be even more important to what the student learns. Those processes must be included as part of the teacher's creative thinking when designing composition lessons.

Three Kinds of Compositional Thinking

Students should be engaged in three modes of thinking within each task: analytical thinking, critical thinking, and creative thinking. The teacher can play an advisory role in each of these. Initially, teachers may need to explicitly teach these modes of thinking by modeling them in various other activities or on whole-class composition tasks.

Students need to analyze what was included in the directions and then in the resulting composition. This analytical thinking is the basis of the structure of the composition. As a result of analytical thinking, sometimes students make deliberate decisions to alter the stated directions for expressive purposes. This should be encouraged by the teacher and used as a teachable moment for other young composers as well.

Students need to evaluate the appropriateness and effectiveness of their craftsmanship and aesthetic concerns within the composition. This evaluative thinking helps the students create and improve the expressivity of their music. Often it occurs spontaneously in young composers. Long before they have the technical language to explain their choices, they tell questioners that something simply "sounded right" or "just didn't fit."

Finally, they must also think creatively about the possibilities for alternative ways of accomplishing the same tasks. They need to be encouraged not to rush to judgment by accepting their first idea as the best one, even if sometimes it does turn out to be the most appropriate solution. Teachers can model this for students. Student can role-play situations that address valuing everyone's ideas and entertaining several possibilities at once.

Encouraging multiple answers to quick improvisational exercises can be one way of demonstrating this. One example of this is given in chapter 6, in the section on developing music ideas (p. 116–117). Another example could occur in a small group lesson. The students have mastered some short piece from their method books and can play it by ear or from memory. The teacher models a jazzy rhythmic variation on the tune, and then each child takes a turn doing the same. As students become more fluent with this activity, it can lead to more idea generation in other musical settings. This musical brainstorming creates multiple options as young people simply generate as many ideas as possible in a short period of time.

The Role of Sharing

Teachers often believe it is important for students to share their compositions with audiences. However, is this a compositional need or an artifact of educational practice? Educators may need to hear some of the music that a student has created for the purpose of assessment or to determine the course of future instruction. Nevertheless, a piece of music can exist simply in the mind of a composer, or in the composer's own notebooks or recordings. It does not need to be shared publicly in order to be a "real" composition. Students and their teachers should understand that a composition is a means for making meaning, whether it is shared or kept personal. Creations do not need to be shared to be of value. The act of composing is an act of meaning making in sound that assists in the development of the self. It is that personal meaning making that makes the act of composing so valuable and precious to humankind.

Writing Task Guidelines: A Quick Summary

Here is a quick summary of the things teachers should consider when designing task guidelines. Decide on the intended product—is it a compositional étude or a composition? Determine a minimum and maximum length, if any. Specify the musical considerations: are there principles, techniques, or elements that must be included? Determine the allotted work time and class time that is available. Specify the mode of preservation. Decide on the details of sharing or performing the piece and who the intended audience is.

ASSESSING COMPOSITIONS

Chapter 5 deals with this topic in detail, but deciding whether or not student compositions will be assessed or evaluated formally should be part of a teacher's planning process. Here are some things related to assessment to consider while planning:

- Should these compositions receive only feedback or commentary, or should they be assessed more formally?
- If the compositions will be assessed, will they be assessed by composer, the teacher, the composer's peers, or other individuals or groups?
- What tools (checklists, rubrics, etc.) will the assessors use?
- Will the assessment be based on accurate task completion, the musicality of the resulting product, or both?
- How will the assessment be used? If the composition will be subject to formal evaluation, what purpose will that evaluation serve? If the composition is to receive only feedback or commentary, to whom will that be given—the student, the teacher, or both?

All of these issues are considered in greater detail in the next chapter.

MAKING CONNECTIONS: LINKING COMPOSING TO OTHER AREAS OF MUSIC INSTRUCTION AND TO OTHER DISCIPLINES

The section of this chapter on co-compositional activities suggested some ways to connect other areas of music instruction to composing. More suggestions are included in each chapter of part III of this book. Children studying instruments learn the techniques of their instruments more readily, play more expressively, and read notation with more fluency when composition projects are included in their lessons. Young children sing more readily when the teacher listens to and values their songs. Students seem to listen more intently to the works of others when they have created works of their own.

When thinking about composition projects, a wide range of extensions may be possible. Extensions may be found by considering what students could do in the next class after the projects are finished that might be closely related to their projects or a logical extension of their work. Similarly, teachers can consider what the next composing project might be. While it may be easier to think about this after completing the project and consulting the students for their ideas about the next project, the teacher should make a note of any thoughts she has on the topic as she plans.

Finally, there may be a way of extending the work at home. The simplest of these is the request that the child play a recording or perform the piece for the members of his or her household. Completed projects can be sent home with students with an accompanying note from the teacher. Alternatively, the projects can be posted on a school website. Then an e-mail or text message can be sent to parents informing them that the project is available and encouraging them to listen to the piece and support their student's efforts with positive comments.

Sometimes classroom teachers and others have children create new words to familiar tunes and consider that composing. Creating new lyrics is not music composition, but lyric writing. However, many times those activities could become real composition projects if they were done collaboratively between the classroom teachers, the music teachers, and the students they both share.

Many projects involve creating and presenting some sort of assembly or show to demonstrate some area of learning. It is possible for the various teachers who share students to collaborate on such a project. Creating Original Opera, sponsored by Education at the Met in New York, is one process that accomplishes this. This program requires formal training and collaboration between at least one music teacher and one classroom teacher. Students have done productions at various ages from six-year-olds upward and at locations all over the United States. The end result is a public performance that is predicated on original music composed by the children. (See www.metoperafamily.org/education/educators/creating_original.aspx for more information about this program.)

Music teachers are often expected to produce assemblies or shows that are related to some school theme. How much more entertaining these might be to audiences when the children create at least a portion of the materials being presented. Moving-up ceremonies and graduations are perfect opportunities for this type of collaboration, but they require plenty of advance planning and cooperation from everyone involved.

One end-of-year project with primary grades in a first- and second-grade school was called Camp Skeeter (short for mosquito). During the final week of school, the students in grades one and two participated in activities that resembled those one might find at a summer day camp in the woods. Part of the exercise was designing cabin logos for the various camper groups and creating camper theme songs as well. Similarly, kindergarteners can create songs for their teachers (see chapter 7 for details) and sing them at kindergarten graduation ceremonies. Adding music to established and valuable school programs is a wonderful contribution for young composers to make to school life.

While composing is the most intellectually demanding of the musical arts, it is also the most intimate. It draws on all the personal musical experiences that the student has previously had to create a piece and alters the nature of future experiences once the composition has been created. Composing is not a journey into the music, but a journey within music that ultimately leads back to the composer. The nature of music does not change, but the self, the creator, does. The composer has accomplished something and expressed something that alters the way she or he views the musical world.

A SCENARIO: MS. JONES PLANS A PROJECT ON CREATING A SCHOOL SONG

Ms. Jones turned to her bookshelf and removed her copy of *Minds on Music: Composition for Creative and Critical Thinking*. She flipped to the page where the blank composition-planning template was located. As she looked at it, she began to think about the various issues involved in composing a school song. Most of her students were at the beginner level of composing. She decided that the competition would be open to anyone but that she would focus her efforts on her fourth and fifth graders, who were the oldest students in her school.

She would plan some lessons that were co-compositional lessons but would allow the children to work independently on their pieces at home if they wished. Ms. Clement was hoping to have a song as soon as possible, so Ms. Jones decided six weeks would be about right. This would give about two weeks to plan thoroughly her lessons and locate materials, and two weeks for instruction. The children would have to turn in their songs on December 1, and the voting for the winning song could take place before the winter holiday break.

Ms. Jones decided to take this opportunity to introduce most of the musical principles to the children and not to focus on any one principle specifically. She decided to encourage the children to work on their songs individually or with a partner. She also decided to talk about famous song-writing teams such as Gilbert and Sullivan and Rogers and Hammerstein and to play some examples of their work as a co-compositional activity.

The children would be allowed to use any tools they wanted to create and preserve their compositions. Because Ms. Jones had a good ear and a strong theory background, she felt she could transcribe whatever the children created into standard notation. She did feel that the song would have to be singable and able to be written down so that others could perform it. She knew the children would need some experiences with school songs to help them understand what made a suitable school song. She also knew they would need help with text setting. She decided that all classes would try to write a song as whole classes in the next few weeks so that she could help them with some ideas about how text fits music.

For guidelines, she decided to limit the songs to no more than eight phrases, that the range should be from middle C to fourth-space E, and that most of the notes should be on the lower end of that range. The words should be an original poem about the school that rhymes and that would be understood by the youngest children, but not too simple for older children.

Ms. Jones decided to brainstorm possible topics to include in a school song before singing songs from other schools and to add to the list as appropriate ideas came up while they were singing. This list would remain posted in the classroom, and copies would be available for the children to take home. The children would be reminded weekly about the contest. They would be encouraged to bring Ms. Jones a recording or score of their songs when they were finished or to come in and sing them for her if they could not write them down or record them at home.

The children would be told that a panel of judges who were musicians and teachers would be listening to their songs without knowing whose song was being heard, and would select five songs that the school would then vote on to select a winner.

The chorus would "premiere" the song ("What a great way to teach this musical term," thought Ms. Jones) at their February concert.

Ms. Jones sat back and smiled. Tomorrow she would begin planning the specific lessons to introduce the project to the children. She would e-mail a few of her colleagues from other schools to see whether they could send her copies of their school songs, and she would find a copy of the song from her previous school. This was beginning to look like a great way to teach the children a lot about singing, songs, and composition.

SCHOOL SONG FOR OUR NEW SCHOOL

Unit: Composing a School Song Project: School Song for Our New School Level: Intermediate	
Planning Elements	*Thinking Guides*
Composer Characteristics	Grade level: Third through fifth Skill level: Better for intermediate and advanced Setting: Classroom and home Time allocation estimate: Two classes and work at home Completion in one month
Focus Principle (Supporting Principles)	All will apply. No specific focus.
Compositional Capacities	Intention: Teacher directed but student involvement Expressive: Feelings of school pride and solidarity Artistic craftsmanship: Text setting; qualities of a march
Compositional Context	Probably mostly individual, but allow for partners
Tools	Instruments: Whatever the student can play, including voice Preservation: Invented or traditional notation, recordings as suits the skill level of the child
Prerequisites	Concepts: What is a school song, lines that rhyme Musical skills: Performance skill helpful, text setting Intuitive understandings: Balanced phrases, sense of tonality and meter
Co-compositional Activities	Singing other school songs
Task Guidelines	Product: A song with lyrics Length: Eight lines Spec: Range from middle C to fourth-space E; easily sung Time: One month Preservation: Recording or score or both Performance: Must be able to perform it for the teacher
Assessment	What: By a panel of judges who will pick four–five finalists. School will then vote. How: Discussion among the judges and within classrooms; voting
Connections	Chorus to premiere the song at the winter concert. Older classes may help create the arrangement. All classes will learn the winning song after it is chosen.

5

Assessment

It is the human, value-edged, perceptual response to stimulation, to the being or doing . . . that is the essence.

—Robert Stake et al.

Many educators might suggest that assessment, evaluation, and grading are synonyms, but this chapter distinguishes among them and suggests appropriate school-based uses of each in the composition program. Assessment comes from the Latin *assidere*, which means "to sit beside." Assessment in the composition program is formative. It helps the student and the teacher form an opinion of what has been accomplished thus far and points to possible next steps. The primary purposes of assessment are to improve learning and determine progress. Assessment can also help determine the appropriateness and effectiveness of instruction.

Evaluation, by contrast, summarizes achievement to date. It comes from the Latin *ex*, "from," and the French word for value, and so its meaning is "to take value from." It is the process of determining the quality of some achievement or of some product. Evaluation is done at a stopping point and may lead to a rating or a grade. Evaluations are used to determine winners of some type of competition, for example, a composition contest. Formal evaluations may also be used to determine grades.

Grades are a process for symbolizing the results of an evaluation. Not all evaluations lead to grades, nor must they necessarily lead to winners and losers. Grades can only summarize a complex and lengthy process. Often they are not the best way to convey information about student progress to the various stakeholders in the educational process. This is especially true of the compositions children create. A grade does not begin to convey the ideas and values that direct contact with the children's work can communicate. Still, grades are widely used in schools, and teachers may be expected to assign grades when composition is taught in a school setting. However, this chapter suggests some rich alternatives to traditional grading practices.

THE ROLE AND USES OF ASSESSMENT
IN TEACHING COMPOSITION

All students need to feel capable of learning. A supportive community of composing peers can help motivate them to learn. One of the most valuable parts of the community of learners is the availability and frequency of constructive, useful feedback on works in progress. This directly involves them in the learning and assessment processes.

The sharing of partial pieces often leads to teachable moments for the teacher and to valuable suggestions from the other young composers. Assessment is a seamless process in a workshop setting. All composers can have a turn to present their creations to date, discuss their intentions, and see audience reaction.

This may be best accomplished in small groups while others continue to work. Several composers sit with one another and the teacher. A composition is performed, and the group asks questions and offers comments. After several different performances, the composers return to their work and another group can assemble with the teacher. While this can be done with a whole class, small groups seem to work better. Five seems to be about the maximum effective number for keeping everyone focused on the task at hand. Three is even better. Everyone is usually eager to get back to work on the pieces. Asking them to listen to and comment on too many pieces frustrates that desire. Much more is said about composing communities and the feedback they provide in chapter 6.

Teachers must also constantly assess where the composer is going with the piece, whether guidance is warranted, and how to guide that process. Sometimes this includes doing a lesson for the class (or a small group) with appropriate co-compositional activities that can present ideas or techniques for composers to use. This requires that the teacher listen very carefully not only to the young composer's piece, but also to what the composer has to say about that piece. For example, if a student is trying to create a duet for two instruments and has assigned the melody always to one part, a teacher might bring in examples of two-voice writing that have a more equal distribution between the voices. These might be used for a listening lesson and analyzed for the techniques the composer used. The suggestion could then gently be made that this is a good idea in duet writing. All of this is predicated on the teacher's assessment of the student's composition so far.

However, it would be up to the child composer whether or not to incorporate those techniques. It is the teacher's role to suggest, but not to request. Those decisions must be made by the child in order for the child to continue to feel ownership of the composition. When offering suggestions, teachers should probably almost always end with, "But it is really up to you. It is your piece, and you need to decide."

Another use of assessment can be to see whether the students have mastered particular content that the teacher has presented. This can sometimes be done through the use of compositional études. These are short exercises that the teacher asks the students to complete to demonstrate competency. Using the duet example above, the teacher might request that everyone in class create a two-part recorder duet that has at least eight measures and shares the melody between the two voices in one of the ways used in the examples presented in class. This technique could also be used before the presentation of the co-compositional activity to see for whom the lesson might be helpful. Students who already can complete the étude successfully might not benefit from the instruction or might be offered more challenging content.

Compositional études often are used for the purpose of assessment. Students usually do not regard these as true compositions because they are being done for some specific external purpose and at a teacher's request. However, they can be added to a sketchbook for later expansion or some other use. If the students cannot accomplish the task, the teacher soon knows that the instruction was not clear. Other examples can be developed and new materials can be presented in other ways. If the students demonstrate competency, the teacher can move on to teaching other concepts and skills. It is the results of the assessment that allow this determination.

TYPES OF ASSESSMENT

At the very beginner levels of composing, assessment needs to be the most encouraging and positive. At first, it is useful to reward effort on each student's part. This can often be accomplished by assessing only how well the student complies with directions. For example, children in early childhood settings can be asked whether they would like to sit in a "composer's chair" and make up a song. When a child volunteers and proceeds to sing, the effort should be praised and encouraged, regardless of the technical mastery shown in the product. Similar results can often be obtained by offering a young child a puppet and asking the child to help the puppet make up a song. With beginners, it is attempting the process that is most important. Simply creating something is an accomplishment.

Self-Assessment

Older children in beginning instrumental classes might be given parameters to follow in making up something using the first few notes they have learned on their instrument. While technically this is a compositional étude, it can lead to self-directed composing if the process is encouraged and valued by the teacher and others. As new notes are added, new works are created and valued until the process becomes natural and rewarding for the composer.

Self-assessment is especially valuable and important for middle-school-aged students. While they also value positive reaction from their peers, their compositions are often highly personalized and deeply expressive of what they feel. Skillful teachers help them grow from composers of music within a limited range of expression to grappling with more extensive musical gestures and more wide-ranging technical means. A great deal of sensitivity to the composer's intent is needed. Co-compositional activities that expand their sonic palettes while appealing to their growing self-awareness may be very useful.

As students become more experienced composers, they begin to notice what makes one piece more effective than another, and that is when self-assessment becomes even more important and more obvious. It is sometimes difficult at first for children to regard their own work critically. The processes of self-assessment develop throughout the composer's life, and these first efforts benefit from the support of the teacher and the learning community as a whole.

Self-assessment may begin simply by deciding whether the directions have been followed, possibly by the use of a checklist. As the composer develops, scoring rubrics may be useful for self-analysis. Eventually, the composer often becomes the most ruthless critic of the work and may need encouragement to see the good in what has been created. The long-term goal is to see the piece as others see it. That is often facilitated by peer feedback in the composing community.

Peer Assessment

Children must be taught how to offer constructive peer feedback. One technique is to ask children to offer three stars and one wish. The stars are things they like about someone's piece, and the wish is something they wish they knew about it or something they wish to suggest. This can lead to a discussion of composer intent. Another focus can be to ask the composer to describe the piece and the peer group to offer specific comments on how that description appears to them to fit in the piece.

Teachers also must determine how receptive to feedback the young composer is. Some students have great difficulty accepting any notion that their pieces are not perfect just as they are. Others are unable to ignore inappropriate suggestions from peers. Teacher modeling and role-playing can have a very positive impact on process because the teacher can demonstrate multiple appropriate ways of responding to feedback.

It is important to focus peer feedback on the piece and not on its performance. In some manner, the teacher must direct the comments toward the work itself. This is particularly important when the composer is the performer. When assessing a performance, musicians often can separate technical skill from expressivity. This ought not be done with composition and may not even be possible (see Green, 2000, p. 102). When the discussion veers in the direction of the qualities of the performance, it may be helpful to have the teacher or someone other than the composer perform the piece.

Similarly, the focus of the feedback should not critique compositional skill. In any learning community there are many levels of skill. All levels should be accepted. The focus should be on the composition and its expressive qualities, and not the technical skill level of the composer. Every composer can always improve his or her skills. This is also a lifelong process. Finally, the focus of comments should not be on the ideas behind the piece or the composer's choice of content. The music and its expressive content always should be the focus.

Teacher and Professional Composer Feedback

Another way that teacher modeling can improve feedback is by showing how to give highly descriptive, specific comments. These comments need to be carefully matched to the developmental age and compositional skill level of the child. Role-playing this in class before using the small peer groups gives the students ideas for appropriate comments. As the groups meet, if the student peers offer stars and wishes first and then perhaps the teacher offers comments, this reinforces the appropriate model. Over time the peers imitate the teacher's manner of offering comments. Of course, the teacher may need to intervene when unacceptable comments are made, but role-playing and modeling often can eliminate those types of comments. In time, the feedback groups may be able to convene and operate without the teacher. At this point they are well on the way to being an independent music learning community.

Ultimately it is feedback that helps the young composer refine his or her skills. When the audience members comment on the work and their perceptions of it, and the composer comments on what effect he or she was attempting to create, the two can be compared and the degree of success of the attempted sonification usually becomes apparent.

Similarly, feedback from teachers and from professional composers needs to help young composers think reflectively about their work. The first task for the teacher is to decide what aspects to assess. While no list can address every possibility, the list in chapter 6, beginning on page 120, is a place for teachers to begin when working with young composers. Those suggestions help the teacher understand the composer's intentions and lead to suggestions without dictating the end result.

While the teacher may often be part of a feedback group or learning circle, the same questions can be used in one-on-one feedback sessions with a student. These sessions should be like private composition lessons and focus on the specific student's needs. Again, the teacher needs to decide upon which aspects of composition to focus. While these times can be difficult to arrange in school settings, the value for the composer justifies making the time for them to happen. This may have to be done at times outside of class or on a very limited basis in class. By working with one or two individuals per class, eventually a teacher can provide individual attention for each student at least once in a while.

Regardless of the type of assessment session that has been attempted, the teacher needs to structure the session so that it ends positively for each participant. When done correctly, these assessment sessions should provide the impetus for returning to work and should leave the student eager to do so. Ideally students will be bursting with new ideas to try and be more motivated to continue to compose.

Learning from Assessment

One thing students should learn from all types of assessment is what works in composing. At first, this may be a matter of what seems satisfying to them. Next they may experience the reactions of peers and the ways their pieces affect an audience. A positive reaction to something they have created can be very satisfying. However, students also learn from the reactions they have to the compositions of others and then begin to notice what causes those reactions. As they work to find words to express their reactions to the pieces others have created, they often take increasing care as they create their own pieces.

Composers also begin to realize that not every piece has to be their best one. Sometimes compositions just do not work. The composer may be attempting something beyond his or her current skill level, and the lack of those skills may make the piece unsuccessful. For example, a child who lacks a basic understanding of harmony might experience difficulty in creating a round. The composer may have created a piece that cannot be played on the intended instrument or performed by the intended performers. Sometimes problems can arise if the piece is created on a computer and the composer intends to perform it personally.

All of these issues can arise during the process of assessment and may lead to discarding ideas and seeking new beginnings. Less-than-successful attempts need to be couched as opportunities to learn by the teacher. They should not be represented as failures, but as steps toward learning to use materials and ideas in other ways. Sometimes the scientific model is a good one. Scientists often do unsuccessful experiments many times before finding the cure for a disease, and inventors make many prototypes before creating a successful new invention. Students may have to create many pieces before one emerges with which they are truly satisfied and that their audiences find expressive.

EVALUATION: SELF, PEER, TEACHER, EXPERT

Evaluation ideally takes place at some time a little distant from the completion of the composition. Evaluations, as used in this book, are summative ratings of the composition—and sometimes of the processes used to create it—to determine some level of quality. Ideally they are based on several examples of a composer's best work, but often they are determined based on a single piece. Statewide and national composition contests are usually done that way. Most grading should not be based on a single work, and that is discussed further in the next section.

The skills of self-evaluation are similar to the skills of self-assessment except that this thought process is not designed to lead to re-envisioning the piece so much as it is to lead to new ideas for future compositions. Young composers frequently want to create something quite different from the previous piece the next time they set to work. Often this is based on their own reflections and evaluations of the works they have previously completed.

The youngest composers often create new pieces each time they begin to work. When the piece is finished in their eyes, it is time to move on to something new. Helping them to evaluate their work and to hear the evaluations of others may extend the length of time they are willing to work on future pieces.

Peer evaluations can often take place following a public performance of a variety of compositions by young composers. Students can be asked which pieces they enjoyed the most, which ones they like the best, which they thought were the most difficult to perform, which was the most exciting, which was the most relaxing, and so on. Younger students can respond orally, but older students might be encouraged to respond in writing. However this happens, the results eventually should be shared— possibly anonymously—with the composers. If the concert was recorded, the selections can be replayed and further discussed or annotated. The skills of music criticism can be taught and musical vocabulary reinforced by this exercise. It is one thing to know that one likes a piece and quite another to be able to describe why.

Similarly, teachers should evaluate the final product and write a brief commentary on the piece. This may take the form of a description of what the teacher found evocative about the piece and possibly include some questions for the composer to consider as he or she begins work on a new composition. The point is to think deeply about the children's pieces and to provide formal written feedback to children who are old enough to read. If possible, this feedback should be based on a recording of the work and possibly a written score if one was created. Publishing the children's work in books, on recordings, or on protected websites increases its value to the students and provides the fixed entity that makes evaluation possible.

Students should be encouraged to submit their best work for evaluation by outside experts. While the teacher has been aware of the progress of the piece all along, an outside set of ears is reviewing it for the first time and should be able to provide fresh insight. Statewide composition contests sponsored by music education organizations and by others are appropriate forums for this type of feedback.

Like the teacher's commentary above, ideally outside evaluators provide not only a rating, if this is a contest, but also a commentary on the successful aspects of the piece and some questions for the composer to consider. Especially at the beginning stages, the outside expert must respond in the manner of a gentle critic. The expert should be able to make discriminations among many subtle qualities of the work and be able to find useful things to say about any child's piece. The emphasis should be on what works about the piece, what questions the expert has about the piece, and on encouraging the composer to continue to compose.

In many ways, it is the opinions of experts in a field that most often determine the quality of a work. While the questions listed above in the discussion of assessment and the tools described below can assist in the process of assessing and evaluating, experts can often recognize and describe quality in the absence of formal guidelines. The important aspect for young composers is the feedback these experts can then offer. They need to make explicit the reasons for their evaluations in order to help the students progress. A simple rating or grade does not usually have that effect.

A Few Words about Grading

There are several reasons why grades are given in schools. Most often it is to communicate with parents or others about student progress. However, a simple letter grade is rarely adequate to convey what has happened in composition classes. Anecdotal records and comments sent to parents in the form of letters and accompanied by recordings of the child's work can convey much more information. Even more effective are conferences with the child and the parents where the work can be displayed, performed, and discussed.

Another purpose of grades is often said to be to improve learning. This is also rarely effective in music composition classes. The threat of a low grade is unlikely to convince a young composer to work harder. Composing, like writing or painting, has to come from some desire or need to communicate. Low grades do not create true desire. Quite the opposite is often true.

Grades or at least some type of rank ordering is often necessary to make awards or give prizes in competitions. As students begin to enter this type of activity, they should begin with those competitions that provide expert feedback for all entries. While some ultimately receive the top ratings, all should receive encouragement to continue composing and comments on the positive aspects of their pieces.

In many cases there are no compelling reasons why grades must be given in composition classes. Perhaps the model here should be more like the private lessons students often receive on piano and other instruments. Assessment is ongoing and available at every lesson. Recital performances provide public opportunities for peers, parents, and others to evaluate and reward progress.

If teachers wish to grade composition classes, they should think carefully about what they want their students to know and be able to do in composition classes. Next they need to think about how the children can demonstrate such knowledge or skills. Several tools for use with this process are discussed in the next section. Only after those things have been decided can the teacher think about how he or she intends to teach those skills and concepts. Obviously this can be decided for individual children, groups of children, or whole classes of children. This depends on the learning situation. The more individualized the instructional setting, the *less necessary* a summative grade is and the *more important* ongoing assessment and guidance are.

If grades are to be given, everyone involved should know what is expected in order to receive a top grade. This includes parents, the students themselves, administrators, and the general public. Everyone should be able to earn an "A" or whatever the top mark is.

Not all work done in classes should be graded. This is especially true for first efforts and for things that are done simply for practice. Ideally, children should be allowed repeated attempts at assessment tasks and be provided with feedback focused on improvement between the attempts. Like any skill, composing improves with guided practice.

Consider reporting several things in relation to composition classes. First, report progress. Is the child making progress in skill development and conceptual understanding? State specifically what skills and concepts are progressing and the level of accomplishment. Then report separately on the process skills. This includes such things as attendance, work habits, and participation. Finally, report the results of any formal evaluations, demonstrations, or other compositional products. This should include a grade for any formal compositional études that were required.

TOOLS FOR ASSESSING, EVALUATING, AND GRADING

In order for students to be successful and make progress in their learning, they need a clear concept of what constitutes good work. When composition programs have been a part of the schools or other programs for a number of years, those expectations are built into the culture, and children can often determine quality independently. They recognize unusual and creative work on their own. At the beginning, it may be important for the teacher to find examples of fine work done by other children and to share that with the class.

Rubrics and Rating Scales

In evaluating any complex project, a scoring rubric can be helpful. Additionally, teachers may find rubrics helpful for encouraging certain skills. Certainly for compositional études done to practice specific skills and techniques, the students should be given explicit directions. The rubric for scoring their work should be shared with them in advance and thoroughly explained. Ideally, there might be something similar used for rating any final products. This can lead to more reliable scoring. Table 5.1 is an example of a scoring rubric for a group compositional étude.

Table 5.1. Assessment Rubric for a Small Group Compositional Etude

Assessment Rubric for a Small Group Compositional Etude
Done by Fifth-Grade Students

Task directions: Think of a story that starts out simply and quietly and becomes more and more exciting until it reaches a climax at the end—maybe a mystery story or a ghost story or a spy story. Decide on a short rhythmic motive that can be played on the various instruments in your group. You do not have to use all the instruments. You can also decide whether or not to create melody on the pitched percussion instrument in your group. Create a piece that tells the story your group chose, but that also demonstrates your ability to use the following musical elements. Use *all* of these elements to create repetition, unity, contrast, and variety in your piece: crescendo, accelerando, more instruments, short sounds, sudden crashes. Be sure your piece has a clear beginning, a middle section that builds excitement, and a clear ending. Below is the rubric we will use to rate your pieces.

	Excellent	*Very Good*	*Okay*	*Not Clear*
Beginning, Middle, Ending	Has a creative beginning or ending	Has a clear beginning, middle, and end	Beginning or ending not clear	No clear plan or form
Repetition	Repeats without being boring	Uses lots of repetition	Uses some repetition	Uses little or no repetition
Crescendo	Uses gradual and controlled crescendo	Uses crescendo	Gets too loud too soon or too suddenly	Doesn't crescendo
Accelerando	Uses gradual and controlled accelerando	Uses accelerando	Gets too fast too soon or too suddenly	Doesn't get faster
Adding Instruments	Adds instruments creatively and appropriately; entrances are clear and can be heard	Starts with few instruments and adds many gradually	Adds too many instruments too soon or at once	Uses the same instruments
Short sounds	Yes, and creatively used	Yes, and often	Yes, sometimes	Few or more
Motive	Clear, interesting motive	Clear motive	Some use of a motive	No clear motive

Compositional Portfolios

Portfolios of compositions that a child has completed can serve several purposes. Some of those purposes can be best served by a process portfolio. Process portfolios demonstrate progress. This portfolio should include early drafts of pieces, subsequent efforts, notes to the composer from peers or teachers, revisions, and completed pieces. It is an ongoing record of the composer's attempts covering at least one school year and sometimes continued for several years. Since it serves as a useful record of progress, reviewing it periodically can be very informative for students, parents, and teachers. The sketchbooks mentioned in the next chapter are a type of process portfolio.

Completed pieces of the best of the student's efforts may be kept in a separate best work portfolio. This may be used for evaluation and often is what is shared with parents at a student-led conference. In this portfolio are pieces that are ready to be shared with a wider audience. Best work portfolios can serve a gatekeeper function to allow someone to qualify for something such as admission to an advanced program or to more specialized programs for students with exceptional interest and ability.

Another type of portfolio that might be kept by teachers is a class portfolio. This portfolio should contain examples of the same type of work done by the members of a class at approximately the same time. It can be used to rank or sort people and functions, much like taking a test. Again, this type of portfolio can be used for gatekeeping functions.

Finally, teachers should assemble program portfolios. This should be a collection of the best work of a group of students in a particular program. This should take the form of a self-published collection, CD, website, and/or a collection of scores. All composers included in the program portfolio should receive copies. This might be done as part of an end-of-year recital. A subsequent use of these collections might be to justify additional resources or programs.

Assessment ultimately happens each time we listen to a piece of music. Opinions are formed, and eventually judgments are made. A collection of children's compositions and recordings of the pieces often speak for themselves to anyone who encounters them. Assessment is a very natural part of the process for all involved in creating and sharing music.

6

Designing and Working in a Composing Community

Regardless of where a composer may rest on the spectrum of development, his or her purpose remains constant—to create sounds that communicate the feeling of living.

—Michele Kaschub

The primary goal of education is to build a bridge extending from the child's wonder-filled self-discovery to the adult's curiosity-driven lifelong search for new things to learn. The strength of the bridge is strongly influenced by the activities of formal schooling. Lessons must be designed to pique students' interests while capitalizing on the natural learning processes of the brain. The intersection of these two influential factors is found in the daily activities of vibrant learning communities.

Learning in a community-oriented setting differs from the common conception of school. Traditional settings often feature a teacher presenting information to students with the expectation that they promptly report the same information back during formal testing. In learning communities, teachers purposefully design and create opportunities for students to ask questions critical to the discipline so that they may discover multiple answers. Learners encounter new knowledge and develop needed skills as they participate in activities that require them to seek out multiple sources of information. Community-based environments are inherently attractive to students who seek to develop their own interests, knowledge, and beliefs within a supportive atmosphere.

BENEFITS OF BELONGING TO A COMMUNITY OF LEARNERS

Learning communities are made up of people who assist and support one another as they work toward their learning goals. Group members may be students, teachers, professional composers or performers, critics, or others eager to interact with the world of music. Through collaboration within the community, students are able to encounter ideas and outlooks that may differ from their own. Over time, communities develop a form of shared cognition (Vygotsky, 1978) in which everyone contributes to a complex dialogue of give and take.

The skills of content acquisition, meaning construction, and critical inquiry are developed as community members share information and experience. Pondering how sounds become music, how music can be shaped and molded, and how composers craft feeling and sound together is foundational work for any developing composer. Contributing to such critical inquiry allows students to find examples of how content, history, or crafting skills found in one situation can have application in a wide variety of musical settings.

Communities are comprised of composers and other musicians from a wide range of skill levels. Each composer wishes to learn new crafting techniques, develop artistic elegance, and improve his or her overall abilities. Community members with the greatest compositional expertise are often sought as leaders, but they also are expected to identify and solve compositional problems appropriate to their own level of skill. Novice and expert composers learn to work smoothly side by side as equal expectations for progress are held for each student. Recognition of individual progress contributes to students' elevating the achievement expectations for the entire group.

As communities grow and take shape, they quickly develop a localized culture. Students adopt a healthy degree of within-group dependency. They seek out one another as projects unfold. Although there exists a wide range of personal goals and agendas among students, transformative dialogue becomes common. Conversations among students provide numerous, rich opportunities for teachable moments. Student interactions often result in questions about how some particular aspect of music works or how a technique can be achieved. At these times, teachers can encourage students to draw on the varied resources and strengths of their peers and other community members. This allows them to recognize that community members are resources for both personal and group goals.

Ultimately, learning communities are built at the microcosm level through the creation of smaller relationships. Ideally, pairs and small groups of students interact and help each other learn new information, test new skills, generate new knowledge, and share and perform their works. When students interact over a significant period of time, habits of behavior and interaction become integrally woven into the fabric of the community. Community life adopts a natural rhythm.

Of all of the benefits of learning communities, perhaps the most important is that community-based learning allows for flexibility in curricular design and implementation. Specific learning goals are easily tailored to the needs of the individual composer. Attention to the development of the individual allows teachers to guide projects and activities that arise organically from the interests of the student. Goals and activities can easily be adapted to meet the needs of the individual as each composition reveals new dimensions of personal musicality.

ROLES WITHIN THE COMMUNITY

As in any community, there are multiple roles to be played. Each role serves an important function in supporting the overall health of the community. As the composing community exists within the larger framework of schools, the roles of the student must be considered paramount. Students may act as composers, collaborators, critics, performers, audience members, and artistic agents. Experiencing each of these roles allows students to consider the workings of the musical community from a different vantage point.

The Roles of Students

Ultimately, students who participate in a community of composers are interested in composing. Although they learn much from the musicians around them, they are eager to create their own music. Students need sufficient time to engage in the processes of composition. They need time to think and reflect on their own works, and on the works of others. Time devoted to composing and thinking about music is often undervalued, but is a key component in the development of artistic awareness.

In order to successfully explore all that composition has to offer, it is eventually necessary for composers to collaborate. They join forces with teachers, professional and peer composers, performers, and others to bring to fruition a musical vision that they hold. Collaboration requires a careful balance of momentous energy and patience. Students need to learn to work with a variety of people. Some collaborators may share a single vision, but at other times, collaborators may need to compromise individual visions to reach larger goals. Like the skills of musical craftsmanship, the skills of collaboration take time to develop and benefit from gentle guidance.

Musicians grow through exposure to constructive criticism. Learning to offer and accept criticism is an important part of each member's experience within the community. Composers learn to consider how audiences experience their works by listening to the verbalized reactions of other members of the community. Similarly, the comments they offer to their peers reveal how they perceive the music they hear. Learning to offer criticism that is constructive and useful to other composers is an important skill that contributes greatly to the establishment of trust between community members.

While it is true that music can be performed by humans or by computers, fulfilling the role of performer is an important experience for developing composers. Participating in the preparation and performance of a score allows the performing composer to understand how his or her own work (scores) might be interpreted by others. The experience of being inside the sounds of music as they are being produced allows the composer to experience music from another vantage point. The wider the array of viewpoints available to the composer, the better he or she is able to make future artistic decisions.

The world of musical engagement is often described as a triangle consisting of creator, performer, and listener. While the composing community focuses highly on the creation of music, it does take both performers and audience members to balance the triangle. Audience members give of themselves and their time to receive the gift of sound. When the audience is made up of composers, they receive this created and packaged gift from someone they understand in a unique way. Hearing the performance of an original work is a great reward for a composer. Sharing that moment with others who understand the efforts made to create music makes this experience that much sweeter.

Getting a composition to performance is a long journey. Pieces need to be conceived, crafted, and preserved. If the composer desires to share a piece with others, then rehearsal and performance become necessary as well. Young composers need to act as artistic agents in representing their own work in its preparation for performance. Convincing others that their creations are worthy of an ensemble's time and efforts is rarely an easy task, even for professional composers.

While the teacher should facilitate performance planning so that every composer has an opportunity to have a public performance of his or her work, it is beneficial for students to learn how to promote their own pieces. Composers should be able to justify why their piece is suitable for a particular ensemble, why it should be included in a particular concert, and what it has to offer to an audience. The ability to speak articulately and convincingly about a composition can be one measurement of a degree of musical understanding.

The Teacher's Role

In a composing community everyone, including the teacher, is engaged in the process of learning. Teachers working with students in a community-based setting often report that they feel as if the students are the driving force of the learning activities. Students identify their own questions and turn to the music itself, instead of the teacher, to determine what their compositions need, suggest, or demand in order to be artistically satisfying. In such environments, the task of the teacher is the creation of opportunities for students to engage with music in as many ways as possible. It is through these interactions with sound that students discover more about the invisible work of the composer.

Students encountering new music may not know how to detect what the composer has done to craft sounds. One important role that teachers fill within the community is that of analytical guide. Teachers can guide students to observe the subtleties of music that might otherwise go unnoticed. Young composers who learn to listen to music artistically and analytically have found an inextinguishable resource for expanding their own compositional palettes. Time devoted to the development of attentive listeners contributes significantly to the overall quality of the compositional products produced by the community.

Teachers also fill the role of nurturer. Every composer develops a unique manner of crafting music that is recognized as the composer's *voice*. Voice is what allows the listener or performer to distinguish Handel from Bach or Haydn from Mozart. Each composer has unique sound inflections that are distinctive. Teachers can nurture the development of voice by listening to what young composers say about their work. Their thoughts and reflections on their own experiences and choices should be honored and built upon as their pieces are discussed. This approach requires the teacher to listen intently to children and think deeply about what they say about their music.

Most importantly, children need more than invitations to learn. They need models to guide their actions. Teachers who are active composers within the community can model all manner of compositional behaviors. As students watch their teacher seek an initial idea or work through a challenging musical transition, they are able to identify processes that they then can use in their own work. Further, children who are invited to offer feedback on their teacher's music are more open to receiving the teacher's comments on their work. Students are ever aware of issues of fairness. When teachers and students share an equality of opportunity, an educationally safe environment is created. Students come to understand that every composer faces similar struggles, criticisms, and challenges and can enjoy equal successes.

The Professional Composer

Young composers need opportunities to interact with professionals. These interactions allow students to understand the wide variety of people who aspire to compose music, the varied styles that composers pursue, and the different working styles that individual composers adopt. However, bringing a professional composer into a school-based compositional community requires careful planning.

Professional composers offer a wealth of musical knowledge to a composing community. They are often eager to share their passion for creating music with younger composers, but they may need assistance as they plan their interactions with young composers. Composers are rarely trained as educators of school-age students. Offering such guidance is a task that the teacher must be willing to adopt. Professional composers may participate with a school-based composing community in three primary ways: as continuous active participant, as visiting guest composer, or as the facilitator of a single project. Each form of participation offers students glimpses of how composers function with the larger musical community.

Composers who are constant members of a community may be present in a number of ways. Some composers are actual teachers in school settings. Others want to regularly attend community functions and participate in composer workshops. They may offer one-on-one composition lessons.

Composers may also participate in the community virtually. It may be difficult to find a composer in every community who is able to be physically present within the school community, but computer-based audio and visual communications allow students access to a wide range of composers without the usual geographical challenges to participation.

Composers with an interest in young people who live in the same geographic area should certainly also be encouraged to participate in school composition communities. Sometimes these professionals can be found at local colleges that have music departments. Other composers may be part of local pop music performing groups. This is a particularly good way to find singer-songwriters. Still other composers may work for advertising agencies, religious organizations, and other community groups. Any of them might be interested in an invitation to visit with young composers.

Some professional composers make single visits. Community-based arts organizations often sponsor preconcert lectures by composers when their works are to be performed by symphony orchestras, opera houses, music theater companies, or other ensembles. Composers visiting cities for brief engagements can sometimes schedule a visit to schools between rehearsals of their pieces. These composers offer very special teaching opportunities in that students can study their pieces, talk with the composer, and then attend a live concert to hear the composer's work performed by musicians of their own community.

Another collaboration that is often possible is to bring a composer into the community to guide work on a single project for a considerable length of time. This working arrangement offers students a "case study" view of the work of one composer throughout the creation of a single piece of music or perhaps a multimovement piece. Students contribute ideas to process and work with the composer to develop the piece over a specified period of time. The students may then participate in the performance of the work as performers or as audience members. This depends on the unique requirements of the composition they have created.

Composers invited to participate within a school-based community should be reflective of the broader world of professional composers. Invited guests might represent interests in different genres, might be from different ethnic backgrounds, or might represent other social or musical diversities that need to be appropriately modeled for a given community. It is important that children be able to find role models who resemble themselves—physically, socially, and musically.

TOOLS FOR COMPOSERS

What do composers need to work, to create their music, to interact with other composers and musicians, and to preserve their music? A toolkit. Composers need a collection of resources, materials, vocabulary, and preservation tools that allow them to work to their fullest potential. Composers need spaces in which they can work. Whether the space is a classroom, a rehearsal hall, a notebook, a computer, or some other comfortable area, composers' workspaces should be filled with the tools and materials necessary for composition. Composers use instruments to think in sound and about sound; they use particular words to describe their intentions and techniques; and they use notations and recordings to preserve their ideas.

Music Vocabulary

In order for children to discuss music with one another and others members of the community, they need to develop a common language for explaining what they imagine, hear, intend, and desire from the sounds they are forming. From the youngest ages children can learn to use the vocabulary of music. They acquire this vocabulary in the same way that they acquire all new words: from hearing terms in use and attempting to use those words for themselves. The use of musical language should not prevent children from responding to music, but should foster new ways for them to increase the precision of their responses. Providing applicable terms serves that purpose.

Children are more apt to use music vocabulary if they hear it modeled by other members of the community. Whenever discussing music, students should use words that are comfortable to them. The teacher may then rephrase student answers to model music term usage. For example, if a child observes that, "The music gets louder and louder," the teacher might respond with, "Yes, Thomas, the music crescendos over time," or, "Yes, Thomas, it does. Do you, Thomas, or does anyone else, remember the musical term for 'getting louder'?" In this way, children are not prohibited from making comments because they lack terminology, but are constantly exposed to more precise musical language.

Placing vocabulary in plain sight is another useful learning tool in any music classroom. Creating a word wall covered with music terminology allows students to reference the wall when they are trying to think of a word. If words are posted in different colors by like category (tempo words in red, expressive words in blue, note durations in yellow, etc.), then the wall can also serve as a go-to hint site. When students are stuck for a word, hints such as, "The answer can be found in the red words," can be very helpful.

Notational Literacy

In addition to learning the words to precisely describe musical events and sounds, composers also need to develop a repertoire of preservation tools to help them as they create, work through, and share their musical ideas. These tools usually take two forms: graphic notations or recordings.

Traditional notations are the most common written symbols of western classical musicians. However, it takes considerable time for children to learn to read, write, and think with these symbol systems. Young children often have little need of notation at all. They create pieces so brief that they can remember them from start to finish. Their performances are repeated many times in the process of creation, allowing each composition to become fixed in memory. As children's musical thinking continues to develop, they begin to create increasingly complex pieces that require multiple performers or that simply exceed their personal memory capacity. At this point, children begin to invent notational systems.

The symbols that children use to represent their musical ideas can range from letters and numbers to squiggles and pictorial drawings. It is important to remember that these scores are not music, but blueprints for the sounds that children have conjured in their heads and usually made with their bodies. These scores are the first steps to understanding how music is notated and shared with other musicians.

As children continue to compose, they discover that they need to use a common notational language in order for other musicians to understand their intentions. At this point, it is beneficial for students to engage in lessons that allow them to create mixed scores that allow for both invented and traditional notations to be included. By using both types of notation, students are free to imagine all the wonderful musical ideas they can but also begin to explore traditional notation to discover how it might serve their goals.

While written scores are certainly used widely today, they are also historical artifacts from a practice that evolved prior to recording technology. Written scores are not the only means that students have for preserving their musical ideas. Indeed, children usually are able to create music that far exceeds their notational skills. In such cases, students can turn to recording devices to preserve the music they have created.

It is important to remind students that recordings do not usually allow for direct performance by other musicians. As such, recordings are best used in three situations: (1) as a way to preserve musical ideas under development across class meetings, (2) to preserve performances of pieces when composer-performers do not yet possess notational skills, or (3) when the composer considers an electronic version of a piece the "composition proper." Recordings offer students the opportunity to save musical compositions that might otherwise be lost. Specific suggestions for how students may use notation at various levels of compositional skill appears in part III of this text.

Although most composers have given up quill and parchment, they still need a system for organizing their work that allows them to manage multiple projects simultaneously. The composer's sketchbook, whether it is bound paper or thumb drive, is a tool that accomplishes just that task. Sketchbooks are ideal repositories yielding easy access for monitoring student progress on individual projects or assessing skill development over time. Sketchbooks may function as a type of process portfolio or may be used in partnership with other portfolio projects.

Creating Sketches

Composers use descriptions, drawings, and musical notations to represent ideas that have passed through their minds as possible components of larger musical works. Sketches are not about precision, but are meant to save ideas that captivate the composer's imagination before they are forgotten. Sketches may grow from a single fragment of two or three notes to jotting that suggests how the idea may develop throughout a piece of music.

Students need a variety of tools to capture their musical thinking. Recording devices, blank paper, lined paper, staff paper, markers, pencils, or other implements can all serve in the creation of sketches. While computers with notation or sequencing software may also be used to preserve ideas, portability is key. Composers never know when a good idea might strike!

Flexibility is also very important. Children who process information visually may find creating a drawing or series of drawings helpful. Others may use existing texts, photos, or pieces of art as organizers for their work. Some children draw squiggles to represent how music moves, while others draw literal pictures of instruments. Composers who possess advanced notation skills may chose to notate their ideas on staff paper. Regardless of the form that sketches take, any and all jottings that help students to preserve their ideas are acceptable.

Structuring a Sketchbook

Sketchbooks can be used to help young composers organize their work. Composers often undertake multiple pieces simultaneously. To make sure that project materials are not lost or shifted between projects, a simple notebook (either paper or computer folders) can be organized into seven headings.

The "My Ideas" section of the sketchbook contains collections of musical thoughts that might grow into something bigger. These ideas may have arisen at any time and may be stories, poems, photographs, drawings, or anything that motivates or intrigues the composer. Composers often come up with several ideas when working on one piece, choose one to use, and forget the rest. Those once forgotten ideas may be handy to have at another time when the composer is hard pressed to find a starting idea.

The "Sketches" section of the sketchbook holds all the little musical gems in one place until the composer is ready to polish them into a piece of music. Initial ideas and jottings go here. These ideas are available for the composer to play with when he or she begins a new piece. Sketches may include the permutations of motive that might unfold during a development. Themes and variations can be worked out in this space. The sketches section ultimately represents the imagination's interplay between divergent (brainstorming) and convergent (idea selection and development) thinking.

Once a composition has starting to take substantial form, it may be moved from "Sketches" to "Sharing." Pieces moved into the "Sharing" collection are ready to be performed for members of the composing community. Such music is shared in order to elicit feedback from peers, more advanced composers, and teachers. Once shared, pieces in this section of the sketchbook are accompanied by notes written by the composer and capturing the essence of the constructive criticism offered about the work. Notes offered by teachers, peers, and other composers may also be included in this section. These comments give composers points to ponder as they continue their work or begin a revision process.

Sometimes when a composer returns to work on a piece that has received substantial constructive criticism, he or she opts to re-envision the music. This is not a surface edit or changing a few notes here and there, but a substantial reconsideration of how a piece of music comes together. Pieces under this type of construction are placed in the "Revising" section of the sketchbook. While here, the composer makes significant choices about the direction of the work. The pieces are refined and choices are made that reflect the composer's response to feedback. Composers do not have to accept feedback wholesale but are free to pick and choose from the comments they have been offered. Pieces may move between "revising" and "sharing" several times before progressing to the "editing" folder.

Compositions arriving in the "editing" folder are nearly done. These pieces need to be thoroughly checked for accuracy and for correlation of parts in multipart works. Any minor musical problems must be resolved. Notational accuracy must be checked for those pieces that are preserved in notation. Depending on the nature of the piece, editing can be a very quick and easy or a very challenging process. Students working with notation software can hear and see their works in a manner that can reduce editing time considerably. Once editing is complete, pieces are ready for performance.

Music filed in the "performance" section of the sketchbook is ready for final planning. The composer needs to determine a performance date and venue, secure performers, and plan rehearsal of her piece. This process may take many shapes, depending on the age of the composer. Teachers may establish protocols for the performance of pieces. A regular series of in-class recitals can be used to offer every student an opportunity to hear her pieces performed, or recital nights may be held at various points during the school year. Most importantly, young composers need to hear their works premiered in settings supported by their families, friends, and peers. These performances allow the efforts of students to be acknowledged and honored.

The "published/recorded" section of the sketchbook is often a separate folder in which the student keeps copies of works that have been published or recorded. The compositions found in this folder have been through all of the process steps and have reached a point where they are ready for circulation to other musicians and audiences. These pieces may be featured in print in a larger collection of student works or may appear on a class CD or website in downloadable form.

FACILITATING THE COMPOSING PROCESS

One role that teachers fill within a composing community is to facilitate the compositional process of the child. This includes traveling with the child from idea generation to performance—a journey that can be smooth or bumpy. Each step of the process has unique features and challenges. While the finale choices made must be the composer's, the teacher can help students to discover the many options available to them as they craft and shape their music.

Idea Generation

Inspiration may be a form of super-consciousness, or perhaps of sub-consciousness. I wouldn't know. But I am sure it is the antithesis of self-consciousness.

—Aaron Copland, American composer

I just don't know where to start. I can't find my first idea. I'm running out of time!

—Xavier Q., fourth-grade composer

As we can see from the quotations above, experts and novices alike feel the pressure to find inspiration and wonder from where it might come. Time to ruminate and hope that an idea might strike is not often available to students in school settings. Students are often presented with a task to complete on a tight time line. They are encouraged to work quickly and may even need to complete projects or activities within a single class period.

Given these circumstances, students benefit from directed teacher guidance when challenged to determine composition type, find a first idea, select sounds, or determine which comes first: text or music. These are the most common problems that students encounter when entering the process of composition.

Student Challenge:

What kind of piece am I going to compose?

Teacher Guidance:

Encourage students to imagine a larger project by thinking through its bare bones. By identifying the main idea of the piece (musically or verbally), describing what might happen in the middle, and sketching a few details about how the piece might end, students have divided a seemingly giant task into three smaller sections. They can continue to divide the project into manageable units by taking one larger section and detailing it further. This process could be repeated for each major section of the composition. As working units become smaller and smaller, the composer feels that work is moving forward. This energy is self-propelling.

It is not important for composers to rigidly adhere to this early plan. Maintaining flexibility allows new ideas to emerge in the process of composing. Dividing a larger composition into several major sections allows the composer to track how ideas move from section to section and how new material is added. Through this process, longer pieces become more memorable and manageable.

Student Challenge:

How do I find and pick a musical idea?

Teacher Guidance:

When students say "I don't know what to do!" it may not mean that they lack ideas. Just as often, it indicates that they have so many ideas that they find it difficult to select just one to use. The following activities can be used to prompt imaginations.

1. Name the composition. A name provides a sense of identity and a degree of ownership—two things that are very motivational for young composers.
2. Use pictures. Encourage students to imagine that they are in the picture. Ask them to tell you what they see, hear, feel. Stretch the idea further by prompting, "If this picture were in a movie, what would the soundtrack be for this scene?"
3. Consider taking a trip. Fill three suitcases covered with world destination stickers with several objects that would be packed for a trip to a specific destination. Things like tropical-print shirts, suntan lotion, snorkel masks, and flippers, or safari vest, bug netting, camera, field guide to jungle animals, and so on, prompt the imagination. Ask each composer to peer into one suitcase and then create a piece of music for a television campaign to entice visitors to the destination.
4. Receive visitors. We have sent recordings of our music into space in hopes that if one of our satellites were to be found by other beings, the music would represent us as humans. Ask students to imagine that they have found an alien satellite in the middle of the school commons. It is playing alien music. What would it sound like? Compose it.
5. Check the funnies. Provide students with a few frames of comics or a series of drawings that imply action. Encourage the composers to create music that sounds like the story. For example, a series of pictures showing a hungry frog, a frog with tongue extended toward bug, and then a happy frog would yield lots of sound possibilities. Have the students perform their pieces with and without sharing the pictures. Can the audience describe the pictures if they haven't seen them?
6. Describe a situation or read a story and ask children to describe the feeling of the story or of a character within the story. Create the music

that would be the soundtrack for the movie (or CD and read-along book) version of the story.

7. Have students ponder the musical thinking of inanimate objects. Students select two (or more for older students) objects and make up a list of things that the objects might sing to each other. What would a fancy high-heel shoe say to a soccer cleat? What would a New England snowman sing to a cactus in the Arizona desert? What would the cactus reply to the puddle?

Offering novel situations makes it difficult for students to fall back on previous experiences. They have to think creatively and differently to meet the challenges. Providing a wide variety of prompts such as these frees students to try things that they might not otherwise have considered.

Finally, when observing students working either independently or in groups during idea generation, a certain degree of seemingly off-task behavior may be present. It is important to recognize that what may appear to be "fooling around" is actually a critical component in the generative process—idea testing and formation. Teachers often approach students engaged in this phase of composition and ask them to focus on the task. This action can bring generative thought to an abrupt halt. What is lost when the teacher intervenes?

When leading creative work in the classroom, we must consider with great care how behavioral boundaries may stifle artistic processes. Classrooms must always be safe and well managed, but flexibility in other areas may be beneficial to the creative process. Allow students the creative freedom they need to generate a series of ideas by being aware of the need to explore and experiment before narrowing their focus.

Student Challenge:

What sounds do I want to use?

Teacher Guidance:

Encourage students to explore as many sound sources as are available to them both in and out of school. Students need to consider the sounds that instruments can make—both sounds they were intended to make and sounds that can be made beyond those intended. Everyday objects offer a wealth of sound opportunities as well. Composers should not be concerned with just traditional or ethnic instruments or voices, but with all the sounds that the world has to offer. Students can create collections of sound resources through amassing instruments, inventing instruments, and recording environmental and other sounds. They should also consider their reactions to sounds.

1. Create a sound resources list. Divide the list into categories: fabulous sounds; worst ever, makes-me-cringe sounds; humorous sounds; weird and wacky sounds; delicious sounds. Encourage students to list at least five sounds in each category. The list can grow over time and become a handy resource.
2. Top five. Encourage students to keep a list of their five favorite sounds. Have the students consider using all of the sounds in a single composition. Challenge students to avoid using any of the sounds for one piece. What do students discover about their personal preferences through interaction with their list?
3. Sometimes students are trying to create music for a special instrument choice but aren't really sure of what to write. Suggest that the student might imagine himself or a performer who he admires onstage. Ask the student to describe the music that is being played. Record the student speaking this description and then challenge him to follow his description and bring the sounds to life.

Student Challenge:

Which do I write first, text or music?

Teacher Guidance:

Text or music is the songwriter's "chick and egg" dilemma. Of greatest importance is emphasizing to students that there is not a single correct answer to the "text or music" question. Ultimately, composers tend to think with whatever music-making tool is most comfortable to them. Singers and singer-songwriters may conceive of lyric and melody as one inseparable unit, whereas instrumentalists often hear melodies and write the words to fit them later.

To help students make the choice, ask, "Which is most important for the listener: to hear the words or to feel the emotion?" This decision does not diminish the importance of either music or text, just prioritizes their roles within this one piece. If the emotion of the song is of primary import, then creating a description of the emotional journey to unfold in the piece may be beneficial prior to considering text. Attention given to the emotional impact of principle relationships can help the composer to convey feeling before the words are even heard and digested by an audience.

Conversely, if the transmission of information is the primary goal, then the text might need careful first consideration. If a song serves to present information, like recitatives in opera, then creating lyrics that include all the necessary story line details prior to creating melodies and accompaniments may be helpful.

Teachers and students may find that additional questions arise at the beginning of a composition process. The most important thing to remember is that for every question there is at least one answer. Start searching for a solution by asking as many questions as you can think of which address that particular compositional challenge. The process of generating additional questions when faced with a challenge often allows solutions to reveal themselves.

Developing Musical Ideas

Composers, like everyone else, can sometimes fall into patterns of behavior. They repeat the same idea over and over, fall in love with the comfortableness of the "old shoe," and dance again and again to a tired old song. Now, if the composer is practicing conventional minimalism, repetition is fine. Lacking sufficient distance to judge a composition objectively can result in stunted musical growth, however.

The skills of objective analysis and the provision of models are necessary for beginning composers to learn to develop their musical ideas. Without these tools, students tend to use up their creativity in proportion to the direction of their piece. Pieces that are primarily horizontal tend to be written for single instruments with musical ideas strung in a linear fashion. Works written for larger ensembles tend to be short and musical ideas stacked vertically over the range of instruments. Both types of composition are promising. Students who create these types of compositions simply need to learn to stretch their ideas out so that they unfold and develop over time. They also need to learn to lead their ideas to musical conclusions. The teaching challenge is to get students to expand in both directions as they develop their crafting skills.

The development of objective distancing needs to be both modeled for and experienced by young composers. Modeling can often be accomplished in large group settings. Each student should be able to see a score (invented, traditional, or otherwise) of the example to be analyzed. Students should hear the music, or even perform it themselves, if possible. The relative merits of the example should be questioned. Does it have identifiable motion? Is there a primary point of tension? Is there balance between unity and variety? Is sound used effectively? What would change if another instrument were used to offer this idea? These and other questions can be used to guide students in determining how a musical idea works on its own or how it might fit into the context of a larger work.

Debate about the relative merits of musical ideas often is found in small group or partnered composition projects. Disagreement about the inclusion or exclusion of musical ideas in a group-generated piece is common. Students in such settings often have to justify why the idea they have presented is the best idea for the problem at hand. Through the action of generating and defending a musical idea, students experience objective distancing. While they may not be fully objective about their own ideas at this point, they may object rather strongly to the ideas of their peers! Given time, students are able to critically analyze their own creations as well as those offered by their partners. Once this begins, students can take on individual composing projects that require more objective thinking.

Actively engaging students in compositional études to explore development is also an important experience for young composers. This exercise is easily accomplished by beginning with a song or tune that students know well. Students may work aurally or in written notations. Ask students to sing through the original melody. Once it is firmly in mind, ask students to make just one change to the original. Ask for a few volunteers to sing the modified piece, and ask audience members to identify how the music was altered. Continue along this process, making more and more changes. After several changes have been made, compare the original to a modified version. Lead the students in a discussion of how the character, emotional energy, tension points, and other key features have been altered.

Students can also excerpt just a few notes or a rhythmic snippet from a tune. Using the same process as described above, students can create variations upon the motif. They can try to make new music, play original and new material together, or experiment with other uses of their new creations. When students have created their own primary ideas in their future work, they can be reminded to employ these gradual shift techniques to develop and extend their musical material.

Reflection

Once students have a completed score, it is time to engage in a period of reflection before moving the work toward public performance. This is a period of product assessment in which composers measure their completed works against their own personal standards. As mentioned in chapter 5, the word *assessment* comes from the Latin verb *assidere*, meaning "to sit beside." Students may desire to push their pieces to completion, but they should be encouraged to sit beside their music so that they may observe the quality of their work.

Students may find the process of purposefully assessing the merits of their own work to be very challenging. They should begin by gaining objective distance through time. Setting pieces aside for a few days allows composers to transition from an "in-process" to a "critical-analytical" thinking mode. After investing much time in the close work of crafting note after note, viewing the work in its entirety is a new experience.

When encouraging students to critically assess a draft of their work, suggest that they listen with questions in mind: Does the piece fit within conventional practice (stable/unstable)? Does the piece have a good balance between sound and silence? Are unity and variety used in good proportion? Does the piece flow (motion and stasis)? Is the listener drawn to expect certain events or surprised by how the piece unfolds (tension and release)? These broad questions can help the composers assess the affective potential of their work. Although students may discover any number of compositional challenges through this questioning and critical reflection process, two problems commonly arise: a lack of ideas or too many ideas.

Above all, students who find their pieces to be overly repetitious should remember that they are intimately familiar with their own compositions. Ideas that they have heard over and over in the process of crafting music are new to the ears of the audience. Repetition, however, contributes to the balance between unity and variety. In assessing this balance, composers must try to hear their pieces as if encountering them for the first time. Some repetition is good and can help listeners quickly feel comfortable with new pieces, but sometimes repetition is simply tedious. Composers should consider that the first time a listener hears an idea it is new; the second time it is familiar; and the third time they know what to expect—so composers might consider doing something unexpected.

Opposite of repetition is the problem of presenting the listener with too many ideas. Some pieces offer an onslaught of musical ideas and material that is disconnected. Such pieces are unstable and offer only tension to the listener, who cannot figure out what is important and what is supportive within a piece. When the problem of too many ideas arises, remind students that music can survive with fewer ideas. Indeed, Beethoven's Symphony no. 5 in C Minor is composed of a simple four-note gesture powerfully and thoroughly developed. Students might consider selecting one or two of the best of their many ideas to serve as focus points for future work.

Providing Feedback in Sharing Sessions

It is important for every child to receive meaningful feedback on compositions that they invest time in creating. To do less is to suggest that their work is not important. Sharing sessions offer opportunities to elicit a critique of works in progress. Accepting critical feedback can be difficult for anyone, but particularly so for children who have made a personal investment in the creation of music that is uniquely their own. Careful consideration should be given to the idea of welcoming criticism. Composers who invite feedback from the peers, performers, and audience members attending a reading are armed with information that can guide their continuing work.

Providing meaningful feedback need not be a daunting task. Feedback should be drawn from multiple perspectives: the composer, peers, teacher, and other community members. When feedback from all of these perspectives is gathered over time, composers begin to develop a sense of their audience. Such feedback not only helps young composers to refine their pieces, but also expands their understanding of how different people listen to and receive their compositions.

Working in conjunction with each composer, the teacher should determine what type of feedback is needed. At times it is appropriate for listeners to comment on any aspect of a work. At other times, feedback focused to address one or two of the musical principles is helpful. Composers may also have very specific questions to ask of a workshop audience. These questions might be about instrument choice, how sounds are working together, whether a particular passage is effective, or whether another compositional technique or device might enhance the overall quality of a phrase, passage, or larger section.

The delivery of feedback is often more important than the specific comments. Young composers are sensitive about their work, and it takes time to develop the ability to brush aside criticisms that are unjustified or inappropriate. Some guidelines for offering feedback can help ensure a positive learning atmosphere when compositions are offered in workshops.

Peers offering feedback should follow the "three and one" rule: identify three things that were successful or well done and one thing that might be revisited. It is important that all feedback be accompanied by an explanation of how something was well done or why something needs attention. Constructive criticism is helpful only if it includes suggestions of how changes might be approached or accomplished. Also, in peer commentary all attention must be given to the music. Criticism of individual performance skills or compositional skills should not be allowed. Respect is the key ingredient in successful peer feedback interactions.

The feedback offered by teachers and professional composers must be highly descriptive in nature. Detailed information about what works and what might be reconsidered within a composition is much more helpful to students than percentages or letter grades. Creating tools that allow for conversations between teachers/professional composers and students is one option that works well with composers upwards from grade 3. By this time students are able to write in journals or create multiple-track recordings that allow the music, the students' questions, and the teachers' questions or comments to be heard in any combination. Software or equipment that allows students to hear their music while hearing comments about their music may be very helpful.

Questions that may guide critical reflections on compositions include:

1. What part of this composition works well? What flows the best?
2. What part of this composition is most challenging to create?
3. How do the instruments selected complement or contrast with each other?
4. What is particularly imaginative about the way the song text and accompaniment are fitted together?
5. If you were to change one thing about this piece, what would it be?
6. If the computer ate nearly every bit of your work, what is the one thing you would hope would still be there for you to use in starting over?
7. After children have shared several pieces—What musical trait(s) can we describe as the student's compositional voice?
8. Is there a main idea in the piece?
9. Does the main idea change over time?
10. Is there a message in this piece? What is it?
11. What are the main things that happen as this piece unfolds?
12. Can I always guess what is going to happen next?
13. If I were to revise this piece, what would I do differently?
14. How do I feel as I hear this piece? Why do I feel that way?
15. What special sounds do I remember when the piece is over?
16. What did the composer have to know to create this piece?

Additional guiding questions may be developed to match the developmental needs and capabilities of different composers or to specifically match compositional objectives in specialized projects. Regardless of the approach adopted for the provision of feedback, one thing is certain: students do not progress to their full potential without careful assessment of their musical successes and future goals.

Finally, sharing sessions should conclude pleasantly. Composers need to thank conductors and performers for their efforts. They should also thank those who offered constructive criticism. The process of acknowledging the contributing and supportive efforts of other member of the community strengthens the bonds that allow for open and honest musical feedback to occur.

Re-visioning

Re-visioning is the process of literally creating a new vision for a piece of music (Smith, 2004). The composer conceives of either a new or substantially altered product that is built from ideas contained within the work that has been critically reviewed. The ability to engage in the process of re-visioning a composition for greater power and economy is one of the higher forms of musical thinking. It requires students to hold existing musical ideas in memory while juggling and swapping them in and out to try new combinations and arrangements until the right fit is discovered. Along with all of this juggling, composers may also invent new material to blend with the old. The process is laborious and best suited for students who thrive on challenge.

Students may think of re-visioning as a process similar to arranging furniture upon moving to a new home. At first, the furniture is placed anywhere; the goal is just to get it out of the moving truck. Slowly, pieces are carried into the right rooms and eventually placed into the right spots. The flow of the house begins to take shape. But then it is discovered that the couch won't fit into the living room. Now, the dining room becomes the living room and vice versa. The contents of the house get juggled about. Finally, when the bigger pieces are best placed, the final touches are brought in. Although all the pieces were present from the outset, a heavy investment of time and energy was required to create a home.

The process of re-visioning can mean completely dismantling a piece or simply excerpting the sections that worked best to repackage them more fluidly. Regardless of the type of re-visioning needed, students should take time to think objectively through the material they have created. Frustrated students may be tempted to throw out an entire project, but no work should be discarded in haste. Being objective about being objective is what allows composers to recognize that music that is not working in a particular situation may work well in another setting at a later date. Generous amounts of patience and discretion must be applied during the process of selecting and cutting material from existing pieces.

Refining and Editing

The processes of refining and editing compositions mark the transition from generating music to preparation for performance. Composers who consider their composition to be complete often engage in a period of refinement during which they introduce certain subtleties or distinctions to their work. While the final touches given to each piece are largely dependent upon the nature of the work, every piece should be offered at its best. These final adjustments may involve minor tweaking to phrases or the addition of instruments to achieve just the right timbral balance in a passage. This is also the point where teachers may choose to notate pieces for young composers who lack sufficient aural skills to notate their own work independently.

Students engaged in the process of refining their work may benefit from hearing their pieces performed by instruments or computers. The ability to hear music externally allows students to adopt the role of composer-listener—hearing the music as a first-time listener, but evaluating with the prowess of a knowledgeable craftsman. From this position, composers can identify the minor refinements that a work requires to fulfill their artistic vision.

Once the composer is sufficiently satisfied with a composition, the editing process begins. Compositions created for computer performance may need attention in the areas of track balance, panning, or other effects, so that artistic choices made in the crafting process are not lost in the transition to headphones, room-size speakers, or other media delivery systems. Ample time should be allotted for composers to become familiar with specialized software as they create and complete the final editing of their works.

Music to be performed from written scores requires special attention in the editing process. Composers who have invented notations need to be sure that they have created notation keys that are highly descriptive. Explanations for newly invented symbols often appear on the first page or two of a printed score and parts. Conductors and performers should not have to puzzle excessively over squiggles and symbols that have not been thoroughly described by the composer. Keys may be edited to correspond directly to each part, or each player may be provided with a full set instructional notes.

Composers who have used traditional notation systems need only verify that score and parts correlate and are easy to read. Many notational software programs print parts directly from the full score. However, computer-generated parts may not be human performer friendly. Adjustments to printed pages that facilitate page turns or other navigational issues should be a priority. It is difficult to have a fine performance of a work if the performers are wrestling with their parts. Reviewing individual parts for missing pages, incorrectly numbered measures or rests, rarely used key signatures, and other oddities is simply a good policy. Any error found before the rehearsal maximizes rehearsal time and moves the composition closer to its premiere performance.

Preparing for Performances

Composers must take responsibility for presenting their work. Compositions intended for computerized performance may require no more attention than what is given by the composer, but music that is performed by people other than the composer requires additional care. Composers and performers share a unique relationship that may or may not be mediated by a conductor. Composers often choose to conduct or perform in their own works. In either case, the ability to communicate musical ideas effectively is very important.

The composer communicates with the conductor and performer through the score. Notation serves to provide conductors and performers with specific guidance as to the sounds desired by the composer. Unfortunately, notation can equally detract from that vision. The composer must give careful attention to the creation of score and parts. Readings of pieces prior to public performance offer the opportunity for the composer to hear from performers. Performers, having expertise that the composer may not possess for every instrument, are able to share valuable information regarding how a composer can best achieve the sounds he wishes to hear. These interactions prior to the premiere of a piece allow the composer to enter into the editing process with an eye and ear to the experiences of the performer.

Another important challenge composers face is the job of graciously welcoming new interpretations of their works. Composers, having spent considerable time and energy in the crafting of their music, are often surprised to hear their pieces performed in a manner that does not match their own internal model or even the computerized model to which they have grown accustomed. Composers must be aware from the outset that the creation of music for others to perform is going to lead to new interpretations and new renditions of the sounds they so carefully crafted. Hearing new possibilities within your own work should be considered an exciting surprise and welcomed for the new insights it offers.

KEY POINTS FOR SUCCESSFUL LEARNING COMMUNITIES

Communities are made up of those to whom we give our time. Within every community there are givers and takers. Givers contribute to the growth of the community by offering their time, talents, and resources as they forge supportive relationships. Takers, on the other hand, usually offer little effort, but great complaint. As community leaders, it is important to help redirect the energy of takers so that the entire community moves forward together.

Communities offer students an opportunity to belong to something greater than themselves. Strong communities emerge when individual members adopt a responsibility for one another. Each member needs to be included, have opportunities to contribute, and share responsibility for supporting the efforts of his or her peers. Students who feel appreciated recognize that their contributions make a difference. This realization leads to a deeper engagement, and every student is given an opportunity to flourish.

Community-based learning acknowledges that teachers do not have to solve every problem. Rather, teachers suggest questions, guide projects, and help students learn the skills of self- and group organization. Musical problems can be thrown to the middle of the room because students believe that they are capable of finding solutions for themselves. Independent learning is the norm.

The rich resources of community-based learning make it easy for students to actively search out local resources (each other, books, recordings, etc.) and distant resources (community members, other classes, other teachers, etc.) to find solutions. Communication and content knowledge interact seamlessly as students and experts exchange information and experiences.

Learning in community-based settings is often characterized by strongly focused student behavior. Students prefer to be on task because they are working toward self-defined goals. There is fluidity between making music and the conversation about music. Talking between group composers often serves to offer peers performance or technical instruction.

Communities must have a sense of history, time, and place. Built upon the foundations set by past composers and reaching toward the work of future composers, communities stand as essential bridges. Those that acknowledge rich histories and honor current diversities invite innovative music making to occur.

III

TEACHING AND
LEARNING COMPOSITION

7

Composing in
Early Childhood

Young children are wonderful contributors to any creative activity in the music classroom. Helping young composers transition from informal and playful composition experiences to the formalized activities that often take place in large group settings does take considerable forethought and planning. The activities that young children naturally pursue in their music making provide a starting place for composition instruction. This chapter offers a profile of prekindergarten through second-grade composers that provides a foundation for planning instruction. Key considerations for guiding composers of this age and ability are outlined, and lesson exemplars are offered as models for future curricular development.

A PROFILE OF PREKINDERGARTEN THROUGH
SECOND-GRADE COMPOSERS AND COMPOSITION ACTIVITIES

In order for instruction to be designed appropriately for young children, serious consideration must be given to the nature and needs of the learner. A profile is a tool for encapsulating this general knowledge. It includes a multidimensional snapshot of the general characteristics, musical tendencies, knowledge, and experiences of young children. Each dimension of the profile is like a piece in a puzzle. It is singular in nature, but contributes significantly to the complete picture.

The profile offered in this chapter highlights the behaviors and thought processes exhibited by young children as they create, perform, and listen to music. Each puzzle piece offers additional insight to the child's creative process. These pieces of the puzzle include the child's understanding of musical principles, the learning environments most conducive to compositional activity, and the types of tools children naturally seek out in their own musical play. Each one also plays a crucial role in informing the professional work of the teacher, who sets forth to design a meaningful and engaging composition curriculum for students in the preschool through early elementary years.

Composer Characteristics

Prekindergarten through second-grade composers may have no formal experience in composition, but they most likely have been creating music as part of their play activities for three to six years. The activities that naturally elicit music making in children should provide the direction for formalized composition instruction. Children make music as part of their daily activities rather than stopping everything else to make music. Similarly, music-creating activities should weave seamlessly throughout the child's day. Inventing songs to sing, making up musical games, creating sound effects and background sounds for stories, and enjoying the music of others should all be included in a child's school-based musical activities.

Children construct their own definitions of what music is and how music works as they encounter it in daily life. Every interaction a child has with music offers information about the world of music as well as about how music works in the world. When children notice someone singing a lullaby, the energized sound effects behind an exciting cartoon, or a crowd rising to its feet to sing the national anthem at a sporting event, they are collecting from each of these experiences sounds and contexts that allow them to make sense of the music they hear, feel, and experience. Over time, children develop a repertoire of familiar musical practices against which they measure and evaluate new sounds.

Listening to music involves the absorption of the language and the conventions of a particular type of musical practice or practices. Children begin to absorb the rules—as well as the exceptions to those rules—from the music around them. Many of these conventions and understandings are built upon biological realities (Damasio, 1999) and occur regardless of the music the child hears within his or her home and culture. However, a musical environment rich with a variety of music heard repeatedly over time is necessary in order for children's understanding to expand. Just as a child's speaking vocabulary is dependent on the language and vocabulary to which he or she is repeatedly exposed, so, too, are forms of musical expression limited to those with which the child is most familiar. Parents, music educators, and other teachers play a vital part in developing and expanding that repertoire of familiar music.

In addition to the conventions of musical practice, listening to music is a key factor in the development of an internalized sonic palette. Establishing a sonic palette within the child is a critical component in his or her compositional development. Formal composition instruction is useful for refining and extending a basic ability that must already be present—the ability to imagine sounds. The work of the composer starts with the knowledge of the sounds that can be shaped into a composition. The young composer begins from a concrete conception of sounds that have been heard before. The child then can move to an abstract conceptualization of what might be heard if sounds are altered or used in combination. This type of abstract thinking cannot occur or develop unless a basic palette of sounds has been internalized through listening.

The final characteristic of the young composer is the progression made from simple to more complex musical products. The compositional evolution from the assembly of previously known works to the creation of mixed and then original music reveals itself in each child. The earliest compositions made by children are often constructed through the repetition of a simple motive or brief musical fragment. These early works quickly give way to the mixing and matching of bits of familiar songs or tunes that have been retained in memory.

The creation of completely original works begins as children become consciously aware of the conventions of the song forms that they hear and sing. Often these early compositions provide the *soundtrack* for the games that children play. Their creations may take the form of background music behind flying spacecraft or may be the songs sung to favorite teddy bears. Regardless of the exact nature of the musical play, music is a constant companion in the discovery of the world and of self for young children.

Understanding and Use of Compositional Principles

As discussed earlier, the principles of music help composers plan their pieces and think about how other people respond to their music. The primary principle of *stability/instability* is achieved though the supporting principles of *sound/silence, repetition/contrast, unity/variety,* and *tension/ release.* Composers approach each one of these dichotomous continua their own way. The unique interpretation that each composer brings to his or her crafting of principle relationships becomes an identity and is often referred to as the composer's *voice.*

The supporting principles of sound/silence, repetition/contrast, unity/ variety, and tension/release are used in ways that are psychologically comfortable to the young composer. Very young composers tend to gravitate toward the "stability" side of the stability/instability principle. Familiarity and comfort are very important to young children. They often prefer the safety of known boundaries and may follow traditional or familiar forms without being consciously aware of their actions. Although children occasionally experiment with something that challenges stability, the majority of their work is within their own comfort zones and emulates the musical sounds that are well known to them.

Experiments with sound and silence are probably most evident on a large scale. Children either are creating physically audible music or not. This is easily observable as children create play songs and then pause between repetitions of their created songs. However, simple observation can be misleading. It is important to remember that an outwardly silent child may be creating or listening to created music internally. Silence used to create effect is discovered as part of their play. This often occurs as they cease their singing, pause, and then begin again in a way that is unexpected and surprising or startling to their playmates.

The "surprise" element of sound and silence is very intriguing to young composers. Indeed, older composers make use of the principle as well. A perceptive teacher who notices the "surprise" element in children's musical play may want to use the second movement of Haydn's Symphony no. 94 in G Major for a structured listening lesson that explores and highlights this technique.

Young children love repetition. Making the same music over and over again is a way to create familiarity and comfort. It also exercises and affirms the capabilities of the musical memory. This is also a way in which children begin to experiment with their own compositional thinking. Just as young babies coo the melodic contours of speech before beginning to speak their own sentences, young composers mimic and echo familiar songs and song fragments as they begin to test their own song-making abilities. These creations often comprise short fragments of several songs in the child's musical vocabulary. They usually evolve and change with each performance. The changes that children make from one singing to the next constitute both experimentation and variety.

This pattern of experimental repetition can also be observed as children play with classroom instruments. Playing familiar patterns and making slight alterations to those patterns allows children to carefully test and control the changing conceptions of their pieces. Through these self-initiated activities, young composers discover that their music becomes increasingly interesting when changes are made and contrast is present. Children then begin to generate original tunes with sections that offer both repetition and contrast.

Unity is achieved as children string together similar ideas. Indeed, some children may find it difficult to create two ideas that are dissimilar.

Children learn what things are by noticing their characteristic features. However, definition by comparative analysis requires that children identify how newly encountered objects differ from previously known objects. As children develop these skills their compositional practices begin to shift. Initially, children draw known musical material together, selecting songs of same meter, similar instrumentation, or similar text (e.g., "Old MacDonald Had a Farm" and "Bingo"). The addition of pieces with less obvious similarities signals that children are ready to create music with parts that have same/different features. This is the first step in generating musical unity and variety.

Children enjoy creating tension but are most likely to use it in brief episodes. Heavy tension in music for an extended period of time is similar to watching a movie that is visually scary. Young listeners may not be able to maintain focus when tension becomes too thick. Prekindergarten through second-grade children are likely to match the tension/release energy flow of their music to their play activities or to the events that they envision as organizers of their music. Tension may appear as sudden loud sounds or might be achieved through motivic repetition. Sometimes children simply sing a short song over and over in a manner that they find comforting and then realize that the endless repetition causes others to experience tension. The excitement of discovering the many ways in which music can be assembled is very important to this age group.

Compositional Context

Young children greatly benefit from experiences that allow them to observe a model or demonstration before they attempt new activities for themselves. Formal composition instruction for young composers often begins with teacher-facilitated whole-class activities before children undertake work in small groups or with partners. The teacher-facilitated instruction is beneficial in guiding students to discover particular features of music or for modeling specific compositional techniques or strategies. Teacher-guided composition activities involving the entire class provide an opportunity for the teacher to model the composition process, to engage students in guided decision making and reflection, and to establish procedures for selecting instruments, taking turns, and working together. These activities lay the musical, social, and behavioral groundwork for small group and partnered projects.

While whole-class activities are ideal for prekindergarten through first-grade students who benefit from teacher leadership in completing the steps of a project, students in grade 2 can usually organize themselves as long as the group size remains manageable. Ideally, students work in groups of three to four (Cooper et al., 1986). This group size allows each student to be highly involved and to contribute to the work of the group. Group sizes may be altered as necessary to fit the needs of the compositional projects or performance, but adding more members to a group increases the opportunity for students to "hide" (Kerr & Bruun, 1983) and let others tackle the work. Small groups are most successful when students have strong social and organizational skills (Kagan, 1992) that allow them to self-direct their work in fulfilling task guidelines.

Small projects or projects with specific guidelines and performance requirements are often best suited for pairs of beginner students. Pairing students is a particularly effective way to generate compositions requiring two parts or two instruments. Likewise, projects that involve the use of a computer are often best suited for pairs of students (Trowbridge & Durnin, 1984). Working in partnership allows students to discuss their compositional choices and make decisions quickly as fewer people are involved in the process.

Tools of Creation and Preservation

Composers work with two types of tools: those used to assist in compositional thinking, and those used to preserve a record of compositional thoughts or creative products. Prekindergarten through second-grade children are most concerned with tools that help them to make compositional decisions by allowing them to hear external sounds. Instruments, voices, and computers are all tools that children can learn to manipulate to serve their compositional intentions.

Many young children are willing to use their voices as sound sources for their compositions. Children's own voices are fun to use in making all sorts of sounds and easy to transport and store. However, some children are hesitant and self-conscious when asked to perform or share their compositions if they realize that it is their own voice that is taking center stage. Teachers can offer support and encouragement within a psychologically risk-free environment. Most youngsters respond to this approach over time and eventually perform without hesitation. For those who cannot overcome this psychological barrier, it is important to have a variety of projects and sound sources available. Including a wide range of possibilities for engaging with sound allows all students to participate fully and create their best work with or without the use of their singing voices.

Classroom instruments offer a broad palette of sound choices that children can utilize in their compositions. It is important to remember that young children are just learning the sound capabilities of these instruments along with the proper technique for playing them. Including lesson time to demonstrate the sound capabilities of each instrument as well as offering instruction on performance technique helps students prepare to use the instruments in their work. Providing a few minutes for children to test and try the instruments also reduces the amount of off-task behavior experienced later as students seek to test and experiment with the new sound sources. Because children may not yet be bound by an idea of "the right way to play it," they may find other interesting ways to generate sounds with newly introduced instruments. Encourage this sound exploration as long as student and instrument safety are maintained.

Additionally, do not be limited by the term *classroom instruments*. Use small percussion from many sources and cultures. Whenever possible, buy professional percussion instruments rather than the less-expensive and lower-quality sets often sold as "classroom sets." There is a noticeable difference in timbre between a toy triangle and a professional one. Moreover, interesting sound sources can be found in the world around you. Very young children often delight in banging on pots and pans with a wooden spoon and then a metal spoon. This is sound exploration at its best. Encourage students to find and bring in interesting sounds to share and add to the classroom collection.

Computers constitute yet another sound source available to young composers. With computers, students are able create music that is not limited by the composer's personal performance skills. This is freeing to some children. However, computers do not require the same type of bodily knowledge (Reybrouck, 2006) of music making that playing an instrument or singing might require. Bodily performance can help children develop pitch and rhythmic capabilities that are not supported by pressing keys on either an interfaced typing or piano keyboard. It is important to consider a balance among the tools used by young composers as tools offer both freedoms and limitations. Just as a steady diet of only toasted cheese sandwiches would not be healthful, working with only one set of compositional tools (voices, instruments, or computers) leads to limited musical development.

Finally, tools of preservation deserve consideration. Music may be preserved in memory, in notation, or in recordings. All three serve different purposes and work in different ways. Prekindergarten through second-grade composers tend to create works that directly correspond to the length of their own musical memories. In these cases, musical memory may serve as a form of short-term preservation for compositions that are going to be shared immediately and for which longer preservation is not necessary.

Reliance on memory, however, begins to fail when children engage in projects that extend beyond the single class period. Instructional sequences of longer duration tend to result in lengthier or more complex products and thus require more permanent modes of preservation. While notational systems may offer the most detailed written documentation of compositional thoughts in process, the acquisition of notational skill can be cumbersome.

Ideally, notational systems, either traditional or invented, are meant to assist a composer's work.

When the young composer is forced to shift focus from musical thought to notational thought, creativity can be lost as students wrestle with the rules and finer points of notation. Further, young composers performing their own works lose fluidity of performance as they pause to read their own notations. The processes of composition, notation, and performance can be complementary, but the developmental pace of skill acquisition in each area is not strictly dependent on the others. Formal notation systems as part of composition need not be emphasized until the young composer finds that he or she "needs" a system for maintaining a record of compositional thought. When this desire to notate has evolved within the composer, then it is time for the formal introduction to notational rules to begin.

Ultimately, the most time-efficient and reliable record of children's compositional work may be recordings. While recordings are often thought of as a record of final performance, recordings can also be used to track progress and remind students of what they have previously created. Often students simply need to have their memories refreshed when a break has occurred in the compositional process. Recording student work on day one and listening to the recording before work on day two is usually sufficient to continue the process. Again, when this system no longer fulfills the needs of the student, it is time to introduce notational tools.

Considering Prerequisites

Exactly what students should know prior to a composition project depends on the requirements for the successful completion of the project. It is important to consider what principles, elemental concepts, and crafting techniques students can identify and use in their compositions. Equally important is the realization that students bring a wealth of informal knowledge gained through everyday experiences to any musical study. Most children know, at some level, what a piece of music should sound like. They possess their own definition of "a song" or other forms from exposure to the music of their culture.

In the early stages of compositional development great attention should be given to filling the child's world with sounds. Music of the highest quality representing multiple styles from around the world and from all historical periods should play an important role in music education settings. This is a critical step in the development of informal musical knowledge that can be attained through listening. Making music available to children and encouraging their interests and physical participation in generating music ensures that children will never be at a loss for something to say musically.

Children are able to draw on their intuitive knowledge about music long before they have developed the formal terminology to fully verbalize their understandings. It is important to remember to balance informal and formal knowledge in the preparation, design, and implementation of composition lessons. Students should gradually acquire the terminology and skills needed to create their own compositions and discuss their pieces in meaningful ways. This process should unfold naturally with students' questions of "What is it called when . . . ?" leading the way to more formalized instruction. Following the child's recognition of a "need to know" allows for stronger connections to be made between prior and new knowledge as children learn about the world of music.

Co-compositional Activities

Direct music-making activities allow students to experience a concept that they may eventually explore compositionally before actual generative work begins. These activities include singing, playing instruments, listening, moving, exploring sound sources, and improvising. These musical behaviors are the ways children gain firsthand knowledge of a musical concept before they are able to weave it into their own compositions. Opportunities to understand sound deeply and broadly through musical activities are critical in the development of young composers. Each engagement with these musical behaviors can allow children to experience sound and then ponder why and how other composers have used the principles and elements of music expressively.

It is also important to remember that instructional opportunities arise in which it may be better to engage children in creating their own compositions before presenting the works of other composers for comparison. For example, in the lesson entitled "Sonic Snowstorm" in chapter 4, children may create their own pieces and then listen to Debussy's "Snow Is Dancing" for comparison. This model allows the children to make their own compositional decisions before considering how other composers may have dealt with similar challenges.

Equally worthy of consideration, it is possible to engage students in a guided listening lesson examining the structure, sounds, and affect present in Debussy's piece. With this approach, Debussy's work would be used as a model for creating a composition inspired by a snowstorm. Debussy would serve as a point of discussion through which the principles and the elements used to achieve the expressive qualities could be discussed, analyzed, and evaluated. Each approach has its merits, and the selection of one or the other must be made in relation to the needs of the students engaged in the lesson.

Task Guidelines

The simple directions to "make up a song" or "write a piece of music" are such open-ended tasks that they may be daunting to a young composer. Given the freedom to use any instrument in any way for any period of time to create any piece of music that might be termed a "song" is quite likely to be paralyzing. Folkestad (2004) and Regelski (1981) have both noted that too little task structure can cause students difficulty as they face too many possibilities. On the other hand, Wiggins (1999) has noted that too many details in the task directions can inhibit creativity and personal expression. Given this natural conflict, the question for the teacher becomes, "What should be the nature and degree of specification within a set of task guidelines?"

For teaching purposes, task guidelines are an efficient way of proceeding with instruction. Guidelines serve the same function as the edges of a painter's canvas: they define a musical space and product. It is important to note, however, that children may feel differently about an étude created to master a particular crafting technique and a piece that they have decided to create because they have something to communicate in sound. Educators need to carefully consider the impact that specified directions or procedures for composition tasks may have on the efforts of the children and on the resulting compositions. Presenting opportunities for children to study compositional techniques as well as opportunities for children to self-define compositional products creates a balance that maintains motivation and enthusiasm as well as the development of compositional skills and musical understanding.

Composition activities that are teacher facilitated may simply list the steps of the creative process. These lists serve as an organizer in guiding group work and for modeling one approach. When students begin to work in small groups or with partners, it may be helpful to offer guidelines that are more specific. Task guidelines for small-group and partnered work ideally list preparatory, musical, and performance expectations. Here is an example that might be considered a balanced offering of guidelines. It specifies criteria but leaves room for the composers to make creative and personal decisions.

GRADE 2—REPETITION AND CONTRAST/PATTERN WORK

Working with a partner . . .

1. select and use one pitched and one nonpitched percussion instrument.

2. create an interesting one-phrase rhythm that you can remember and play more than once the same way.
3. create a one-phrase melody that you can remember and play more than once the same way.
4. develop—use the two phrases that you have composed to make up a longer piece. Use what you know about patterns and repetition and contrast to make your piece interesting to hear. (Avoid simply taking turns playing your rhythm and melody.)
5. rehearse—practice your piece until you both can play it easily.
6. perform—pieces will be recorded as you share them with our class.

Guidelines offered for young composers can be read to the students and written on a board, displayed on a projector screen, or offered on a project sheet. Students may need to refer to the guidelines multiple times during the course of their work. The guidelines should be discussed to be sure that each student understands the assignment. Task guidelines may also serve as a checklist that students can use to determine whether they have completed all parts of an assignment prior to more formal assessments.

Assessment

While students should not feel the weight of endless assessments, evaluation of learning is an important tool for planning future instruction. To fully measure what children understand of music composition, it is important to create assessment strategies that include an examination of both compositional processes and products. Assessment of compositional processes should reveal not only what, but how, a student is thinking about composition.

In large group settings this may be accomplished as individuals ask or answer questions during teacher-facilitated group composition activities. It is important to remember that the types of questions children ask reveal as much about their thinking processes as do the answers that they offer in response to teacher questions. Children's questions and comments reveal the associations that they are making between concepts, skills that they are exercising as they suggest crafting decisions, and their developing awareness of the expressive capacities of music.

In the sample lesson, "A Song for Our Teacher," children are asked to supply information about unity/variety and melodic direction. As this activity unfolds, it is easy to assess what individual contributors understand about the topic of melodic direction and the use of variety within melodic structures.

Another opportunity to glimpse how young composers are thinking can be found when students are working in small groups or in teams. Success in small group or partnered work usually occurs when the teacher circulates between the composers acting as a resource and checking student progress. These walkabouts offer the teacher an opportunity to listen to the conversational exchanges taking place among children composing together. The nature of these exchanges reveals how children define and solve compositional problems.

Process information can illuminate the assessment of student products. Conversations may reveal composer intentions that are not evident in final products. This may help in identifying the gaps that students often experience between musical imagination and skills of artistic craftsmanship. The identification of such a gap helps the teacher to plan instruction to introduce and reinforce the development of technical skills. Although such gaps are observable with prekindergarten through first-grade students, they become increasingly noticeable by grade 2 as students engage in more small-group and partnered projects and work with increased independence from the teacher.

Students working in pairs or small groups should be guided to identify their own compositional processes. These students generally have sufficient reading and writing skills to be able to record their answers to simple questions about their own working styles. Additionally, these students can utilize a simple three-point scoring system—NY: not yet, M: meets, or E: exceeds—for evaluating their own products against specific task guidelines. Students become very adept at using these systems to check their own work. These systems are also simple enough to be time efficient for teachers who need to record assessments for large numbers of children. Given the highly general nature of these tools, it is important to plan and utilize periodic assessments that offer a more detailed analysis of student work.

Teacher-generated feedback contributes significantly to the development of compositional skills and understanding in young composers (Webster, 2003), but they must also learn how to evaluate their own work. Students should always be encouraged to evaluate the results (products) of their musical decisions (process). Listening critically to their own compositions and to compositions created by their peers can inform their future processes. In every class where compositions are shared, there are pieces that stand apart from the others in their effectiveness and musicality. Skillful analysis of why these pieces are especially musical helps everyone in the composing community to increase their understanding of what constitutes music of higher artistic quality. The "Snow Is Dancing" beginner lesson offered earlier provides an excellent opportunity for students to consider the effectiveness of their own pieces as well as those created by other kindergarten classes. The compositional process is not complete until children have been engaged in a critical reflection on their work.

DEVELOPING THE THREE BASIC COMPOSITIONAL CAPACITIES WITH YOUNG CHILDREN

Composing is not a single task or skill, and music does not result from a singular process or outpouring of musical thought. This popular myth, often assigned to the great composer Wolfgang Amadeus Mozart, does him and music no honor. We now know that Mozart, like so many other composers, had sketchbooks and worked out his ideas over varied lengths of time. While Mozart may have possessed sufficient musical memory to retain longer episodes and more details of music than some of his contemporaries, few, if any, of his works were truly turned out effortlessly in a single work session. Composition takes time and effort.

The process of composition comprises a multitude of activities that are interwoven as the composer makes decision after decision to bring a piece of music into being. Depending on the length and complexity of the piece, the composer may make thousands of decisions. Considerations range from selecting a single note to be played by a single instrument to the selection of a large ensemble to perform a multimovement work. In some ways, the more we consider what is involved in the act of composition, the more amazing it is that any person is able to create music—let alone that young children can do it.

The skills and abilities that young children must develop to take them beyond their natural inclination to make music can be described as *basic compositional capacities*. These capacities, as previously discussed in chapter 2, include (1) *intention*—the ability to generate and execute ideas, (2) *expressivity*—the ability to think about the impact of musical sounds, and (3) *artistic craftsmanship*—the ability to shape sounds to achieve affect. They are often discussed and employed simultaneously. However, it is important to consider the unique developmental path of each of these compositional capacities and to be aware of how they take shape in young composers.

The Growth of Compositional Intention in the Prekindergarten through Second-Grade Composer

One of the first decisions that any composer must make is the decision to create music. This decision may be direct, as in, "I'm going to make up a song," or indirect, as when children create music or sound effects (a precursor to film scoring) that accompany their daily activities or play. These *intentions* find root in feeling and action. They may arise from the memory of feeling or be drawn from a particular context or recalled event. Intentions may be the result of something being experienced at present or the projection of a future feeling or experience. Regardless of what gives rise to

Table 7.1. Compositional Capacities in Prekindergarten through Second-Grade Students

Compositional Capacities	Novice	Intermediate	Advanced
Intention	Music arises in the course of play and other daily activities. Music is often organized in parallel form to the activity in which children are engaged. Games, toys, pictures, and stories are often springboards for music making (often song based).	Young children shift from storied to expressive pieces of music as their awareness of their own and others' feelingful response to music grows.	Young children now possess the ability to predetermine product intention. They purposefully select whether to create programmatic or absolute music. Children are better able to evaluate the effectiveness of their compositional choices against their envisioned product.
Expressivity	Young children become aware of how different types of music are used in various settings. This awareness forms a foundation for creating music that conforms to cultural norms.	Young children begin to consider the expressive impact of their compositional decisions. Choices are shaped by the child's own response to the affective potential of a sound.	Young children can imagine and compare how different gestures will impact the expressive capacity of their music. Compositional choices are directly tied to the affective potential of each gesture. Choices are dominated by self-awareness, but audience awareness begins to emerge.
Artistic Craftsmanship	Technical skills begin to emerge as young children play with sounds. They may use familiar songs as a basis for their own songs by borrowing excerpts of melodies and/or rhythms and adding their own lyrics.	Young children may base original songs on the melodic structures of familiar pieces. These new pieces are often ornamented or extended as children intuitively experiment with how elements impact principle relationships.	Young children's compositions take on increased length, detail, and internal connectivity. They begin to transition from borrowing material to creating original songs or compositions.

intentions—either direct or enacted—a composer must choose to act. But just how do these actions take shape as intentional capacity develops in the prekindergarten through second-grade composer?

Novice Composers

Very young composers tend to experience their compositions as they are created. These composers may not have a direct musical intention at the beginning of the creative process, but such intention may evolve as children play with the sounds within their environments. The development of direct intention is often preceded by *enactive* engagements. In the process of enactive composition, children create sounds that partner or accompany what they are doing and experiencing or have done and experienced as part of their activities. These actions lead to intentions that result in *storied compositions*—compositions that are about something.

Storied compositions play a critical role in the development of musical understanding. Inspired by transactional engagements within the child's daily activities, these creations may be based on the composer's play, the actions that a particular toy might take in a given situation, interactions with other people, or even the sounds that could be performed to accompany a picture or painting. The target ideas (games, toys, pictures, stories, etc.) arising from such activities are the springboards for creative music making. Children use these ideas and experiences as frames of reference to offer organizational boundaries for their work. Although such boundaries are extramusical in nature and perhaps difficult to ascertain by observation alone, they still possess the same characteristics and serve the same functions as musical forms by providing limits to be explored.

Intermediate Composers

As young composers move beyond the direct experience of enacting their compositions and toward a more objective stance, they begin to develop an awareness of their own interests and feelingful responses to music. This growth in intrapersonal awareness equips composers to consider a range of compositional intentions for their work. Composers may begin to experiment and test how different sounds and approaches to organizing their music impact their final products. These experiments may be purposeful and intended, or they may simply arise as composers explore and experiment with the musical materials at hand.

The young composer's catalog at this stage continues to include pieces that are *storied*, but also expands to include works that are *expressive of* something or evocative of a particular emotion. In this way, the young composer is able to consider and demonstrate a range of possible intentions. As

children develop at different rates and maintain different sources of inspiration and intention for their compositions, the shift in catalog from *storied*
to *expressive of* pieces vary from child to child. A child who has amassed an
extensive collection of a singular type of intended piece (e.g., a collection of
astronaut adventure songs) may need guidance to expand their intentional
capacities. Children may be prompted to consider new ideas and products
through the use of guided listening and teacher-prompted compositional
activities.

Advanced Composers

The ability to establish a particular compositional goal for one's work
is the mark of advanced development in intentional capacities. Advanced
composers give careful consideration to the outcome of their compositional processes. They establish a vision of an "end product" that serves to
guide the decision-making process during composition. Although young
composers may present a limited range of intended products, the ability
to envision products grows and expands with compositional experience.
Like all compositional skills, initial abilities vary from child to child and
develop over time.

The ability to decide whether to pursue *programmatic* or *absolute* music
enables the young composer to give additional attention to other compositional questions. Once the composer has determined an intended product,
he or she is better able to define his or her own work. The contributions and
roles of time, pitch, and expressivity can be considered in greater detail because there is an end goal against which decisions can be measured. While
the definition of the intended product may change and shift over time, and
perhaps even evolve into a completely different product, possessing an initial intention allows the composer to set his or her own boundaries more
effectively than when enacting compositions.

Encouraging Expressivity in the Young Composer

Discovering the relationship between sound and feeling is a key component in musical development. Children first notice this relationship as
it unfolds personally before beginning to think about how others respond
to music. Over time, children can learn to imagine how a feeling might be
felt if it were experienced as sound. To transition to compositional thinking,
children must be able to draw upon their formal and informal understanding of how the principle relationships within a piece of music relate to feeling. Once these realizations are made, the young composer can explore how
musical language can be shaped to invite an array of human responses.

Novice Composers

All composers begin developing an awareness of expressivity by noticing the feelingful impact of sounds as they are created. In the young composer awareness is often awakened as the composer enacts, or possibly imagines, music. This initial realization is the first step on a journey of exploration that allows the composer to acquire an understanding of the parameters of cultural norms and expectations. The music that accompanies daily living— that is, music found in supermarkets, malls, restaurants, television shows, movies, religious worship services, and even school settings— informs children as to what is culturally accepted as "scary," "silly," "dangerous," "energized," and so on. These experiences lay the foundation that allows the young composer to question how music can achieve those broad emotional characteristics. When children reach this point of questioning, they enter into a transitional stage where they sometimes desire to control music's expressive power.

Intermediate Composers

As children's perceptions of expressivity in music grow, they become increasingly able to consider the impact of the sounds they choose. Purposed experimentation is used to explore sounds with the intent to discover what invokes human response. Much of this work may fall into the "trial and error" category for the intermediate composer. However, it is through these experiments, and an increased curiosity about the music of their world, that young composers continue to expand their vocabulary of expressive sounds.

Another critical development in the expressive capacity of the intermediate composer is marked by the transition from reacting to external sounds to imagining sounds internally while composing. Predicated on the development and use of musical memory, the skills of audiation allow composers to imagine and manipulate musical ideas internally. The fluidity of the process increases as composers are able to conceive of musical gestures without pausing to perform the sounds externally. The acquisition of these skills marks the beginning of sustained and meaningful expressivity in composition.

Advanced Composers

Prekindergarten through second-grade composers exhibiting advanced skills in the use of expressive gestures are those who are able to give detailed consideration to how sounds can be used, connected, organized, and presented to achieve the greatest affective response. These composers have developed the capacity to imagine the impact of their compositional choices in the near absence or complete absence of external sound. The ability to consider how a feeling might be captured in sound and to imagine how those sounds might be organized for the greatest potential impact on others encountering the composition marks the full development of the advanced expressive capacity in the prekindergarten through second-grade composer.

Developing Artistic Craftsmanship in the Young Composer

Composers armed with intention and expressive purpose are unable to share their musical vision unless they possess the skills of artistic craftsmanship. The ability to use the elements of music to shape principled relationships for affective impact is at the heart of this capacity. However, craftsmanship leads to musical results only when tempered by the artistry that arises from knowledge of intention and expression. Artistic craftsmanship begins simply and grows into an ability to shape music in meaningful ways within particular stylistic systems or to extend beyond the rules of a particular system. The artistry needed to temper craft stems from the careful contemplation that composers give to the feelingful impact of their crafting choices.

Novice Composers

Novice composers are most frequently engaged in the process of discovery through experimentation. They revel in trial and error as they create music. Through this process, the young composer may accidentally create sounds that are musically satisfying. These pieces are probably best termed "fortuitous accidents." Yet the discovery of a single sound or set of sounds that are pleasing or in some way appealing to the composer tends to spawn repetition. Such repetition may be within a single piece or across a collection of pieces generated at roughly the same time. Revisiting successful musical ideas (those that have been expressively assembled) allows children to develop a basic awareness of the importance of artistic craftsmanship.

Intermediate Composers

In the early stages of developing artistic craftsmanship, young composers discover that the repetition of compositional success is enjoyable. With this realization in mind, children moving into the intermediate stage of development may borrow thematic material, consciously or subconsciously, to serve as the foundation of their work. Indeed, several researchers have commented on the tendency of children to use snippets of things they know well in their own pieces (Smith, 2004; Stauffer, 2002). Imitation, direct quoting, and the piecing together of familiar tunes may all be in evidence across the range of the pieces created by intermediate composers.

This approach is clearly a natural step in the development of craftsmanship. Our histories are full of composers, poets, dancers, artists, and writers who copied or imitated the work of others to develop their own repertoire of creative skills. Indeed, J. S. Bach spent hours literally copying the works of other composers to familiarize himself with their compositional techniques. It is important to remember, however, that Bach lived in a time without recordings; the score was all that was available as a record of the sounds of performance. Now children can learn about the music that surrounds them through a much wider range of activities. Attempting to imitate the music with which they are familiar (Campbell, 2005) is but one approach.

Ultimately, the intermediate composers set out to create music that they enjoy. This is what they can most readily imitate and adapt. They place greater emphasis on creating music that fits preconceived norms rather than pursuing more innovative forms and styles. Imitating and quoting successful compositions of others changes over time. Intermediate composers transition from creating compositions quoting familiar material to the creation of pieces that also feature extended sections into which original material is added or woven. Some composers will advance to creating fully original works with formal organizations that carry many of the characteristic features of known forms.

Advanced Composers

As children's artistic capacities and skills grow, they begin to exhibit a strong familiarity with the tools and forms of convention. Some of their compositions adhere to the rules of a particular style, while others seek to challenge the rules and use sounds in new and unconventional ways. Children's compositions begin to change in shape. Some children create pieces that unfold over a longer span of time. Other composers continue to create shorter pieces, but extend the detailing within the piece or expand on the number of instruments, ranges, textures, or other parameters in their compositions.

As compositional products grow in detail and intricacy, the potential for increased internal relationships grows. Advanced composers begin to generate material with an increasing number of linkages between ideas within the same piece. Compositions that were once easily memorized are now of such length and detail that they require some mode of preservation (notation or recording). The teacher's role in the production of pieces (prompting and reminding children of what they have heard previously) diminishes as the young composers begin to find their own *voice*. Emphasis on developing the young composers' sound palette becomes increasingly important so that they may continue to embrace new compositional techniques that may eventually be utilized in their own work.

TOUCHPOINTS FOR TEACHING

1. Draw inspiration from the child's natural interest and curiosity when designing composition activities.

Transitioning children from creating as part of their self-determined play to composition in a stylized setting such as school requires a subtle approach so that the joy of creation is not lost. The activities and interests of children as they invent their own music should be preserved in formal instruction. Talking with children about the things in their lives that fascinate them provides entry into their world.

Children who love to share stories about their dogs are going to love writing songs about their dogs. And, if "dogs" is too narrow a topic, then a song about "pets in my family" is usually a good fit. Asking children to think about the sounds pets make (meowing, barking, whining, clicking toenails, chirping, and even silence), the ways those pets move (jumping, sliding, crawling, swimming, running, darting, snuggling), and how those sounds and movements might be made with music is a conversation sure to engage every child in the room.

2. Offer plenty of opportunities for children to explore, create, and share their musical work.

The first try at any new activity is likely to be filled with a few bumps and rough spots. Children need time to explore the sounds that musical instruments can make as well as to consider how those sounds might be used. Children need time to make up an idea, test it out, discard it, start over, revive the last idea, change it a few times, and just walk away. These explorations are the building blocks of musical thinking, and the creators are making mental notes of what works and what doesn't work quite so well.

As these playful exploratory forays grow to reveal completed compositions, children should be invited to share their work. Just as young visual artists' work is displayed on refrigerators and bulletin boards, so should the works of young composers be given an audience. Teachers should give careful consideration to how these works can be preserved and shared. Music class websites where compositions can be posted for parents to hear and download are easy to maintain and give parents and children an opportunity to share together the joy of music making and listening.

3. Supply children with a wide and varied sound palette for both listening and creating.

Children need to be introduced to a variety of instrumental and vocal tone colors from within and beyond their own cultures. Not all children encounter these sounds (let alone be able to identify them by name) outside of school. Students may begin by learning about families of instruments or individual instruments and then progress to learn about the myriad ways in which instruments and voices may be used in music.

Although recordings are a wonderful resource, invite skilled performers into the classroom (physically or virtually) to demonstrate instruments and different styles of music whenever possible. These performers need not be professionals. Older students, parents, college musicians, other teachers, or community members may be willing to share their knowledge with young composers. Many local orchestras have educational outreach programs available as well. Visiting performers are able to address students' questions and curiosities through discussion and modeling that is not available from recordings.

Find ways to make learning about instruments fun with sound games. For example, when presenting a classroom instrument, pass it around the room, challenging students to discover how many different sounds can be produced with the instrument. Later, hide several instruments from the view of the children, and play them one at a time. Ask the children to identify each instrument first by pointing to pictures of the instruments and later by saying the name of the instrument. A more advanced version of the game is to challenge the students to identify instruments when two or more are played simultaneously.

4. Follow the child's lead in musical interests and instructional pace.

Children are naturally curious about the world of sound. Filling classroom spaces with a variety of instruments and scheduling time for children to explore those instruments is developmentally appropriate for the young composer. Up to about the age of seven, many children engage in music making without adult prompting. They sing to themselves, make up songs, and create versions and variations of songs they have learned.

Unfortunately, in most American schools this is not recognized, encouraged, or rewarded. Some researchers feel that the disappearance of this spontaneous music making may be more directly related to the process of schooling than to any developmental condition (Barrett, 2006). How much more musical our society might be if this spontaneous music making could be channeled into a lifelong habit of creating with sound. After all, for the vast majority of people, music is described in terms of "songs." Wouldn't it be wonderful if people created songs as easily as they converse?

5. Be encouraging.

Inspiration for hard work is easy to find when praise for hard work is close at hand. Children need to hear that their compositions are musical, expressive, exciting, gentle, fun to perform, interesting to hear, and so on. An invitation to share their work and to applaud the work of their peers is a critical element in the creation of a supportive composing community. A simple, "That's wonderful music. Let's record it!" does a lot to help children feel good about themselves and the music they create.

6. Engage in exercises and games that foster the development of musical memory.

The best way to encourage children to learn and remember sounds is to engage in games that require those skills. Games help young children develop skills of attention, analysis, and recall that are the foundation for artistic craftsmanship. These games begin simply and increase in challenge as children develop their memory skills.

One game that children enjoy involves recording the voices of each adult in the school that the children encounter. The adults say a simple phrase, such as, "Hello boys and girls. Have a wonderful music class!" First as a class, and later individually, have the children try to identify the adults from the sound of their voices. This is a good game to repeat when someone new joins the class.

Another game that children greatly enjoy is the "radio game." This game is based upon a song that children know very well and are able to sing independently. The children are told that they are being turned into a giant radio. When the "tuner" (the teacher or an appointed child) turns on the radio, they should begin to sing. When the radio is turned off, they should stop singing aloud but continue to sing the song in their musical imagination. When the "tuner" turns the radio back on, they need to be at a new place in the song, just like when they turn their own radios on and off at home.

The teacher may need to model this a few times at the beginning of the game. Guiding the children to keep a steady beat by patting their legs or tapping a finger gently may also help. After a few times with the teacher controlling the radio, allow children to take turns being the "tuner." The teacher can assist the class by singing softly when the radio is on. Eventually the children can play this game unaided.

7. Introduce musical terminology as it arises from the student's musical observations or creations.

Students should be introduced to musical terminology when a word will be most easily attached to its meaning as experienced, created, or performed by the child. When students discover they can play something backward, teach the word *retrograde*. When they are searching for a word to describe something in their music, briefly explain the term used by professional musicians. Keep in mind, however, that there are musical terms relevant to nearly every composition as well as those so specialized as to mainly exist in the dominion of the professional theorist. Balance attention to these details accordingly when introducing musical terms to children. Be sure that focus terms are words that children will have many occasions to use.

8. Offer instruction in music notation when the student has determined a "need to know."

Many of the initial works created by novice composers are so brief that they can be held in memory. Once children have exceeded the capacity of their own musical memory, they will either ask to record their compositions or invent their own notational systems. These systems may allow children to function for a significant span of time before a more traditional system of notation becomes necessary if, indeed, it ever does. It is important to remember that musical thinking, not notational skill, is the goal of composition instruction. The confines of learning notation may impede creative thinking as children opt to set aside complex musical ideas that are simply too difficult for them to accurately notate.

9. Provide theoretical explanations in relation to music created by the student.

Music theory documents the historical evolution of compositional practice. In short, theory has followed creation. In educational practice this should not change. The logical application of theoretical rules usually requires an understanding of exceptions. These practices can be confusing for novice composers and are not necessary for successful compositions to emerge from children's work.

10. Keep it real. Compositions are compositions, not exercises to teach something else.

Composition activities created for children to execute should mirror activities regularly undertaken by composers throughout history, across cultures, and representing multiple genres. These real compositions are meaningful to children because children draw connections from context, their efforts, and the resulting products. Examples of real compositions that young children can successfully create include making songs for specific purposes. These might include songs to celebrate special events like a school tournament or fair, a special day such as the one hundredth day of school, or a special person such as a retiring teacher or a new baby in their family. Children can also create class songs or school songs that they sing at the start or end of the day.

Another activity that is engaging for children is in the addition of sound effects to stories. This activity can take two different forms. First, children may use a story as the foundation for a composition. In this case, the children create the story in sound, capturing as many details and events as possible through the sounds they select and organize. The story may then be set aside or used as score to organize performance. In either case, emphasis is given to the sounds of the composition, and the narration is set aside.

The second approach closely resembles the work of film score composers in that the children create sounds to accompany a story as it is read. While the most novice of composers may generate only the sounds that are literally presented in the story, with practice the musical landscape will expand to evoke the settings, moods, characters, and actions. Children easily understand the concepts of leitmotif and soundscaping from cartoons and can employ such techniques in their own works. These types of projects are ripe for development into interdisciplinary units that engage literacy skills in both language arts and music.

11. Honor each student's work by resisting the urge to "fix" it.

Music has evolved over thousands of years because those who create it are not always aware of or tied by the rules of their predecessors. It is important to hold judgments of quality in reserve. Rather than measuring a student's work against a preconceived notion of "what music is," ask questions of the composer that help to reveal his or her thinking by provoking reflection. As one very apt second-grade creator noted, "Whenever I make up a song that nobody tells me to fix, it comes out perfectly!"

A TEACHING SCENARIO

The following teaching scenario and lesson plans illustrate how the methods described in this chapter play out in the classroom. Each lesson plan is summarized on the planning grid template as developed in chapter 4.

A SONG FOR OUR TEACHER

Unit: Songwriting Project: A Song for Our Teacher Level: Novice	
Planning Elements	*Thinking Guides*
Composer Characteristics	Grade level: Prekindergarten through first grade Skill level: Novice composers General music class Four classes, ten minutes per class
Focus and Supporting Principles	Unity and variety using melodic direction, phrase structure
Compositional Capacities	Teacher-directed intention, melodic direction as intuitive expression, artistic text setting
Compositional Context	Large group
Tools	Instruments: voices, small percussion Preservation: Invented notation, recording
Prerequisites	Concepts: Melodic contour (smile, frown, up, down, same) Musical skills: Familiarity with verse/refrain form Intuitive understandings: Awareness of same/different
Co-compositional Activities	None
Task Guidelines	Product: Song about classroom teacher Length: One verse, one refrain Specs: Write eight-line poem about teacher; create 8-mm AABA verse, 8 measures AAAB refrain; use variety of melodic direction; add instruments to punctuate text Time: +/– ten minutes per class Preservation: Teacher notes/invented notation for kids to read; record for teacher and class Performance: Full class for teacher
Assessment	What: Composition is the tool for the summative assessment of melodic direction
Connections	At home: This is a year's end project. A copy of the composition is sent home with instructions for parents to ask their child to sing the song for them and tell them about making up the song for their classroom teacher.

Week 1

It is nearing the end of the music class for Mrs. Linnehan's kindergarten class. As they finish putting instruments back on the shelf, Mrs. McRae calls for the class to gather in a tight circle near her chair.

"Boys and girls, we are going to begin a very special project today. We are going to compose, or make up, a song for Mrs. Linnehan. We will perform this song for her during the last week of school in just a few weeks. It is important to remember that our song is going to be a surprise for Mrs. Linnehan. Let's make sure not to tell her about it! Today we are going to begin to write the words of our song. Could someone please raise your hand, wait to be called on, and then tell me one thing that Mrs. Linnehan does for you or does with your class?" Hands fly up around the room. "Clara?"

"Mrs. Linnehan, um . . . she . . . she helps us with our reading."

"Thank you, Clara. Let me write that down in my notebook. Brandon?"

"She takes us out on the playground."

"Yes. That's a fun one! Lorinda?"

"Mrs. Linnehan helps us with math. You know, two plus two equals four and stuff."

"Got it. Let's have a few more." Mrs. McRae continues to jot down the thoughts that the students offer about their year with Mrs. Linnehan. Mrs. McRae then reads back the list to the students and tells them that she will turn it into a poem about Mrs. Linnehan that she will read to them next week. She calls for the children to line up just as Mrs. Linnehan arrives at the music room door. The children line up, giggling at how close they came to being "caught" at work on the surprise.

Week 2

Mrs. Linnehan's class enters the music room, and a few kids start to whisper about the "surprise" project. Mrs. McRae hushes them gently and reminds the children to find their seats as she closes the door.

"Good morning, class. Raise your hand if you remember the special project we began last week." Most of the children excitedly raise a hand. "Well," begins Mrs. McRae, "I took all of the wonderful things you told me about Mrs. Linnehan and made them into a poem. Let me read it to you."

Mrs. McRae reads with a strong sense of rhythm:

> "Math, reading, work, and play
> Mrs. Linnehan, you're okay
> Stories, snacks, books, and swings
> Mrs. Linnehan does great things!

Oh Mrs. Linne, Linne, Linnehan
Oh Mrs. Linne, Linne, Linnehan,
Oh Mrs. Linne, Linne, Linnehan
You're the best teacher in all the land."

"Well, what do you think? Will Mrs. Linnehan like it?" The children nod and respond positively. "Let's take a minute to learn the words then, so we can make up the music." Mrs. McRae taps the beat quietly on her knees and states the poem line by line. The children echo her. After a couple of minutes, the class says the entire poem all together.

"If we are going to turn this poem into a song, we are going to need to make up a melody. We have talked about how melodies are made up of musical shapes. Does anyone remember one of the shapes?" Mrs. McRae collects answers and prompts the kids as she draws a smile, a frown, an arrow pointing up, an arrow pointing down, and a straight line.

Mrs. McRae then asks, "Can anyone use one of these shapes to make up a melody that we could sing for "Math, reading, work, and play?" As they think, Mrs. McRae reminds the children that there are no wrong ideas. Slowly at first, children begin to sing ideas. After each idea is sung, Mrs. McRae echoes it in a strong voice and asks the class to repeat it, too. She jots each idea in solfège in her notebook. She is also recording the class so that she can focus on what the students are singing. After collecting a few ideas, Mrs. McRae asks the children to try each idea. The class then discusses which of the two or three ideas suggested best fits the line.

This process is repeated for each line of the song with Mrs. McRae moving things along. The children are encouraged to consider when ideas should repeat and when new ideas should be used to create interest. After about ten minutes of work, Mrs. McRae says, "Boys and girls, very nice work making up our song melody today. I will take all of your ideas and polish them up into one song for us to work on next week. Let's move the center carpet and sing "Put Up Your Umbrella."

Week 3

As Mrs. Linnehan's class enters the music classroom, Mrs. McRae is drawing on the board. She has drawn 2 + 2 = 4, a storybook with a picture, a stick figure with a hammer, and a pair of stick figures tossing a ball. When the class is seated, Mrs. McRae points at each picture as she says, "Math, reading, work, and play" in rhythm. She invites the children to suggest pictures for the remaining text and quickly sketches it on the board. "Children, please chant our song lyrics quietly."

As the children whisper-chant, Mrs. McRae sings a melody. "Children, please listen to the first line of the song. Does it go up, go down, or stay the same?" The children listen to Mrs. McRae as she models each line of the song. The class takes a few minutes identifying the melodic contour as smile, frown, up, down, and straight. Contour shapes are added to the score that has been drawn on the board. After a few minutes, the children are able to follow the invented notation on the board to sing the full song.

"Children, our song has come a long way. We can really sing it very well now. I think we are ready for the last step. Let's talk about how we can add instruments to our song. Does anyone have an idea? Stephen?"

"I think we could add a steady beat."

"Yes, that might work. What instrument would you use, Stephen, to play a steady beat?"

"I'd like to use the drum."

"Who else would like to play drum with Stephen and keep a steady beat for us?" Hands fly around the room. Mrs. McRae names four children and instructs them to each get a small drum.

"How can we draw the drums on our score?" Mrs. McRae takes several answers and then draws a round drum at the beginning of the score with a hand raised above it. The class continues to discuss how classroom instruments can be used to add accompaniment to the song, with each new instrument being added to the score as students are assigned to play.

Once all of the children are holding instruments, rehearsal commences. Mrs. McRae helps each group of players master their parts and then reminds the children to sing as they play. As the children put the instruments back in their places, Mrs. McRae takes a quick digital photo of the whiteboard that is covered with the score of text pictures, melodic arrows, instrument cues, and performer names. She thanks the children for their hard work and moves to the next step of the lesson.

Week 4

As the children enter the music room, Mrs. McRae invites Mrs. Linnehan to return to hear a special project that the students have been working on and would like to share with her during the final ten minutes of class. (Mrs. McRae has made this invitation to Mrs. Linnehan earlier but repeats it for effect before the children.) Once Mrs. Linnehan has left, the children spend a few minutes working on a folk dance and then begin to set up for their performance. A chair is placed in the front of the room for Mrs. Linnehan. Mrs. McRae turns on the projector, and the score for "Mrs. Linnehan's Song" appears on the pull screen just to one side of the chair. The children collect their instruments and position themselves near the chair by instrument group.

Mrs. McRae sits in the chair and helps the children rehearse their performance. She begins by asking questions about the score to prompt the children to remember where they play. The class sings through the song once, then again, adding the instruments. After one more rehearsal Mrs. Linnehan appears at the door. Mrs. McRae explains that the class has spent the last month working on a special project, a musical present for Mrs. Linnehan. Mrs. Linnehan is escorted to the seat of honor. The class performs the piece.

Mrs. McRae asks the students, "Can anyone tell Mrs. Linnehan how we made up this song?" Different children reveal bits and pieces of the process, and then Mrs. Linnehan asks to hear the song one more time. Mrs. McRae turns on the microphone, and the children perform the song again. Later, Mrs. McRae posts the recording on the school music website so that the children can share their work with their parents.

SUGGESTED LESSON

TIK TIK TAK

Unit: Creating an Arrangement
Project: Arranging a Vocal Piece: Form Based on Tik Tik Tak
Level: Advanced
Overview: For several previous lessons the children have been listening to "Tik Tik Tak" sung by Glykeria, from the album World Playground: A Musical Adventure for Kids, published by Putumayo World Music. They have focused on dynamics, vocal tone color, tempo, and form. They have created listening maps and followed listening maps of the piece. For this piece, the students work in groups of three to create an extended piece following the same form as "Tik Tik Tak." See the task guidelines following the chart.

Note: This same lesson can be done with older children to assess understanding of major and minor by asking them to create the entire composition instead of just the instrumental sections and instructing that one section of the vocal piece must be major while the others are minor. This works well when at least one student in the group has instrumental music experience and can play in a few minor keys.
Task guidelines as given to the students:

1. Select a short song that your group can sing which has both a verse and a chorus. (Brainstorm some possibilities: "Yankee Doodle," "Rocky Mountain," "Angel Band," "Jingle Bells.")

2. Practice the song several times until your group can sing it smoothly.
3. Create an introduction for the song.
4. Think about the way the song sounds, and create an instrumental piece that is about the same length as the verse to contrast with the singing. Your new piece may or may not have a melody.
5. Put your composition together using the pattern of "Tik Tik Tak": intro, instruments (and repeat), verse, chorus (and chorus repeat), instruments (and repeat), verse, chorus, chorus repeat. It is helpful to also use the shapes that the children used in the listening lesson to define the form.

   Triangle for instrumental part, circle for verse, square for chorus.

   The form then looks like this and can be read by nonreaders and beginner readers:

Figure 7.1.

Intro △ △ ● □ □ 2 X (two times)

6. You may also have the instruments accompany the singing as well as play their own part.
7. Different people can play and sing, or everybody can do everything.
8. When you have finished your composition, practice it with your group so that you can play it easily for the class.

ETUDES

1. Observe at a preschool or nursery program. What musical materials are available to the children? What use is made of them?
2. How should music programs for kindergarten and first grade differ from those for older children? How should they differ from nursery school programs?
3. What could you do to foster creativity in your classroom, or how will you do so in the future?
4. Develop an equipment list and budget for a well-equipped prekindergarten through second-grade music classroom that would allow for the types of activities recommended in this chapter.

Planning Elements	Thinking Guides
Composer Characteristics	Grade: Second, spring of year Skill level: Advanced Setting: Classroom Time allocation estimate: Two thirty-minute classes
Focus and Supporting Principles	*Repetition/contrast*—Instrumental solo versus accompanying a vocal line
Compositional Capacities	Intention: Teacher-directed, with student choices Expressivity: Student choice based one songs used, plus tempo changes Artistic craftsmanship: Verse and chorus form and expressive use of tempo changes
Compositional Context	Small group
Tools	Instruments: Various nonpitched percussion, melodic percussion, and voices Preservation: Invented notation, from chart, recording
Prerequisites	Concepts: Introduction, coda, repetition Musical skills: Tempo changes; verse and chorus form Intuitive understandings: Balanced length of sections
Co-compositional Activities	Listening activities based on "Tik Tik Tak" 1. listening to a rembetika 2. listening for voice versus instruments 3. listening for repetition 4. listening for major versus minor 5. creating a form chart 6. creating a formal listening map
Task Guidelines	Product: Piece that has both vocal and instrumental sections that follow the repetition pattern of "Tik Tik Tak" Length: Various because of composer choices Specs: See task guidelines Time: About thirty minutes spread over two class periods Preservation: Recording, invented Performance: For the class
Assessments	What: Follows the form requested, creates a piece of about the same length as verse of song. How: Rubric
Connections	Ask the groups to make up a song instead of using one they know. Can they do this in a minor key? The words to this rembetika are about being around someone you like so much that it makes you nervous because you want to make a good impression. Who might this person be? Where would you see them? Can you make up a song about it? Will your song be major or minor? Or both?

5. Explain why space for physical movement is important in order for this age group to develop compositional skill.
6. Using the "Sonic Snowstorms" lesson in chapter 4 as a model, design a similar lesson for kindergarten that would create rainstorms.
7. Make a list of the issues relating to teacher-imposed task structure and children's compositions. Which side of this argument do you favor? Should children be free to compose without guidelines?
8. It could be argued that the ability to use a concept or technique in a composition demonstrates true understanding. Should compositions be used to assess conceptual understanding? Is that type of composition an authentic assessment?
9. Select a particular piece of music and use it as the basis for co-compositional activities. Design instruction using the planning grid that would include as many of the co-compositional activities listed in this chapter as possible, as well as a compositional activity.
10. List some characteristics of advanced second-grade composers. What distinguishes them from novices and intermediate-level composers at the same grade level?
11. Observe a classroom composition lesson, or teach one yourself. Then write a teaching scenario similar to the ones in this chapter to focus on the techniques of teaching this type of lesson. Reflect on the process and how it might be improved.
12. Find several stories from different cultures that could be used as starting points for compositional activities, and complete a planning grid for each of them that includes music from that culture as part of your plan.

8

Composing in the Upper Elementary Grades

Children in the upper elementary grades and from about ages eight to ten often begin formal musical instrument instruction. This presents many opportunities for exploring the sounds their chosen instrument can make and for organizing those sounds in ways that they find personally meaningful. They may also be singing in children's choirs and can explore composition in that setting. However, composing in classroom settings also should continue, since not all children have access to these additional opportunities or choose to participate in them. Also, the technical limitations of their skills on their instruments or their own voices can restrict what students are able to create at the beginning levels of formal study. After suggesting a profile of upper elementary composers, this chapter presents key concepts for guiding upper elementary composers, makes suggestions for working with composition in elementary choral and instrumental ensembles, and presents some lessons as examples for use in curriculum planning.

PROFILE OF UPPER ELEMENTARY COMPOSERS AND COMPOSITION ACTIVITIES

Like any other music class, students in the upper elementary grades bring a range of backgrounds and experiences to compositional activities. Some may have benefited from compositional experiences in the primary grades. These students are at different levels of development in their own composing skill. A few of them have progressed rapidly from intermediate levels to more advanced conceptual and technical skills. Others may be experiencing the freedom to create for the first time. While they are older and possibly more intellectually advanced, they may be novice composers. This profile offers a look at the behaviors and thought processes exhibited by children of this age as they create, perform, and listen to music.

Composer Characteristics

By the time children are in third grade, they may have very well-formed musical preferences. These are often based on the music they have been exposed to at home. They may also continue to enjoy exploring unfamiliar styles in the context of the music classroom and are often more welcoming of unfamiliar music than some older children.

It is vitally important at this age that children continue to be exposed to a rich and widely varying musical environment in order to expand their sonic palettes. This gives them more sounds to consider when they create pieces of their own. Upper elementary students are often intrigued by music from other cultures and by unfamiliar instruments. They continue to be interested in how sounds are produced and can be manipulated. They often revel in the opportunity to explore an unfamiliar sound source and then use it in a composition. Didgeridoos, panpipes, ocarinas, and many other instruments intrigue them and spark their creative ideas.

This is also the age at which children begin to work well in small groups to create compositions. While younger children often work well in pairs and sometimes trios, these children often work well in trios and sometimes in groups of up to about five. They need models and guidance to work together effectively and to make musical choices for their compositions.

Upper elementary students often do not make music as a routine part of their day in school the way some younger children do. Somewhere around age seven or eight children often stop making spontaneous songs to accompany their work or their play. No doubt this is somewhat because school becomes a more serious place and more quiet is expected. As children become more self-aware and aware of what others think, they become more reluctant to sing aloud their own songs. It becomes even more important, then, for music teachers to provide opportunities for creative self-expression.

Composing can become a private way of communicating that which formerly was a more public—and less self-conscious—form of musical expression. How sad it is that so many children stop composing when they stop creating spontaneous songs. Encouragement to keep making their own music is something that could continue to allow them a voice for the rest of their lives.

The upper elementary grades provide a critical opportunity for music educators to encourage people to create music. It seems especially important that music teachers of upper elementary students provide interesting opportunities for these children to compose music of their own. Otherwise, this ability can disappear from a child's life when her singing of spontaneous songs ceases.

Another characteristic of children this age is their developing sense of humor. This is the age where "knock-knock" jokes are often pervasive. Much entertainment can be provided by having children sing "knock-knock" jokes and imitate various musical styles. Operatic style "knock-knock" jokes with improvised melodies and free rhythms are an easy way to get these children to improvise vocally once it has been successfully modeled by the teacher. Country music style also works quite well with many students. Because this is the age where a sense of style seems to have been solidified and a sense of humor is emerging, both of these also can begin to appear in children's compositions.

Understanding and Use of Compositional Principles

One of the interesting aspects of upper elementary–aged composers is their ability to use the compositional principals to craft musical surprises. They begin to understand how to use sudden release of tension or sudden instability for humorous effects. They are often still very interested in the use of silence and of various sounds and continue using these in their compositions. However, notions of instability and tension and release seem to hold more appeal. They are much less inclined than primary students to include lots of repetition in their works, but this is not totally abandoned.

Because children this age often model their pieces on music that is familiar to them, there is still usually a great deal of stability in the works they create. However, as their natural sense of humor begins to appear, more instability also suddenly arrives in their pieces, but usually in rather predictable ways: sudden loud sounds, deliberate "wrong" notes, and humorous sound effects. Stravinsky's *Greeting Prelude*, based on "Happy Birthday," and Lucian Cailliet's *Variations on "Pop Goes the Weasel"* are two pieces by well known composers that upper elementary students often enjoy. Discussion of how these two composers employed the musical principles to create humorous effects in their music often leads to further experimentation with humorous effects by young composers.

As students begin to learn recorder (and possibly use Orff instruments), creating variations on the pieces from their classes and methods books becomes an intriguing way of exploring composition of a different sort. Unity and variety can be the focus of compositional études assigned as part of beginning instrumental classes. This is dealt with more completely in the next chapter.

Similarly, variation assignments can be used with recorders or Orff instruments once the children have acquired the basic playing skills and can play a familiar tune with ease. These compositional études can be used to demonstrate various types of rhythmic and melodic variation. The task then becomes to be sure that students continue to have unifying factors to their works while experimenting with the infinite possibilities of variation.

Related to the ideas of how much variation and how to create humor can be similar struggles with motion and stasis. Continual motion and then sudden stasis is another technique for musical humor. Deliberate repetition also creates an expectation that then can be thwarted with humorous effects. Each of the musical principles can contribute in its own way to sounds that can be perceived by young composers (and often their listeners) as humorous. These young composers make choices based on how they respond to the sounds and how others respond to the sounds they have organized.

This should not be taken to mean that all the music composed by students this age has a humorous intent. To the contrary, many pieces are created that do not include any attempts at humor. It is merely that this penchant for humor usually first appears at this age. This corresponds as well to an increasing sense of audience and of creating music for others to hear. These children begin to make purposeful choices that incorporate qualities of familiar styles that they recognize and respond to and that they expect their audiences to recognize and respond to as well. This, too, is an element of musical humor, but extends beyond humor to pieces intended for other purposes as well. These children often wish to emulate musical models with which they have some personal identification.

Compositional Context

As noted above, this is the age where group composition often begins to be successful. By third grade, students are often able to create satisfying pieces in groups of three. After some experience, groups as large as five may experience similar favorable outcomes. Often the children have had experience working in cooperative learning groups in their regular classroom. If the grade-level teacher has assigned groups, the music teacher may want to use those groupings in her classroom. If the groups have been thoughtfully constructed and if the children in the groups are used to working with one another on cooperative learning tasks, this may work quite well. It can also save time initially.

However, the goals the classroom teacher has for the groups she has designed may not be the same as those of a music teacher. The music teacher needs to consider how groups are formed if she wants to create her own. One way to do this is to allow the children to form their own groups. These are often referred to as "friendship groups" and may be one of the most effective ways to help children begin to learn to work together collabora-tively.

This can, however, present problems if some children do not get selected to work with any others. The teacher must then encourage a group to wel-come a member with whom they initially did not choose to work. Teachers can ask the child who is not in a group with whom he or she would like to work. Then the teacher can ask that group to include the student. Tact, diplomacy, and encouragement from the teacher may be necessary at first in order to make friendship groups work. Role-playing how to work in a group may be necessary before beginning a formal task.

It usually does not work well to take three children who are left over from the choosing of groups and form a group with them. They did not choose to work together, and this may be problematic. Finally, it should be noted that students who regard themselves as a community of learners and who have been encouraged to regard all class members as valuable colleagues and friends usually do not have these issues.

There are many ways to structure groups in classrooms. Composition teachers may want to explore using a variety of groupings across different projects and at different times. It is usually wise not to keep exactly the same groups from one composition task to the next. Working with a variety of people often increases the range of ideas within a class. Some teachers find that mixed-gender groups are more effective than single-gender groups. Others want to be sure to include a range of ability levels in a group. Friend-ship groups rarely form in this way, and so the teacher may choose to assign groups for some projects and allow choice of group members for others.

Part of working in groups is learning to share one's ideas and then accept-ing a group decision on whether and how to use those ideas. Teachers may need to model behaviors for helping groups to actually consider everyone's ideas and for making *musical* decisions on which ideas to use. Children in friendship groups initially may base decisions on factors other than compo-sitional effectiveness if they are not reminded to consider the sound. Many articles have been written on using cooperative learning in music classes, and composition teachers may wish to consult some of these if group work seems to be new to their students.

Sometimes a teacher notices that one child is using the group to work out her own ideas to the exclusion of everyone else's ideas. These are *executive groups,* where one child uses team members to fulfill his or her musical vi-sion. Others in the group are sometimes frustrated, and there is a lack owner-ship of the project. Perhaps this could be an opportunity to provide that child time to work alone rather than in a group. (The child's ideas may still be per-formed by a group.) These strong leaders are occasionally at a more advanced compositional level and need the space to work out their own ideas.

It also can be effective to place several more advanced students in the same group if they can work collaboratively. However, this can lead to less-than-stellar results because each insists on using his or her own ideas. They may use a concurrent group style by working separately and then trying to patch the parts together. This often does not lead to satisfying results.

Cooperation may not always be the hallmark of more advanced students. Teachers can work on the skills of cooperation and collaboration in these groups, but allowing some children to work alone while others are working in groups is sometimes a more satisfying solution. Sensitive teachers make those decisions based on the needs of the child and of the knowledge and experiences of that child. While everyone needs to experience group composition, not everyone needs to use it each time an activity is planned.

By contrast, over time some children definitely come to prefer to work in groups when they compose. These children likely prefer to choose their own group members, but often are willing to accept another member at the teacher's suggestion. Their collaborative skills evolve as their compositional skills do. Their ability to see the value of the ideas of others and to incorporate those ideas into a final product becomes one of the hallmarks of their compositional style. These abilities have their beginnings in the group compositional work done in the upper elementary grades and continue to evolve in middle school.

Particularly for intermediate and advanced composers there is less use of whole-class compositions at this level. It may still occur in some situations with beginner composers and as a way of modeling something the teacher wishes to present. However, just as story charts from younger grades become personal narratives in upper elementary school, whole-class compositions evolve into more personal expressions in upper elementary music classrooms. Teachers may still provide structure and ideas that are then explored more fully in group and individual work.

Tools of Creation and Preservation

Upper elementary students continue to expand their sound palettes. New instruments can be introduced in the classroom. Interesting sounds can be made by instruments invented by third- and fourth-grade students. Some students are beginning traditional music lessons at this point, and those instruments can be added to the available sound sources. It is often interesting to figure out ways to make sounds on instruments in ways that are not the usual method. A related lesson can be to use Henry Cowell's *The Banshee* for prepared piano and to show how the piano sounds can be altered by placing materials on the strings. Students need to be cautioned about using things that can damage their instruments, but otherwise, unique sounds can be found.

Children often have fun playing with just the mouthpiece of the recorder or by taking off the bell or other parts and by trying to play two recorders at once. This is also a good time to make a garden hose horn with a mouthpiece and a funnel or double reeds out of plastic straws of differing lengths. Blowing across bottles holding various levels of water or striking them with a rubber mallet can lead to other sound explorations. Another related lesson could then be about the glass harmonica, how Benjamin Franklin improved it, and how Mozart composed for it. Similarly, children could learn why Adolphe Sax invented the saxophone or Les Paul the electric guitar. Once a collection of student-invented and -adapted instruments have been created and brought into the classroom, they can be used in compositions done by groups or by individuals.

Obviously, the children can be encouraged to create pieces for instruments that they are learning to play. While initially their technical skills may be somewhat limited, creating pieces often leads to better technique and improved notational skills. The children can hear in their minds what they want their instruments to do and work to produce those sounds and to find ways to write them down. Often children simply write down the pitch names and prefer to remember the rhythm of something they have created (Smith, 2004).

Gradually, as they become more fluent at reading notation, they include more and more notational details. After about one year of traditional study, children can often create and notate fairly complex pieces for their instruments (Smith, 2008). Teachers can then assist by creating appropriate accompaniments for the pieces the children have created and by having them performed publicly. This is discussed in greater detail in the next chapter.

At this age, most children continue to use recordings as the primary means of preservation and to use invented or mixed notation as another aid to memory. Teachers should regularly record their pieces and help the children discuss their intentions and the results. It is important not to push the use of standard notation too soon, but to concentrate on the sounds and gradually add the use of written notation as another tool.

The use of computers in compositions can be introduced at this age. Children often particularly enjoy programs that let them organize sounds or create sketches in sound. While these can be entertaining in their own right, a skillful teacher helps the children use these tools to create expressive works that make effective use of what the children already know about musical principles and composition. Morton Sobotnick's Making Music and Making More Music software programs, published by Viva-Media, and his www.creatingmusic.com website allow for this kind of sketching. The doodle pad section of Music Ace by Harmonic Vision, and Groovy Jungle, Groovy Shapes, and Groovy City, by Sibelius, can be used.

Various articles and books on using music technology exist, and lesson plans for using these programs are available on the web. It is a matter of choice as to when and how to introduce technology into the composition program, but it is quite important not to do so too soon before the children have had experience creating in sound and controlling the means of production.

This issue is similar to the one of introducing traditional music notation. The sounds and the techniques of organizing sounds and playing with sounds should precede any work on the means of preserving sounds. Do not introduce traditional notation software programs as a way of composing at this age level. This should come after the children have had experience with inventing notation systems and using traditional notation in part in their own handwriting. Once there is a need for more elaborate notation in their work, and once they have a working knowledge of how traditional notation works, there will be time enough to transcribe and eventually create pieces on a computer.

However, this is a good age to introduce music notation programs to teach music reading and performance skills, and there are suitable software programs that can assist with this. This should simply be taught separately from composition until the children themselves begin using traditional notation in their pieces or until they have some fluency in reading and performing from notation.

Another type of computer compositional activity that can be used with children of this age is working with the various types of looping programs. Again, this should augment work in composition in other more acoustic formats, but it can be introduced effectively with students this age. Upper elementary children are often quite thrilled to be able to use these programs to create music that sounds to them like the styles with which they are familiar. Programs such as GarageBand for Apple computers and Acid for computers running Windows allow children and teachers to begin to experiment with this way of organizing sound.

Children can also create their own loops in some programs and use these to add to the basic loops available. These types of composing experiences work particularly well to accompany poetry readings or as soundtracks for short movies.

Considering Prerequisites

Prerequisites for any teaching plan depend on the experience of the children. Upper elementary children have eight or more years of informal music learning in addition to any formal experiences in school, religious settings, or private study. These children have an intuitive, well-developed sense of style for their own familiar music. Using this interior knowledge as a starting point for composing can lead to more successful initial pieces. Teachers can often determine this type of knowledge by observing how the students or groups of students attempt to create something meaningful in sound. This can then become the basis of future compositional tasks.

Obviously, students who have had previous compositional experiences in the primary grades are able to work from a greater sonic palette and clearer understanding of compositional principles. They are more willing to proceed in their own direction and with less teacher guidance than students who are approaching composition for the first time.

Because their general vocabularies have greatly expanded in the primary grade, upper elementary students are at the appropriate place in their development to acquire and use many more of the terms that describe their compositions. They can discuss their pieces in meaningful ways, but sometimes seem at a loss for a word. This is the best possible time to introduce a term and reinforce it because the student has an immediate use for it.

Similarly, compositional skills should be introduced at a teachable moment. This is especially true for teaching the ideas of contrasting sections and variations on a theme. Students often begin to create contrasting sections for their works at this age and often respond well to the suggestion to consider making the piece longer. At first the most common ways they do this are to repeat the whole piece or a significant part of it, or to add a completely different section. This is often followed by a return to the first section (Smith, 2007). These ways of lengthening the work can lead to discussions of what works well, how to relate the two sections, and how to gracefully lead back to the first section if one wishes to repeat it.

Being able to play simple tunes by ear can lead to the first exercises in creating variations. Sometimes these arise unintentionally because one child knows a different version of the song than the teacher or another child. Variations can be modeled in lessons or classes and assigned as homework. Teachers need to model many ways of creating variations and encourage the children to experiment on their own. Again, this work should primarily be done by ear and created from the sounds and not from the notation. This works best when the child has learned the song well enough to play from memory or when he or she has learned it by ear in the first place.

Once this type of assignment has been completed a few times, it can be helpful to listen to what adult composers have done with simple songs to create variations. In addition to the Stravinsky and Cailliet examples above, there is a humorous set of *Variations on Happy Birthday* done by Gidon Kremer and the Kremerata Baltica in imitation of various styles that somewhat sophisticated young composers can enjoy. Again, be sure to focus attention on what the composer/arranger did to create the effect of the sounds.

Finally, do not make excessive use of theme and variation at this age. Simply present it and do more extensive work with it in middle school. More advanced composers may find it very appealing and include it in their own creations, but most upper elementary students stay with simpler binary, ternary, and rondo forms.

Upper elementary students need to continue to explore the nature of sound. What creates a sound and how many ways it can be modified can be the focus of science lessons as well as composition classes. This leads naturally to the "design an instrument" task mentioned above. Once a collection has been assembled, the instruments should be grouped and regrouped in various ways to classify the sounds. Groups of mixed timbres can then be created, and compositions for the set of instruments can be begun.

Similarly, environmental sounds can take on new importance. One of the best ways to begin a discussion of the nature of music and what it means is to use John Cage's *4' 33"* with older upper elementary students. This often has the effect of expanding their notions of what music is as well as further increasing their notions of what sounds can be used to compose.

Co-compositional Activities

Perhaps no children enjoy music classes any more than typical third- and fourth-graders who like their music teacher. These children are often eager to learn and willing to be flexible about the musical styles they are exposed to in music classes. Their developing skills allow more advanced work with Orff instruments, recorders, and other sound sources. They enjoy singing, listening, playing instruments, and moving to music.

This naturally leads to creating interesting music of their own. Since upper elementary children enjoy many kinds of music activities, teachers can plan a variety of co-compositional activities to teach the basics of compositional principles and techniques. These often can be immediately applied to what the children are creating if the teacher takes the time to teach the transfer of the ideas to compositions.

For example, if the children are interested in the expressive quality of darkness in winter, they could be singing songs about winter nights, reading poems about winter nights, listening to music with dark-sounding themes, moving expressively to wintry music (themes from *The Snowman* by Raymond Briggs and Howard Blake, "Snowflake Dance" from *The Nutcracker*, "Winter" from the *Four Seasons* by Vivaldi), and watching dancers move to music. The teacher could probe their thinking to find out what musical qualities the children seem to associate with darkness and point these out in the musical examples they have been exploring. This could culminate in an assignment to create music that somehow evokes a winter sky, winter twilight, northern lights, winter nights, or a variety of other winter darkness themes selected by the children. The resulting compositions might even be shared as part of a winter concert or other presentation.

Task Guidelines

Task guidelines should always be moving recursively from the specific to the general and to the open. All types of structure should occur at various times. However, when beginning work in small groups, more structure may be helpful. Two important things to remember are to be sure that everyone understands the compositional task and to clearly determine how each person will select instruments or sound sources. Understanding the task can often be very important to the success of the individuals within the group. Similarly, much time can be lost bickering over who plays what. Having a sound source to use that one likes the sound of can also determine how much a student contributes to the group's work. If this is determined initially, work often proceeds much more quickly.

Another thing that groups of students sometimes have to be directly taught is fair and efficient ways of settling conflicts. Traditional counting out rhymes such as "Eeny Meeny" and "One Potato" can be taught as well as the "stones, scissors, paper" game or "pick a number" to fairly choose who gets to use a disputed instrument or settle other conflicts.

At first, simple checklists of task requirements is enough to guide the groups. Teachers may find it useful to have one checklist for the compositional parameters and another for the behavioral aspects of working together in a group. Samples of these types of checklists are included with the "Rondo for Found Sounds" lesson at the end of this chapter. This compositional étude is a beginning-level group composition but an intermediate-level composer activity.

As the students become more experienced with composing in groups, there should be less structure provided by the teacher. The students are able to decide more of the composition's parameters for themselves and often prefer to make their own decisions rather than having to follow too many directions.

For groups who seek assistance from the teacher, more structure can be provided by carefully asking questions about the intent of what the group is doing and what they have already tried. Often simply asking good questions helps the group members solve their issues on their own. Always consider asking leading questions rather than proposing what the group could do. There is more personal ownership of the composition if the ideas are theirs.

Assessment

Similarly, much of the assessment of the group's pieces and the members' ability to work together should be done by the group members themselves. This does not mean that the teacher should not also assess, but that the children should be taught to critique their own work and that of others. Again, a checklist can be helpful for the group to complete, both in terms of the task itself or to assess how well the group worked together. A simple request by the teacher to tell what each person contributed to the group product can often be enlightening. Older children can be asked to list the group members and what each person contributed to the work on a form. Still older children can individually list all the group members and their contributions. The teacher can collect these and compare what the group members said about one another as part of her assessment process.

Gradually these assessments should become more global. They may take the form of discussions among the various groups, discussions between groups and the teacher, or a composer's workshop format. Teachers need to model how to focus on the sounds and the effectiveness of what has been created and not on the skill level of the composers. In most settings there are pieces that are more musically effective than others. These can then be used to help increase everyone's understanding of musical quality.

It is the sharing of their work, the discussion of the work with others, and the reflecting on their own pieces and the comments they received that helps composer grow. However, at these beginning stages, the focus needs to remain on what is well done rather than on what is weaker. The students themselves may be quick to disparage their own work and that of others. They need to be reminded that progress is the intent, and that they are trying to help one another get better. It is not about winning a competition of some type, but about musical expressivity. All composers need to continue to learn and grow. Upper elementary student composers can all continue to do that in a supportive atmosphere.

DEVELOPING THE THREE BASIC COMPOSITIONAL CAPACITIES WITH UPPER ELEMENTARY STUDENTS

Whether the students are novices, composers with some experience, or composers who have done quite a bit of composing, they continue to develop their ability to compose with intention, musical expressivity, and artistic craftsmanship in the upper elementary grades. While compositional études may expand what the students can technically do, true compositions begin with something that the student wishes to capture in sound. At this age they are more able to craft pieces reflective of the styles of music with which they are most familiar. They are very interested in techniques that

Table 8.1 Compositional Capacities in Upper Elementary Students

Compositional Capacities	Novice	Intermediate	Advanced
Intention	Music making may be inspired by cultural phenomena or prompted by school or other activities. Children may desire to emulate the musical models with which they identify.	Children's music making exhibits an awareness of how self and others respond feelingfully to cultural phenomena and events. This awareness then impacts compositional choices.	Musical choices are based on careful consideration of how people will feel when engaged with the final product.
Expressivity	Children are able to incorporate the feelingful qualities of familiar styles into their work.	Children give increasing consideration to the ways that expressive gestures can shape and enhance the expressive capacity of their music.	Children become conscious of the relationship between feeling and musical principles. Their artistic choices become increasingly purposeful as they begin to give attention to how audiences will respond to their work.
Artistic Craftsmanship	Children's abilities to combine sounds evolve. Horizontal organizations usually precede vertical ones. Performance ability (who plays what) sometimes drives process.	Children draw upon their personal bank of musical gestures to create original music that conforms to the stylistic conventions of pieces with which they are familiar.	Children expand their personal sound banks to include conventional sounds made or altered in unconventional ways. Imagining sounds, rather than physically producing sounds, may begin to emerge as a compositional practice.

allow them to imitate those styles in some manner. They are much more interested in audience reaction to their works than primary-age children. Consequently, their pieces often are designed with a specific intent in mind or seek a specific audience reaction.

Compositional Intention in Third- and Fourth-Grade Composers

Novice Composers

As noted before, children this age may desire to emulate the musical models with which they identify. Novice composers may initially be disappointed if their audiences do not react as they anticipated. There may be quite a discrepancy between their intentions and what actually occurs. They are tempted to give up too easily when things do not seem to be working, but they also are eager to learn ways that might work better. They are especially receptive to ideas from more advanced peers and may seek out those individuals as group members.

Their composing may be inspired by cultural phenomena or prompted by school or other activities. Composing for a specific purpose becomes more important to them. Class projects that include video with a soundtrack can be completed at a beginning level. Class songs for particular occasions can be created, such as a "back to school" song or "end of school" song or song for an assembly or concert. Children can be encouraged to write songs for family occasions. The "Song for Our Teacher" project in chapter 7 can easily become a birthday song for a classmate.

Intermediate Composers

Children who have had some composing experience often have a more developed awareness of how they respond feelingfully to music at various cultural events. They are also noticing more observantly how others respond to music. This heightened awareness then impacts their compositional choices. Because they are more aware of how music impacts them and because they are becoming very aware of how their music impacts others, they are making more conscious choices as they create their own music.

Advanced Composers

More advanced upper elementary students consider ever more carefully how people feel when they listen to their music. These young composers often wish to work independently rather than with a group, but are also often concerned with audience understanding and reaction to their work. While they still respond feelingfully to spontaneous ideas and use their own inspirations and favorite sounds, they also want their peers and teachers to like and "understand" their work. They often compose on their own for the sheer pleasure of organizing sound and presenting it to others. Unlike older children, who often prefer to keep their compositions private, these young composers often are quite willing to share their works with anyone who will listen. It also seems that their skills develop by leaps and bounds as they create more and more pieces.

Encouraging Expressivity in the Upper Elementary Composer

Novice Composers

Children of this age are able to incorporate the feelingful qualities of familiar styles into their work, but often need help creating the sounds that they want something to sound like. They hear the sounds in their imaginations, but cannot always reproduce what they hear as closely as they wish. Working in groups with peers aids this process for some children because of the immediate feedback they receive in a group context. Ideas are shared, manipulated, and either used or discarded in the group context. This feedback shapes what the composer does next and also what he or she does at the next composing session.

Intermediate Composers

Intermediate composers give increasing consideration to the ways that expressive gestures can shape and enhance the expressive capacity of their music. Perhaps no compositional étude can help shape this any better than the time-honored compositional study of creating variations. When an entire class has an instrument and knows the same basic tune, it can be very interesting to see what each child does to manipulate the same musical materials.

A brief teacher-led discussion on how one melody can be different from another may be all that is needed to spark ideas. However, some classes may need teacher modeling to help with understanding. This should be done using a different tune than the one the class used. It is often sufficient simply to produce variations based on student suggestions, but usually it is good to include switching meter (e.g., from duple to triple), switching mode (from major to minor), adding notes, subtracting notes, and changing the rhythm. The children can then come up with variations of their own and practice them to present to the class. After each child presents a variation, the child should explain to the class what he or she did to create the variation. Others can then attempt to do the same thing if desired. Discussion can focus on how each variation makes the tune feel different and why that appears to happen.

Advanced Composers

More advanced upper elementary students are quite conscious of the relationship between feeling and musical principles. Their artistic choices become increasing purposeful as they begin to give attention to how audiences will respond to their work. One compositional activity that gives upper elementary students a chance to make many artistic choices is the "Carnival of the Animals a la Seuss" project. Students create invented paper creatures. They can then create biographies about their creatures, including how the creatures move, where they live, what they eat, who their enemies are, how they reproduce, and other elements from their science classes. Next they create a piece of music to depict their creature. As an extension, children can be asked to first create a piece using only acoustic instruments or working in groups and later be asked to create another piece using electronic sounds and working alone. Any combination of these can lead to interesting results and inspire discussion about musical expressivity.

Developing Artistic Craftsmanship in the Upper Elementary Composer

Novice Composers

Children's abilities to combine sounds evolve in the upper elementary grades. Horizontal organizations usually precede vertical ones, but as these children learn to sing rounds and two-part songs, their awareness of harmony also increases. Still, working with combining percussion sounds is often the place novice composers at this level begin to make expressive combinations, and these are usually horizontally conceived. This is often quickly followed by adding percussion sounds to accompany a melody. Sometimes accompanying a melody comes before percussion pieces if the teacher has been using instruments to accompany singing in class. In either case, the beginning upper elementary composers now think about how their sounds fit in with others. They often create a part and then try to make it fit, rather than listening to others and creating a part. Fitting the parts together as they work is one of the indications of a more advanced composer at this level. The ability to think vertically and horizontally as they work requires more skill and craftsmanship.

Performance ability, especially who plays what in a group composition, sometimes drives the composing process. The young composer needs to be content with the sounds he or she is using and needs to be able to manipulate those sounds in various creative ways in order to make choices about the sounds to be used. Children who are assigned an instrument often make less creative choices about how to use it than children who are allowed to choose what sounds they will use. Sometimes it is necessary to limit the number of choices for expediency and so that the work may proceed. After all, too many interesting possibilities can be a little overwhelming to beginners. However, allow for student choice in sound sources whenever possible because their interest in the sound aids the development of their skills.

Intermediate Composers

In addition to the budding ability to think vertically in sound, upper elementary intermediate composers draw upon their personal bank of musical gestures to create music that conforms to the styles of familiar pieces. They are often interested in the rhythms of pop music and begin to include these in their works.

What they listen to outside of music classes influences what they compose. They deliberately copy favorite rhythms and gestures into their pieces. This should not be viewed as plagiarizing those pieces, but as experimenting with favorite sounds, particularly if the students can explain why they are using someone else's ideas and what they found attractive about them. This is similar to creating variations and is a step in their composing development. At a later time, teachers can talk about the various acceptable and unacceptable ways to appropriate someone else's work. At this level, copying can be recognized for its value and discussed as a technique, with mention being made that credit must be given when using materials from other composers.

Upper elementary children often expand their personal sound banks to include conventional sounds made or altered in unconventional ways. Sometimes instrumental study influences their work. A child who has just learned to trill on an instrument often starts putting trills into his or her compositions. Young instrumentalists should be encouraged to use their expanding technique to expand their compositional ideas. Teaching young recorder students to flutter tongue often leads to pieces that include that technique. This often leads to experimenting with other unconventional ways to use the recorder.

Attempting to create something in the style of another culture is one way students become more deeply familiar with how that music works. Students are often fascinated with trying to make something sound Chinese by using pentatonic scales or Middle Eastern by bending tones on recorders or string instruments. What these efforts may lack in authenticity, they more than make up for in the expansion of the composers' craftsmanship and technical skill. A teacher familiar with the basics of these and other styles can lead group improvisation sessions by providing a basic structure. The experimentation may then later appear in works the members of the group create on their own.

Advanced Composers

Among more advanced upper elementary students, imaging sounds rather than physically producing sounds may begin to emerge as a compositional practice. While this is to be encouraged, it needs to come from an extensive background creating in physically present sound. Only then can the composer mentally organize the sounds in meaningful ways. It is important, too, that these imagined sounds then be heard without resorting too quickly to standard notation. Children who write too soon without enough background in composing in sound or in using standard notation often produce less than satisfactory pieces (Smith, 2004).

TOUCHPOINTS FOR TEACHING

1. Work in groups of varying sizes and with varying members.

Begin with work done in pairs if the composers have few previous experiences. Then work in groups of three, preferably several times and using different group members each time. Allow friendship groups as well as teacher-selected groups. Eventually experiment with groups as large as five musicians per group. Allow some students to work alone if they choose to do so.

2. Vary the amount of structure.

Resist the urge to specify so much of the composition that very little remains for the children to decide for themselves. While this may guarantee successful completion of the task, it also practically guarantees a sameness in the resulting compositions. Initial efforts at group composition may need more structure than later ones when the students have more experience working together. Decrease the number of parameters you provide as soon as possible.

Specify how sound sources will be selected/decided, but allow for some student choice. This leads to more work on the composition itself with less time spent arguing over instruments. Teach conflict resolution if necessary.

3. Ask, don't tell.

When the students themselves seem at a loss as to how to proceed or at an impasse in making a decision, ask them leading questions to help them arrive at a solution rather than suggesting options. Ask, "Which option seems more musical?" or "What are you trying to make a listener feel?" Children often are able to reach decisions on their own when redirected to the music itself rather than their own contribution to it. Keep the focus on the sound: "Which sounds more musical to you? Why do you think that is so? How does it fit with the other parts?"

For groups who are having difficulty getting started, ask them to describe the task for you. They may be unclear as to what the compositional problem is. Then have them brainstorm solutions. Whenever possible, the ideas must come from the individuals in the group or their friends in other groups rather than from the teacher.

4. Provide varied sound palettes.

Upper elementary teachers should continue to provide a wide and varied sound palette for both listening and creating. This includes projects with body percussion, vocal sounds without words, found sounds, invented instruments, and musical instruments from a variety of cultures. These sounds often need more than a simple introduction to become part of the child's working sound palette. Experimenting with the sounds, combining them, arranging them, and trying out new ways of creating sounds with the sources all increase the available sounds a child can use and may promote creative thinking.

5. Introduce musical terminology appropriately.

Continue to introduce musical terminology as it arises from the students' musical observations and creations. When children's efforts to describe what they have created lead to descriptions of some appropriate musical term, introduce and reinforce the term. For instance, when the child talks about the music getting faster, use the term *accelerando* and explain that it is the musician's word for tempos that gradually speed up. Then use the work in a sentence later on. If you use a class word wall, add it to the wall (see Hollenberg, 2004, on word walls). Building a vocabulary for discussing their intensions and the qualities of their pieces is an important part of a young composer's music education.

6. Keep music notation separate.

Offer specific instruction in music notation separately from composing. Many children this age are learning to read music in their instrumental classes, in piano or guitar lessons, or in other musical settings. Because the focus in composing initially needs to be on the sound, it is best to work on these skills separately. As the children's notational skills increase, they will begin to use standard notation more and more in their work. This should be encouraged but not required at this level.

7. Explore technology-based composing programs.

An important thing to keep in mind here is that technology cannot completely replace the need to work in acoustic sound. Because the technology makes so many things easier to do, it is easy to neglect the development of the ability to think in sound. Yet the ability to imagine a sound and then create with it is an important compositional skill. The composition programs mentioned above should simply be some of the many tools available for children to use.

8. Offer examples of techniques from adult composers.

The co-compositional activity of listening to music can play a role for students at every level. The examples above were specifically about theme and variation and from a classical music repertoire, but others can be found and utilized in similar ways. They can occur before composing, during the compositional process, or after the students' compositions have been created.

9. Use instruments that they are learning to play.

Much more is said about this in the next chapter. However, if children are already learning to play an instrument at this age, encourage them to compose for that instrument as soon as possible. This usually can begin when they can play three notes on their chosen instrument and can continue throughout their studies. It is not necessary to wait until they have developed notational competency. Once tones can be produced consistently and reliably, they can be added to the students' sonic palette.

Similarly, it is important not to limit the children to composing only what they can play on their own instruments. They need to imagine what the possibilities for their instrument are and to understand its limitations as well. Beyond that, they need to continue to work with an ever-increasing variety of sounds.

A TEACHING SCENARIO

Unit: Creating Our Own Instruments
Project: Rondo for Invented/Found Sounds
Level: Intermediate

Planning Elements	Thinking Guides
Composer Characteristics	Grade level: Third grade to fifth grade Skill level: Intermediate Setting: Classroom Time allocation estimate: Two class periods
Focus and Supporting Principles	The focus is unity/variety; all others are supporting.
Compositional Capacities	Intention: Possibly, if a story line or feeling Expressivity: Depends on group choice Artistic craftsmanship: Tone color choice and contrast
Compositional Context	Small group (trios) for contrasting sounds as determined by classification system
Tools	Instruments: Invented instruments and found sounds Preservation: Recordings

Prerequisites	Concepts:
	    Classifications systems
	    Invented instruments
	    Found sounds
	Musical skills:
	    Rondo form
	    Solo versus group
	Intuitive understandings: Balanced forms

Co-compositional Activities	Creating and demonstrating interesting sounds; classifying those sounds. Both done before composing.
Task Guidelines	Product: Rondo ABACADA Length: Composers determine Specs: A section with Q & A played by all three sounds at the same time. Other sections are solos for each sound. Time: Thirty minutes One class to demonstrate their instruments and to classify several different ways. Next class, fifteen minutes to compose and rest of class for performances. Preservation: Recording Performance: For class
Assessments	What: Following specs, working as a group How: Self-assess on checklist Why: Promote cooperation
Connections	To past or future music lessons: Relates to other rondos; use keyboard sounds for similar task. Older children can do similar task on computers. To other disciplines: Relates to science unit on sound.

Table 8.3. Rondo Checklist

Our Rondo Checklist	Our Group's Checklist
__ Three different tone colors	__ Everyone contributed ideas
__ Eight-beat pattern	__ We took turns speaking
__ Q and A	__ We listened to one another respectfully
__ All three instruments play together	__ We made decisions based on the needs
__ Three solos	of the piece (musical needs)
__ Practice until it works smoothly	__ We asked questions to be sure we
Optional:	understood each other
__ Paired solos	__ We helped each other
__ About something	__ We settled disagreements fairly
__ Specific mood	__ We stayed on task most of the time

Ms. Perez knows that the fourth-graders have been studying sound and vibration in science class. She decides to do a unit on musical instruments. In one class she reviews with the children the typical five families of instruments associated with Western music (woodwinds, brass, strings, percussion, keyboards). In another class the children explore instruments from around the world by using Internet videos and information. The ethnomusicological classification system (aerophones, chordophones, membranophones, idiophones) is introduced, and the children love using the new long words. Ms. Perez then gives a homework assignment: find an interesting sound and bring it to class next week or invent an instrument and bring it to class next week. She discusses the assignment with Mr. Lopez, the children's home room teacher, and he agrees to remind them of the assignment a few times during the week.

During the next class the children demonstrate the sounds they have made or found. Ms. Perez then leads the group in classifying the sounds several different ways (how they are played, the materials they are made of, their size, etc.). They then use their sounds to play along with several different recordings in different styles. Not all instruments play with each recording. They listen to a bit of the recording, decide which instruments would be most appropriate, and play along. If there is extra time, the children add sound effects to a picture book using their sounds, voices and body percussion. They leave their sounds with Ms. Perez for an activity the next week.

When the children come to class the next week, they find their sounds and assemble in groups of similar tone colors (or by what they are made of). Ms. Perez puts the directions on the projector board and goes over them with the children. She reminds them to use their cooperative group skills. She forms groups of three that have three contrasting tone colors and reminds the students that they will have only about fifteen minutes to complete their rondo before performing it for the class. They know that they need to practice their piece once it is created. The children then begin to work.

Ms. Perez moves around the room, observing the groups as they complete the task. If they ask questions, she answers them, but otherwise, she simply observes and takes notes. When most of the children seem finished, they are reminded to fill in their checklist and pass them in to Ms. Perez. They then perform their pieces for one another, and Ms. Perez videotapes them. After each group performs, Ms. Perez asks the class to tell things that they liked about each piece. Sometimes the comments lead to a repeat performance or comments from the composers as well. Later that day Ms. Perez uses the notes she took, her recordings of the performances, and the checklists from the children to assess the students, the success of the projects, and the quality of the projects. Based on what she learns, she begins to design their next composition experience.

SUGGESTED LESSONS

Unit: Theme and Variations
Project: Creating Variations
Level: Advanced
Overview: Students have been listening to themes and variations in general music and have a basic understanding of some ways variations can be created. In an instrumental lesson group, they can play several beginner-level pieces. The teacher reviews several ways variations can be created and demonstrates on an instrument, following student suggestions and using a familiar tune. The student selects one of the tunes from previous lessons and creates a variation on that tune to perform during the next lesson. Encourage students to create several variations and perform the one liked best.

Planning Elements	*Thinking Guides*
Composer Characteristics	Beginner instrumentalists Advanced composers Setting: Classroom or lessons Time allocation estimate: +/– fifteen minutes in two classes
Focus and Supporting	Focus is on unity/variety with possible focus on stability/instability as well.
Compositional Capacities (When?)	Intention: Creating a parallel or contrasting feeling using the same basic material Expressivity: Varying feeling or keeping the feeling while varying the tune Artistic craftsmanship: Ways to create variety
Compositional Context	Individual
Tools	Instruments: An instrument the student knows how to play Preservation: Optional, recording
Prerequisites	Concepts: Same and similar Musical skills: A short song that can be played from memory Intuitive understandings: What sounds interesting

Planning Elements	Thinking Guides
Co-compositional Activities (When?)	Lead a discussion on the various ways to create variations and include demonstrations using a tune familiar to the young composers. Listening to other variations. Cailliet's *Pop Goes the Weasel*, Stravinsky's *Greeting Prelude*, Ives's *Variations on America*, etc.
Task Guidelines	Product: A variation on a tune Length: Same as song, more or less Specs: None Time: Ten minutes in class or as homework Preservation: Composer's choice, but must be on paper Performance: In class the next class
Assessments	What: By self and peers How: Describe how you created your variation Why: Skill building
Connections	To past or future music lessons: Repeat with additional tunes or original tunes. To other disciplines: Look for other examples of theme and variation in the real world. Photograph and bring to class.

THE HOUSE THAT DRAC BUILT

Unit: Adding Sounds to Stories
Project: The House That Drac Built
Level: Beginner
Overview: Expressively read the picture book The House that Drac Built by Judy Sierra and Will Hillenbrand, published by Voyager Books, 1998. Go through the book and audition the children as creators of appropriate sounds for each character in the book. Read through the book again and pause for the children to make the sounds. Then show the pictures only, and do not read the text, but have the children create the sounds. Record this version, listen, and critique. Revise and re-record as needed and time allows.

Planning Elements	Thinking Guides
Composer Characteristics	Grade level: Third; can be first through fifth as adjusted Skill level: Beginner Setting: General music class Time allocation estimate: Fifteen minutes
Focus and Supporting Principles	Unity and variety is the focus; all others can be supporting
Compositional Capacities (When?)	Intention: Teacher directed Expressivity: Fake scary as humor; scariness that is not really scary Artistic craftsmanship: Using sound to tell a story
Compositional Context	Large group
Tools	Vocal sounds Preservations: Recording
Prerequisites	Concepts: Monster vocal sounds Musical skills: Vocal freedom Intuitive understandings: What makes something sound scary

Planning Elements	Thinking Guides
Co-compositional Activities (When?)	None
Task Guidelines	Product: Sound story Length: Same as book Specs: Add sounds, remove words Time: Fifteen minutes Preservation: Audio recording Performance: As created
Assessments	What: Of the recording How: Can we make this even scarier? How? Why: Instruction improvement
Connections	Other sound stories Do in small groups

ETUDES

1. Write a script for role-playing some difficulty a group might have. Brainstorm with your classmates some ways of solving.
2. Ms. Perez knows that she has two very talented students who have trouble working in groups because they are very committed to their own ideas. What are some ways she might adapt the rondo assignment for them to do?
3. Read the teaching scenario again and invent some things that Ms. Perez might have found when she did her assessments. Design the next composing task for these students.
4. Examine a piece of music software (web-based or CD-ROM) that says it teaches composition to young children. Would you use it with students in your classroom? Why or why not?

DISCOGRAPHY

These recordings are only some of the possibilities for this type of composing activity. Teachers may find others they prefer.

Cailliet, L. (1994). Variations on pop goes the weasel. On *Music of the USA, Bowmar Orchestral Library Series 2* edited by Lucille Wood [CD]. New York: Alfred Publishing.

Cowell, H. (1994). The banshee. On *Piano music* [CD]. New York: Smithsonian Folkways Records. Also available on iTunes and Amazon.com as an mp3 download.

Kremer, G. (2003). Happy birthday variations. On *Happy Birthday* [CD]. Gidon Kremer and the Kremerata Baltica. Los Angeles: Nonesuch. Also available on iTunes and Amazon.com as an mp3 download.

Stravinsky, I. (1971). Greeting prelude. On *The essential Stravinsky* [CD]. New York: Sony BMG. Also available on iTunes and Amazon.com as an mp3 download.

9

The Transition to Middle School

Composing in Grades Five and Six

> The middle school movement seeks to improve the education of the adolescent. At the core of this movement lies the realization that adolescent learners are neither mature high school students nor "big" elementary children, but rather unique and special people.
>
> —Brian Moore

For purposes of this chapter, fifth- and sixth-grade students are considered young middle-school students. Some students this age attend elementary schools, some attend middle schools, and some attend junior high schools. While the type of overall school program influences the types of opportunities these children are offered, music classes typically include general music classes, instrumental lessons and ensemble experiences, and formal choral experiences. Additionally, middle-school programs may offer a variety of exploratory classes. Regardless of the setting, there are characteristics of young composers and of their compositional practices that remain similar.

A PROFILE OF PREADOLESCENT COMPOSERS AND COMPOSITION ACTIVITIES

Composition is a critical component of music education in middle schools for several reasons. Composing promotes the development of a musical self-identity that may otherwise never be experienced. It directly provides an artistic outlet for the wealth of emotional growth and development that takes place at this age. The act of composing and of reflecting on that act can create a means of understanding human experience and feeling. Finally, composing gives older children the opportunity for a successful musical experience and the ownership of music that is personal and uniquely their own.

Composer Characteristics

Young middle-school students are often curious, although sometimes they are very guardedly so. While they are adjusting to newly found freedoms, they often need the balance that is created by clear rules, consistently enforced. They benefit from peer interaction and seek peer approval. However, because their compositions are highly personal and important to them, they may not always be willing to share their musical creations. They have a deep sense of ownership of their pieces.

Some older children are eager to share what they have composed and feel successful at what they have done. Still, they often do not want to shine too brightly on the classroom stage for fear of negative peer reactions. They do appreciate and enjoy private compliments from adults, even when similar public praise might be uncomfortable. Written notes and private e-mails often are appreciated.

Young middle-level students can be very intuitive musically and able to create music deeply reflective of their own felt experiences. Moreover, they are able to imagine what feelings might be experienced in a given situation and attempt to sonify those imagined experiences. This ability to project feeling may appear at younger ages in some students, but older children display this ability more readily. They usually are also more able to capture some aspect of those feelings in sound.

Students this age often remain eager to manipulate sounds that intrigue them. This is particularly true of computer-generated sound loops and other sounds that enable them to create music that imitates the musical styles they prefer or that their peers prefer. Those who are studying electric guitar often have access to a variety of sound-altering tools that can be used in their pieces. Similarly, electric keyboards are explored and savored by many children if they are given the opportunity to experience the many tone colors available electronically. They can also experiment with the creation of sounds by altering waveforms.

As with many composition students, older children benefit from being exposed to compositional models and discussing the techniques and devices they employ. These children often can distinguish between a successful model and a less successful one. They also can articulate why there is a difference between the two works. The vocabulary acquired in younger grades can be put to appropriate use. However, if these older children were not previously exposed to music vocabulary, they easily learn it at this level as they describe what they hear and what they have created.

Similarly, it is still best if students acquire skills of artistic craftsmanship on a "need to know" basis. As these older children struggle with issues of increasing independence from adults and finding personal expression, formal lessons may become less and less well received. Once a task has been established, mentoring, coaching, and just plain stepping back and observing until asked for help often is much more successful.

Understanding and Use of Compositional Principles

Even novice composers at the young middle-school stage have quite an intuitive understanding of musical principles as applied to their preferred styles of music. Part of the mentor/teacher's role is to make those understandings explicit and to point out their expressive nature. Students with some compositional background already are familiar with the principles and the ways they can be manipulated to achieve some expressive qualities. The range of expression often increases noticeably from composition to composition at this age level because students become so concerned with the communicative possibilities of their pieces. This is discussed further in the section on compositional capacities below.

Teachers may plan lessons that draw attention to the individual principles by using compositional études when this seems appropriate. While the focus may be on a specific principle, others almost always play a supporting role as well. Often co-compositional activities can lead young middle-school students to a deeper appreciation of how the principles lead to expression. The "Russian Sailor's Dance" compositional étude at the end of this chapter focuses on unity and variety but also makes supporting use of stability and motion. It also draws attention to effective use of tone color changes and tempo changes.

Compositional Context

The variety of compositional contexts may expand greatly with young middle-school students. These students continue to engage in occasional composition projects as part of general music classes, but they also often work on their own at home on projects of their own choosing. This is particularly true for students who are studying an instrument such as guitar or piano. It can also be true for students studying other instruments if they are encouraged by their teachers to create for their instruments and those of their classmates.

Composition can also be integrated into small and large ensemble work. This often leads to deeper understanding of the technical demands of the instruments and of reading notation. Composing for traditional band and orchestral instruments can begin with unison works for like instruments or solos for the child's own instrument. With the guidance of a sympathetic teacher, this can quite easily lead to duets and other chamber groups. The "My Piece" lesson at the end of this chapter provides suggestions for this type of work.

Tools of Creation and Preservation

Young middle-level students who are learning to play instruments in group and private lessons often have a reasonably good command of traditional notation. This is the age to require these students to begin to use those conventions. Doing so improves their abilities to read notation as they learn a standard way of preserving their compositions. Once these instrumental students can use standard notation to communicate their ideas, they should be taught the basics of computer notation programs such as Sibelius or Finale as a time-saving device. Often these students then wish to create their pieces directly on the computer. It is usually better for these intermediate to advanced composers to continue to compose directly on their instruments, at least for a while, so that the focus remains on the way the music sounds. By using a computer, it can be quite easy to exceed the capabilities of the actual instrument and also to drift away from the musical expressivity of the sounds.

None of this need apply to compositions created on computer for computer-generated sounds. When the expressive intent is the use of electronic sound and the techniques of electronic composition, the need for the limitations of a physical instrument and for traditional notation recede. Young middle-school students should be encouraged to explore this possibility as well.

Not all young middle-school students are studying an instrument. These students can work with computers and other sound sources, but they need to continue to use means of preserving their work other than traditional notation. Invented notations, graphic notation, and recordings continue to play a large role for beginning and intermediate composers. Advanced electronic composers may never learn to use traditional notation, simply because it does not fit their work as a means of preservation. However, this is the age where all children should acquire at least the basics of notational skill so that they have an appreciation of its possibilities and limitations.

Considering Prerequisites

The type of lesson and the level of the children's skill and understanding determine the prerequisites for composition lessons. Lessons for beginners may have very few, relying instead on the children's intuitive understanding of how music works. More advanced composers may have more knowledge to bring to the composing task. Some tasks at this level may require skill at playing an instrument or using a computer software program. Teachers need to determine the skill level and other prerequisites on a task-by-task and student-by-student basis.

Co-compositional Activities

Compositional activities continue to play a role in middle-level composition classes. These are more likely to be listening activities than at younger age levels. Middle-level students sometimes are shy about using their voices to sing or about moving to music to demonstrate their understanding. Teachers need to be sensitive to changing voice issues and to the children's comfort level about moving their often rapidly developing bodies.

This does not mean one should never use singing or movement with this age of student, but that the success of such co-compositional activities may vary widely from class to class and with students within a specific class. Teachers who are quite familiar with their students may be able to use materials and activities more successfully than those teachers who are new to their students.

Authentic examples from pop music may be sung and moved to more willingly than music from other repertoires. Movement compositions, where the students create choreography to existing or improvised music, can often be surprisingly successful at this age.

Task Guidelines

Young middle-school students often prefer less teacher-imposed structure for their compositions, but still often need a basic format that they can follow. While they resist "fill-in-the-blank" composing études designed by the teacher to engineer success, they still need to feel successful. The more decisions about the composition that can be left to the students to decide, the more ownership they feel for the final product.

Nowhere is this truer than in tasks that require the students to create a setting of a text. It is quite important that the children create or select the text. One way is to work with a classroom teacher who is having the children create poems. Another version can be to ask the children to bring in a poem they would like to turn into a song. For group or class activities, a variety of poems can be provided and discussed before one is selected.

In any case, the text needs to be one the students find personally meaningful and relevant. This is rarely true of a single text chosen by the teacher. Groups may also have trouble settling on a text since what is relevant to some may seem unfamiliar to others. Friendship groups have an easier time choosing a text than most teacher-chosen groups.

Setting a text can often work well as a paired composing activity, where two children with unequal performance skills help each other create a piece. Two children may be able to come to agreement on a text sooner than a larger group. However, creating a setting with more accompanying parts may require the help of other classmates for the performance. One such beginner-level task is the computer-based poem task at the end of this chapter.

Assessment

Teachers should be very clear with young middle-school students about the role and purposes of assessment in composition classes. If a piece is to be used for a graded summative assessment, the criteria for that grade should be clearly stated at the start of the compositional process. Every student should have an opportunity to receive top marks. Beginners should not be forced to compete against advanced students in order to receive a good grade.

First efforts at composing should almost never be graded on anything except possibly for completing the activity. This is where formative assessment can be most helpful. Gentle guidance from the teacher and supportive comments from the members of the class or of a small group of classmates may be the most effective way of helping young composers learn.

The composing community model discussed in chapter 6 can provide the composer with encouragement and other suggestions. While this is assessment in its best sense, it is not meant to assign grades or rank-order work. Ideally, composing should be an ungraded class where progress is the criterion. Realistically, in most schools, teachers must assign grades. Clear criteria for grading, models of acceptable work, and opportunities to repeat the process until the results are acceptable should all be part of middle-level education. Just as various kinds of writing are done prior to formal testing of writing skills, various kinds of composing should take place before a summative assessment of music compositions.

DEVELOPING THE THREE BASIC COMPOSITIONAL CAPACITIES WITH PREADOLESCENT COMPOSERS

With their increasing ability to think more abstractly, including the ability to think in sound, young middle-school students often demonstrate a quickly growing understanding of music principles and the workings of the underlying compositional capacities. With encouragement, they compose on their own and with deliberate intention. They explore the extremes of expressive gestures, particularly as they relate to their preferred styles of music, and they increase their own artistic craftsmanship through experimentation and asking questions of more capable composers.

They listen attentively to the works of others and often add the techniques and skills they hear to their own artistic palette. Teachers can serve an important mentoring role for these composers by providing the spaces and opportunities for this kind of learning to occur. They can also help the students to reflect on the experiences and the possibilities for musical expression embedded in them.

The Growth of Compositional Intention in the Preadolescent Composer

Novice Composers

Older children increasingly identify with popular music models. They are very interested in how those sounds are created and what they can do to imitate the types of music they find interesting. They intentionally seek to emulate their favorite music and sometimes need encouragement to continue with this when their first attempts are less than successful in their own eyes or the eyes of their peers.

Their musical intentions are often highly personal and focus on themes that are important to them. The dynamics of relationships can be a recurring theme. They write about friendships, fairness, loss, and similar topics, particularly if there is a songwriting exploratory class or if songwriting is included in a general music class. These feelingful intentions may or may not be shared with the teacher or the class, but they are very deliberate on the part of the composer.

Intermediate Composers

The breadth of older children's experiences with performing and listening to music impacts their choices of compositional products. Children who take guitar or keyboard lessons often choose to write songs, while children whose lessons are on wind or classical string instruments may be less likely to create pieces with lyrics. Idiomatic conventions may appear in their pieces that are related to particular instruments or genres. For example, students who have been taught to create in the twelve-bar blues format as an étude sometimes choose to use that genre when creating works of their own. Without this experience, they are less likely to create in this form unless it plays a large role in their listening world outside of school. Their intentions are defined by what they know and are able to do.

Table 9.1 Compositional Capacities in Young Middle-School Students

Compositional Capacities	Novice	Intermediate	Advanced
Intention	Older children increasingly identify with popular music models. Musical intentions are often highly personal and focus on themes, e.g., the dynamics of relationships (friendships, fairness, loss, etc.).	The breadth of older children's experiences with performing and listening to music impacts their choice of products. Idiomatic conventions may appear related to particular instruments or genres.	Older children's product intentions may arise from personal experience but may extend beyond that to consider how less-familiar instruments and ensembles may offer feelingful content.
Expressivity	Older children are able to consider an increasingly broad range of expressive gestures in the creation of a single work.	Older children's palette of expressive gestures is expanding in breadth. Attention is given to how multiple types of gestures can serve complementary purposes.	Older children begin to employ a broad range of expressive gestures in their compositions. They may be able to anticipate an audience's reaction to the expressive impact of particular gestures.
Artistic Craftsmanship	Older children employ intuitive knowledge of stylistic conventions to shape their own compositions. They experiment with nonconventional sounds and often use such sounds as markers of "personal voice."	Some older children prefer to adhere to stylistic conventions while developing personal voice. Other children prefer to deeply immerse themselves in nonconventional sounds and often seek unique organizational forms.	Older children continue to develop personal voice within familiar structures and forms. They are able to imagine the impact of their compositional choices in the absence or near absence of external sound.

Advanced Composers

More advanced older children's product intentions still arise from personal experience. However, advanced composers tend to extend beyond their own personal experience to consider how less-familiar instruments and ensembles may offer expressive opportunities. They become interested in exploring the feelingful content of larger ensembles and unusual combinations of instruments and sounds. Electronic composers become sound source addicts in that they seem to be unable to ever find or create enough sounds to meet their sonification needs. They play endlessly with the possibilities of the sounds they encounter or create and often find uniquely expressive ways to use them.

Encouraging Expressivity in the Preadolescent Composer

Novice Composers

One of the distinctive characteristics of young middle-school children is that they are able to consider an increasingly broad range of expressive gestures in the creation of a single work. They no longer find one idea and use it exclusively, nor do they string together one idea after another in the manner of primary-age children. More than one change to a sound or a gesture is often used to express their intentions.

Intermediate Composers

Older children's palettes of expressive gestures continue expanding in breadth. They seek out intriguing sounds, especially those from computer-generated sources and those from pop music instruments. They consider how the sounds can be used to express their intentions and experiment with unusual combinations of sounds in a search for personal expressivity.

Attention is given to how multiple types of gestures can serve complementary purposes. They are more thoughtful as they consider contrasting sections and how to best express more than one aspect of an idea or feeling by using different tone colors and motives.

Advanced Composers

Some older and more advanced children may be able to anticipate an audience's reaction to the expressive impact of particular gestures. Their ability to think in sound and to imagine sound combinations allows them to begin to employ a much broader range of expressive gestures in their compositions. They often use idiosyncratic gestures in their works that allow an observant teacher to be able to identify whose piece a given work is simply from the sound of it.

Developing Artistic Craftsmanship in the Preadolescent Composer

Novice Composers

Even novice composers who are young middle-school students can employ their own intuitive knowledge of stylistic conventions to shape their own compositions. Driving rhythms, syncopations, and common time are all employed in many pieces.

They also experiment with unconventional sounds and may have personal favorites. They often use such favorite sounds as markers of "personal voice" in their pieces and use similar combinations in new pieces over time.

Intermediate Composers

Some young middle-level students prefer to adhere to stylistic conventions while developing personal voice. If they are instrumentalists, their music often is quite idiomatic for that instrument. Pianists create pieces that sound like piano pieces, and violinists write pieces that sound like violin pieces (and sometimes fiddle tunes). While their pieces are uniquely theirs and they are seeking to convey their own musical ideas, they are firmly grounded in familiar styles.

However, other children prefer to deeply immerse themselves in non-conventional sounds and often seek unique organizational forms. This occurs with both children who do not study a specific instrument and instrumentalists after they have created a few traditional pieces. As part of a composing community, they are exposed to fresh ideas and sounds. They branch out by exploring what interests them and by asking for assistance from peers who can do something that they would like to use in a piece of their own.

Advanced Composers

Advanced young middle-school composers continue to develop personal voice within familiar structures and forms, similar to intermediate composers. However, they are able to imagine the impact of their compositional choices in the absence or near absence of external sound. It is the marked ability to think creatively in sound without the physical presence of that sound that distinguishes the more advanced composer at this level. While they continue to work with the sounds in actuality, advanced composers often report imagining something at home or away from their preferred sound sources and then trying out their imagined sonifications later, when they return to their instrument or computer. Much of their work continues to be done by physically creating the sounds, but they are also able to consider possibilities by mentally manipulating the sounds and imagining the results. Advanced middle-school composers are very much able to be fully independent as they create. They benefit from coaching, from receiving multiple perspectives on their works, and from being exposed to more sophisticated forms and models from within their preferred styles and genres.

PROMPTING REVISION: HELPING YOUNG COMPOSERS SEE THEIR WORKS IN OTHER WAYS

This young middle-school age (eleven to twelve years old) is the age at which young composers often begin to spontaneously revise their works (Stauffer, 1998). Most often this occurs by lengthening a piece that the young composer had previously considered finished (Stauffer, personal communication, 2008). Teacher suggestions can provide scaffolding for even younger composers (nine to ten years old) to revise their pieces, but simply suggesting that a child to revise a piece is not usually sufficient.

Suggesting that the young composer create a longer piece based on a shorter one he or she has completed may be an effective way of encouraging the student to continue working on a composition (Smith, 2007). Helping children consider creating contrasting sections, introductions, and endings are easy ways to encourage extensions, since many children do that naturally when asked to make their pieces longer. However, they may need help with how to make the beginnings and endings and new sections relate to the rest of the piece.

Young composers often do better when asked to extend a piece they like than to change one they are not as pleased with (Smith, 2007). These pieces that the young composers feel are less than satisfactory are usually abandoned or filed away in their sketchbooks. The young composers themselves are reluctant to revisit them. They prefer instead to begin working on new pieces.

Sometimes, though, they are simply stuck at some point in a particular piece. They may ask for suggestions of ways to continue or conclude the composition. This is a very appropriate place to seek peer feedback. Armed with several suggestions from a feedback group, the composer may go back to the piece with several new ideas to try, and work may once again seem to flow easily.

Another way to receive feedback on the piece is to use an anonymous recording. The composer selects a piece to be shared, and a recording is made. The teacher introduces the recording and asks the members of the class (or a small group) to think of three things they like about the piece and one or two suggestions. The reviewers are asked to write their comments on a form provided by the teacher—index cards work well. The teacher then collects all the comment cards. These are anonymous comments. The composer also fills in a card so that her identity is less likely to be revealed.

At a later time the teacher and the composer have a conference to discuss the feedback on the cards. During the conference the teacher needs to do several things. The teacher's role should be to ask questions of the composer as the cards are presented. She should follow the student's lead on revision and let the student decide which suggestions, if any, are good ones. She may also point out inappropriate comments and suggestions or merely remove those cards from the stack before presenting them to the composer. The teacher may also offer musical or technical support as needed for the composer to act on any ideas he or she wishes to pursue.

Only an occasional piece is selected for this type of feedback. Time constraints prevent it from happening regularly in most school settings, although it can be more common in classes devoted specifically to composition. In these classes, the need for anonymity may be less if the composing community has developed into a supportive group. The composer may simply perform her piece and may ask the group for specific types of feedback, such as suggestions for an ending or how to transition between one section and another. The comments may be aural, but often it is better if they are put in writing for the composer to review later.

Young middle-school composers at the intermediate and advanced levels are the ones who most often begin to benefit from being encouraged to extend and revise their pieces. This sets the stage for longer works and more complex pieces in later middle school and beyond.

TOUCHPOINTS FOR TEACHING

1. Embrace social interaction.

Create a composing community where students support one another's efforts. Remember that young middle-school students are very social creatures. Embrace this and use it teach them effectively. They need to learn the skills that allow them to work with all kinds of people and many different settings. Group composition activities, sharing sessions, and positive reflections can help build those skills as well as support young composers. They need to be taught how to do this effectively, but the rewards of doing so can be very long lasting.

2. Balance freedoms with the security of rules.

Begin with structured activities and work toward more choices with fewer requirements. Novice composers are not ready for most unstructured composition activities. More advanced students may need only deadlines. Most young middle school–age students need some structure in order to get started but may quickly be able to proceed on their own. Procedural rules may be all that is needed after some initial groundwork. Each situation and group of students is different. Teachers can quickly recognize the most appropriate structure level for their students.

3. Provide multi-session compositional opportunities.

While single-class composing lessons are better than no composing lessons, middle level students need repeated opportunities to allow for more personally meaningful interactions with sound. Longer pieces often need more than one class session to evolve. Group work may take longer than one class period. One-time composing tasks simply show what the students can do at that point. Skills take time to develop and need repeated opportunities to practice. Doing similar tasks but with increasing amounts of freedom often leads to more rapid growth.

4. Encourage musical independence.

To foster musical independence and personal expression, students should be helped to self-define an increasing number of musical parameters as they become more experienced composers. While total freedom from teacher-imposed task guidelines may be too overwhelming at first, there should be fewer and fewer parameters as the students compose more and more works. Teachers should encourage students to create music that expresses feelings that are important and valuable to the students.

5. Use technology.

This can connect young middle school students to real-world music making. Technology can provide an avenue for creating music that sounds more like the music of their preferred styles and genres without extensive music performance skill. However, it is also important to include activities that do not require computer technology. This allows young composers to develop broader understandings of the processes of composition.

6. Offer positive comments and encouragement.

Teacher modeling and role-playing help students learn to offer appropriate comments to their classmates. These skills take some time to develop and need a vocabulary that allows these discussions to take place. Sometimes it is more appropriate for the teacher or other adults to speak privately with a student to praise her work and offer encouragement. Notes and e-mails can be another way of privately supporting excellent work.

A TEACHING SCENARIO

Mr. Lee smiles at his fifth-grade clarinet lesson group. It is their first group lesson of the year, and the seven students in the group all were in his program the previous year. He knows they will continue to build technical skills this year, and he hopes their abilities to express themselves also continue to develop. Last year in class, the students had done some improvising and had created some short pieces based on their lesson books, but Mr. Lee wants to include composition in a more serious way this year.

At this first lesson, he tells the students about a long-term project they will be doing. The students each will create a piece to play on their instruments that will be their very own. He will help them learn how to do this, and in May, there will be a recital for anyone who wants to play their piece for their parents and friends. For now, he tells them not to worry about writing down their pieces, but just to make up something on their clarinets that they can play. They should come to their lesson next week ready to play something that they made up for the class. It doesn't have to be very long, just a short something that might be an idea for a piece. He then continues with their regular lesson for the day.

The next week at the start of the lesson, Mr. Lee learns that only three of the children have come with something that they have made up and are ready to play for the class. He encourages the others to come up with something for the next week and sets aside ten minutes at the end of class to hear the students who were prepared. He tells them that he is recording them so that he can think about their pieces over the next week. They play their pieces, and he praises each one of them for doing their homework. He encourages them to keep working on their pieces.

The following week he hands a notated copy of what the students had played the previous week back to the students. He asks them to take it home and play it to see whether it sounds right to them. He also records the other two students who came in with ideas. The two stragglers are encouraged to bring something next week. This takes no more than ten minutes.

Once most of the class has a start on their pieces, Mr. Lee sets aside one lesson in every four to work solely on their compositions and does not use lesson time in the other three lessons for composing. However, at each lesson he encourages them to continue working on their pieces.

At the composing lessons, he records the sessions and at the next lesson hands the students notated versions of what they played. The lesson group functions as a community of composers, and members offer comments and suggestions to one another. He often improvises simple accompaniments on the piano while they play what they have created so far. After several months, he also makes himself available before school and at lunch to students who want to bring in their pieces for a "private lesson" or who did not get to play their pieces in class during a particular session. Students can sign up for these times during their lessons.

By March, most of the students in this lesson group have created pieces, and Mr. Lee now switches to encouraging them to practice their pieces so that they will be ready for the recital. At the same time, they are working on producing a clean, notated version of their pieces, complete with dynamics, breath marks, and articulation markings. This will be published in a collection of pieces composed this year. Two of the students have not yet finished their pieces, and Mr. Lee continues to encourage them to finish. Several students are also working together outside of class time to make up duets.

Mr. Lee realizes that his students have made more progress in their lessons than groups from past years in spite of the time that has been devoted to composition. Their work on their pieces seems to have improved their reading skills and their playing technique. The desire to be able to play their own pieces—and sometimes those of their classmates—seems to have led to an increase in their performance abilities.

In early May the recital night takes place. Many sixth-grade students from the lesson groups have chosen to perform their pieces in the recital. The recital is recorded, and the pieces are placed on the school's website. That night they are given a copy of the composition book. This was created with the help of parent volunteers who used the school's copy machine and a spiral binder. The cover was chosen from ones some composers designed and brought in to their lessons. The pages are the final copies of the scores that the students made.

Many of the students are continuing to compose pieces on their own, and Mr. Lee encourages them to work on these over the summer. He secretly smiles at this enthusiasm because he feels it may lead his students to occasionally pick up their instruments when they otherwise might not be practicing them. He looks forward to hearing their new pieces in the fall.

MY PIECE

Unit: Instrumental Group Lessons for Second-Year Students Project: My Piece Level: Intermediate	
Planning Elements	*Thinking Guides*
Composer Characteristics	Grade level: Fifth to sixth Skill level: Intermediate Setting: Group lessons and at home Time: Several months, depending on frequency of lessons and other demands on time
Focus and Supporting Principles	All apply, and depend on composer choices
Compositional Capacities (When?)	Intention: Composer determined Expressivity: Composer determined Artistic craftsmanship: Creating melodies for a specific instrument; notation skills
Compositional Context	Individual
Tools	Instruments: Band, orchestra, keyboards, guitars, recorders Preservations: Traditional notation, recordings
Prerequisites	Concepts: Music is created to convey a feeling. Musical skills: A year of lessons on a wind instrument, melodic percussion, piano, or guitar or the ability to play at least an octave range and read the notation for the instrument. Intuitive understandings: How a piece of music fits together
Co-compositional Activities (When?)	Playing the instrument in classes and learning its techniques are the co-compositional activities. Refining the final product in notation is also a co-compositional activity.
Task Guidelines	Product: Solo piece with piano (or other) accompaniment Length: Student determined Specs: Student creates the melodic line. Teacher creates accompaniment in coordination with the student. Student determines overall length and form. Time: As needed, usually several months Preservation: Teacher records and notates as the piece evolves. Student creates the final notated draft. Performance: Public performance near the end of school year
Assessments	What: Self-assessment and possibly peer group How: From recording or performance by teacher Why: Self-improvement and satisfaction
Connections	To past or future music lessons: Try creating a partnered piece (duet) with another member of the lesson group. To other disciplines: N/A

SUGGESTED LESSONS

Unit: Repetition and Variety in the Arts
Project: Classroom Instrument Piece Based on "Russian Sailor's Dance" by Glière
Level: Beginner
Overview: As part of an interdisciplinary arts unit on repetition, the students listen to a recording and then discuss the "Russian Sailor's Dance" from *The Red Poppy* by Glière. They make a list of the ways Glière changes the music while repeating the tune. The students then assemble in groups of five with similar sets of classroom instruments, only one of which will play a melody. The other instruments are nonpitched percussion and include at least eight other instruments (more than the number of students). They are told to create a melody that will be repeated at least five times. They are asked to create a piece based on their melody that uses some of the same techniques (from their list) that Glière used. Pieces are performed for the class and recorded for further discussion.

Planning Elements	*Thinking Guides*
Composer Characteristics	Grade level: Fourth to sixth Skill level: Beginner Setting: Classroom Time: One to two class periods of thirty minutes
Focus and Supporting Principles	Unity/variety—focus principle; all others apply as supporting principles
Compositional Capacities	Intention: Composer choice in melodic and setting construction Expressivity: Repetition as a way of emphasizing a melodic idea Artistic craftsmanship: Ways of creating variety while using a unifying tune; combining sounds
Compositional Context	Small groups
Tools	Instruments: Classroom instruments and recorders or other melodic instruments played by group members Preservations: Recordings
Prerequisites	Concepts: Same and different; ability to work in groups Musical skills: Steady beat and performing techniques on small percussion Intuitive understandings: A sense of phrase
Co-compositional Activities (When?)	Listening: Before the compositional task, "Russian Sailor's Dance" from *The Red Poppy* by Glière Also may involve concepts of repetition in movement compositions in physical education classes and of repetition in visual art if this is planned as a coordinated unit. Music teachers may want to include these as part of a unit even if it is not jointly taught.

Planning Elements	Thinking Guides
Task Guidelines	Product: Piece with repeated melody Length: Minimum of five repetitions Specs: Use the list generated after listening to the Gliere and your own ideas to make your repetitions interesting and expressive. What is your piece about? Time: Thirty minutes once work has begun. Be sure to include practice time. Preservation: Recording, video if possible Performance: For the class
Assessments	What: Done by group members after performance How: Listen to (and watch?). What worked well? What might be improved?
Connections	To past or future music lessons: Repeat another time using *In the Hall of the Mountain King* by Grieg or a section of Bolero by Ravel as the trigger piece. To other disciplines: Repetition in visual art, dance, and poetry

SOUNDSCAPE FOR A POEM

Unit: Impressionist Music
Project: Soundscape for a Poem
Level: Advanced
Overview: After studying various impressionist art forms, including music by several impressionist composers, the students are asked to select one landscape picture from a variety of pictures provided by the teacher. They create a descriptive poem based on the landscape and then use a computer to record themselves reading the poem. Next they use looping software to create a background soundscape to enhance the evocativeness of the poem and the picture. The teacher may provide examples of completed projects she has created as guides. Once the unit has been taught, models done by other fifth-grade students should be presented to the children before they begin.

Planning Elements	Thinking Guides
Composer Characteristics	Grade level: Fifth Skill level: Advanced Setting: Computer lab Time: One to two class periods of thirty minutes
Focus and Supporting Principles	All apply. Emphasis will depend on poem selected and composer choices.
Compositional Capacities (When?)	Intention: What qualities of the selected landscape does the composer select to convey? (student determined) Expressivity: Student determined, based on the poem Artistic craftsmanship: Effective use of spoken word and loops to enhance the mood of the poem
Compositional Context	Individual or partnered

Planning Elements	Thinking Guides
Tools	Instruments: Computers work best; also possible using classroom instruments Preservations: Computer program as saved file
Prerequisites	Familiarity with sequencing and looping software or time to learn program Poem-writing experience
Co-compositional Activities (When?)	Listening: French impressionist Study visual art examples as well Done before or after composing
Task Guidelines	Product: Poem and soundscape Length: Composer determined, based on poem Specs: Provide students with several visuals of landscapes from which they select one. Students create a descriptive poem evoking imagery. Students create a piece that is the sound equivalent of the poem using computer recording and looping software. Time: Thirty to sixty minutes Preservation: Save file on computer Performance: By the computer
Assessments	Student description of how piece relates to visual following the performance
Connections	Other soundscapes from impressionism and from new-age composers Poems could be created as part of language arts poetry unit.

ETUDES

1. Interview a ten- to twelve-year-old student about his or her musical preferences and the uses of music in his or her life. Write a lesson plan and teaching scenario that would interest this young person in composing based on the information you learned in your interview.

2. Review the "Soundscape for a Poem" lesson. Rewrite the lesson without using looping software or any other computer resources. How do you think this would impact the products the children produce and their satisfaction with them?

3. Using the model for "My Piece," create a unit done over the course of a year that would lead to duets or trios instead of solos. Write a teaching scenario that takes into account how this would need to differ from the model presented here.

4. Create a poem soundscape to a favorite poem of yours (or one that you write) using looping software. Make a list of everything a ten-year-old would need to know or be able to do to use the software.

5. Create a short piece for solo instrument and accompaniment. Share with your classmates and model the attitudes and dispositions of a composing community for one another as you do so.

10

Composing in Upper Middle School

Upper middle-school composers span every imaginable spectrum. They want freedom but would also like some guidelines. They want to write their *own* music but make every effort to sound just like the pop star currently occupying the top of the charts. They want their music to stand out but also to blend in. They are the epitome of "generative tension."

This chapter offers a musical profile of these highly diverse, interesting, and challenging young composers. The unique characteristics that make up their human development play heavily in their broader musical growth as well as in their compositional interests and motivations. Despite the many challenges that this age group presents, one thing holds true: when upper middle-school students find a focus for their energy and imagination, great things happen.

UPPER MIDDLE-SCHOOL
COMPOSERS AND COMPOSITION ACTIVITIES

Composer Characteristics

Upper middle-school students are likely to range from those who have no formal composition experience to those who are adept young composers. Additionally, by the end of middle school, some students may have four or more years of performance study to draw upon and influence their compositional work. As the breadth and depth of prior experiences continues to expand, so must the curriculum created for upper middle-school students branch out to accommodate their needs and interests.

The conceptions of music that adolescents bring to composition continue to shift and change. As many middle-school students are attracted to popular music, their working definition of "acceptable music" is highly influenced by mass media and peers. Songwriting as a means of personal expression is very appealing to some students, while others who are developing performance skills on voice or instruments are equally interested in composing for their instrument or for instruments played by their friends. In both cases, students are seeking to create music that fits into the experiences of their daily lives—what they hear and what they do.

Along with listening and performance skills, students are increasingly drawn to resources for making music on computers. Knowing that good-sounding music can be produced with relative speed and ease makes computer-based music composition extremely attractive. Computers also provide a means for an impressive expansion of the compositional sound palette as sampled sounds, loops, and recordings of acoustic performance can be easily intertwined within a variety of software programs.

The final characteristic of upper middle-school composers is their sometimes conflicted desire to create music that uniquely reflects who they are while simultaneously being acceptable to their peers. This is a personal challenge that each composer tackles in his or her own way. Teacher-assigned tasks can relieve some of the burden by freeing composers to produce pieces that may not be immediately embraced by peers. Nonetheless, young artists eventually have to find their own way and their own voice within the processes of composition.

Understanding and Use of Compositional Principles

Compositions created by upper middle-school students tend to be either daring or conventional. Conventional pieces abound in early work as composers seek peer acceptance. However, as the musical artist grows, there is a tendency to gravitate toward new and unexpected sounds in ways that test and challenge preconceived notions of what is and what is not "good music." This transition marks an important developmental step as the young composer wrestles intentions and strengthens the presence of his or her compositional voice.

Stability and instability are found in the work of adolescents on several levels. First, there is an initial desire to conform to expectations in terms of musical products. Students compose pieces that are recognizable and fall into common forms and styles. However, as composers develop and begin to believe in their own compositional voice, they begin to add musical gestures that challenge the norm and cause instability and surprise. When composers discover the power in challenging expectations, the level of expectation to be challenged changes, and entire pieces are created that often defy categorization.

While experiments with sound and silence often thrill the very young composer, silence can be uncomfortable for adolescents, who tend to surround themselves with music, television, radios, movies, mp3 players, and talkative peers. Upper middle-school composers, therefore, tend to emphasize sound in their work. When silence is introduced, it is used in powerful ways. Silence for middle-school students implies time to be alone, time to be oneself without the judgment of others, and time for reflective thinking—though they may not be overtly aware of this practice. The use of silence, therefore, is always a purposeful decision made for immediate and long-term impact. Its use heralds a growth in expressive awareness.

While unity and variety are certainly present within pieces created by upper middle-school composers, it is perhaps most noticeable at the macro level. Composer sketchbooks tend to feature either a wide range of musical pieces or numerous pieces created within the same style or for the same group of performers. This approach to unity and variety is important because it represents a narrowing of focus in which the composer is seeking to refine a particular set of skills or address a particular area of need. In the case of wide-ranging musical pieces, composers are trying to identify a genre in which they believe they can speak musically. Conversely, in collections of pieces within a single style, genre, or ensemble, composers are trying to determine how many things they can communicate within the restrictions they have imposed. In both cases, the composer may not be aware of his or her personal search. Equally important is the fact that either focus of attention invites and demands compositional growth.

Rather than being tied to personal movement, motion and stasis in the work of upper middle-school students is used to contribute to expressivity or to reflect developing technical proficiencies in the area of personal performance. Composers write music for themselves or their peers that provides the performer with an opportunity to boost technical and musical achievements. These pieces—being performance driven—tend to feature musical gestures that engage speed and range: lots of eighth notes, very high, or very low.

These pieces are informative for the composer on multiple levels. First, they allow the composer to learn what different instruments are capable of doing. Secondly, they allow the composer to learn how different musical gestures work and fail to work with performers of differing abilities.

The words *tension* and *release* could be painted on a sign and placed above any upper middle-school classroom door. The terms are nearly synonymous with adolescence. The tensions that students face on a daily basis (being caught between childhood and adulthood, peer acceptance or rejection, increasing self-awareness, sexual awareness, etc.) are nearly over-whelming to many and completely overwhelming to others.

These same tensions, however, are fertile ground for creating art. When students are led to understand conflicts, personal or external to themselves, they begin to understand how meaning arises from the juxtaposition of ideas and/or experiences. Because the experience of tension and release is so personal and so deeply situated within what it is to be twelve or thirteen years old, students can create pieces that are profoundly shaped by the use of tension and release.

Compositional Context

Whole-class or full ensemble activities remain beneficial for modeling various aspects of the composition process. Nevertheless, upper middle-school students learn best when they identify and solve problems on their own or assisted by peers, with the teacher functioning as a knowledgeable resource. The highly social nature of middle-school students directly relates to their ability to learn in social groups (Kagan, 1992). Peer work, however, needs to take a variety of forms to allow for the growth and exercise of in-dividual skills and understanding.

Upper middle-school composers benefit from working with their friends. Friends are known entities. They are familiar, comfortable, and supportive. The criticism they offer is easier to accept than criticism offered by less-familiar classmates. Friend groups function as a "safety zone" when com-posers are trying something new or unfamiliar and also work well for proj-ects that unfold over multiple classes or weeks. Working with friends can also be motivational (Kaschub, 1999).

Students also benefit from working with peers of equal or near-equal compositional skills. Groups formed by skill level allow for more equalized collaboration as there is no clear compositional leader to be followed. Simi-larly, students benefit from working with peers of equal performance skills. Performers who are excelling on an instrument enjoy collaborating with others who can perform the challenging musical ideas they have included in their compositions.

Performance abilities may vary widely within one class and can impact product perceptions. Therefore, it is important to encourage students to use the skills they have developed and to explore new areas of sound produc-tion as well. Create tasks that place every composer on equally familiar and comfortable footing. One way to do this is through the use of novel in-struments, computers, or body percussion to prevent unnecessary product comparisons between pieces.

Working with peers of varied skill levels can be very rewarding. More advanced composers can model processes and techniques as well as offer objective analysis of products. Less advanced composers also benefit from explaining and justifying their ideas to other composers. When students are grouped by compositional abilities, between-group comparison of products can arise. It is important in these situations for composers to identify their compositional problems and solutions in ways that allow feedback to relate to employed strategies rather than just outcomes. This reduces between-group comparisons and allows each composer to grow in the manner that best suits individual development.

The social nature of learning in adolescence naturally leads to group work, but it is also important for young composers to work independently. Working alone allows composers to fully exercise their intentions without compromise. Peer feedback, however, is often still desirable and can be made available through the use of sharing sessions. The nature of feedback to individuals is very important as perceptions of success or failure will rest squarely on one set of shoulders. Feedback must emphasize things that are working and invite consideration of less successful elements. Framing feedback in "I" statements such as, "When I listen to this piece I hear . . ." and "I find it effective because . . ." presents comments in relation to the listener rather than the composer. This makes feedback about perspectives less confrontational.

Tools of Creation and Preservation

Upper middle-school students need to work with tools that are representative of their growing musical interests and sophistication. Keyboards, guitars, drums, and computers are instruments that are broadly represented within their personal listening and instruments with social appeal. As many middle-school students want to write songs, it is important that they have access to these instruments and others that reach beyond their earlier experiences with instruments traditionally found in elementary general music classes. Traditional wind band, orchestral, and vocal instruments are broadly appealing, and students are usually eager to engage with instruments of different cultures.

The use of computers is very appealing to upper middle-school students. Computers can provide immediate aural information, make sounds easy to manipulate, offer a wide range of sound choices, and separate the composer from the dual role of composer-performer. While the experience of performance complements composition as a way of understanding music, many middle-school students pass through a period of extreme shyness and prefer not to perform for their peers. Computers offer students an opportunity to make music at a comfortable distance from the audience. Further, composers freed from the task of performance are able to write music that is not limited by their own performance skills.

Composers must also determine how they will preserve their work. Middle-school composers may use memory, invented or traditional notation, computers, or other recording devices. As the complexity of their musical thinking continues to develop, computer programs that preserve compositions in a variety of graphic notations become increasingly appealing.

Composers with limited knowledge of traditional notation can use computers to create pieces for human performers, though editors familiar with both software and traditional notation may be needed to proofread scores.

Considering Prerequisites

As every compositional étude or composition project is different, it is important to consider what skills and knowledge composers need to be successful from étude to étude or project by project. Students with limited prior compositional experience may want to hear models before they begin their work so that they can align their intentions with what they have heard. This is a good starting place for beginners. Students with more highly developed internal libraries may desire explanations of specific techniques or skills that they wish to use.

In most cases, students can be prompted to consider these and other questions as they plan their work:

1. Intention—What do you want this piece to sound like or feel like? Why? How do you imagine your piece?
2. Expressivity—Is there a particular mood, emotion, feeling, or experience that is important to this piece? Have you considered how you can achieve that with sound?
3. Artistic craftsmanship—Are there particular compositional devices that you wish to use? What are they? Do you know how to use these devices?

Upper middle-school students are adept at verbalizing their "need to know" once they have been prompted to consider the parameters of their tasks.

Co-compositional Activities

Since middle-school students who study composition are likely to come from a wide range of backgrounds, it is important to consider how singing, playing, improvising, and listening activities may inform their work. Students with limited listening backgrounds may benefit from guided listening that highlights styles, ensemble types, or compositional devices. Some students may need listening experiences that begin with instrument identification, while others may be focused on more technical aspects of construction.

Students considering writing pieces for specific instruments or ensembles might focus their listening efforts on learning about the idiomatic sounds associated with each instrument. By familiarizing themselves with expected sounds, they can capitalize on stability and instability in their work. Further, they may be able to transfer sounds and musical gestures that are the signature of one instrument to another instrument or style of music.

Improvisation presents the challenge of "composing in the moment." Improvisation exercises can be used to explore variation techniques or to learn to develop ideas quickly. Because improvisation happens quickly, students are less able to self-edit. This encourages divergent thinking and is helpful for students who complain that they have trouble coming up with a starting idea. It is important to note that some students find improvisation very uncomfortable exactly because they are unable to self-edit their ideas and ensure peer acceptance.

Although many middle-school students prefer not to share their singing voices, singing remains a valuable tool for the composer. While stunningly beautiful vocal production is certainly nice, the ability to match pitch and sing in a way that can communicate musical intent and ideas is sufficient for the composer. Because of this, middle-level music educators should teach the basics of vocal production and encourage students to continue to develop their voices. Students find the ability to sing ideas very helpful as they communicate with peers in group work or when they wish to convey interpretation to performers.

Task Guidelines

The guidelines provided to upper middle-school students must carry a careful balance of teacher-imposed constraints and composer-controlled freedoms. Tasks tightly prescribed by the teacher can be off-putting to young adolescents who are eager to demonstrate that they can do it themselves. Conversely, tasks that are too broadly sketched can leave students unable to properly self-define the project they are to undertake. Flexibility is key in discussions of task requirements.

There are two basic types of task formation that work well with upper middle-school students: teacher-to-student and student-with-teacher. Teacher-to-student tasks work best for compositional études. Teacher-structured tasks serve to engage composers with specific content knowledge, skills, or experiences. When creating task guidelines for études, teachers should specify exact details for one or two components of the project while leaving other areas less defined. This provides space for students to frame the remaining aspects of the task within an appealing context.

Student-with-teacher tasks fit composition projects that are composer driven. The task guidelines for open composition projects are designed by the composer and presented to the teacher. The teacher, serving as guide and mentor, listens very carefully to the student, asks questions and makes suggestions that the student can explore as the project evolves. The teacher does not try to reshape or direct the project, but presents questions that invite composers to think about the project that they are establishing for themselves. In both cases, student perception of personal agency in the process is a critical determinant of future success.

Assessment

Assessment plays an important role in planning and monitoring the compositional and musical learning of middle school students. The process begins with an assessment to establish a baseline of knowledge for each student. While class baselines can be helpful, the nature of composition study warrants the identification of individual starting points. As learning progresses, formative assessments can be gathered to gauge progress and guide task tailoring to the needs of each composer. Summative assessment can be used to measure overall learning and provide information about the effectiveness of instruction and curriculum.

While students are often eager to share the products and move on to the next project, it is important to take time to gather additional data. Scores, performances, and students' spoken or written verbal accounts of their intentions and their level of satisfaction with their pieces provide additional insight into the learning that takes place as composers create their music. To focus only on any single artifact of the process without the others is to chance missing key information related to student growth.

Middle school students are tested endlessly, and they often resent teacher assessments of their work. While proper documentation and feedback are critical components of both educational practice and learning, gathering information from sources other than the teacher can provide new perspectives. Middle school students benefit from self, peer, teacher, professional composer, and performer assessments.

The assessment of the processes of composition can provide important clues to student learning. Process assessment can be individual, within a group, or performed by the teacher. One particularly effective strategy features the use of a folded piece of paper. A trifold is used for groups of three, quarters for groups of four, and so on. Students write their own name and then the name of each member of their group, one per column. Using just two or three short sentences, students explain their own contribution and the contributions of their collaborators within each named fold of the paper (see table 10.1). The teacher can then take all of the reports from the group and compare perceptions across the group. Groups in accord typically need little attention, but groups in disagreement may need to take a little time to discuss how their group is functioning.

An important aspect of assessing upper middle-school students should be that the students become aware of the progress that they are making as composers. As students move from project to project, it can be easy to overlook new skills. They may fail to notice their increasing level of planning detail, or they may miss improvements in the effective use of compositional devices. Assessment can identify each of these things, but it is the teacher's task to make certain that students are aware of their growth. This can help frame their future goals in relation to what assessment has revealed.

Table 10.1. Trifold Reporting Form

Susan's report:

Susan (reporter)	Eliana	Jake
I entered the drum part and the triangle idea that Jake made up. He didn't know how to move them on the screen, so I showed him how to do that in the program.	Eli was our timekeeper. She played her flute into a live track to make ghost sounds for the movie.	Jake picked out two triangle samples and overlapped them into one part. He also suggested a cool guitar riff and recorded and recorded it himself

Eliana's report:

Susan	Eliana (reporter)	Jake
Susan was really good at the computer and helped us to enter all of our ideas.	I was the timekeeper. I made up a part on my flute and played it into the computer.	Jake worked for a long time with some triangle stuff.

Jake's report:

Susan	Eliana	Jake (reporter)
Sue helped me to put the triangle parts that I liked on the computer. She also showed us how to record, which was really helpful.	Eliana wrote a ghost song and played it on her flute. It fit against the guitar line that I made up.	I made up a really cool guitar lick and recorded it. I also put a couple of triangle ideas together for the middle of our piece.

DEVELOPING COMPOSITIONAL
CAPACITIES IN UPPER MIDDLE SCHOOL

The breadth and range of compositional capacities evident in upper middle school students (see table 10.2) is remarkable. While some young composers are hesitant to reach for new ground, others approach it by leaps and bounds. The diversity of composers found within any group of upper middle-school students would cause even the most eager teacher to pause. Yet it is just this diversity that makes teaching middle-school composition energizing. The potential for intense and expansive music learning is tangible.

The Growth of Compositional Intention

Upper middle school marks a period in artistic development that is often characterized as a plateau (Brophy, 1999; Kratus, 1985). While many factors may influence this temporary pause, perhaps the most influential factor is the all-encompassing shift of awareness that unfolds as children approach their teenage years. Framing nearly every event in terms of how others might perceive them, many preteens are highly conscious of social acceptance and endeavor to blend into—rather than stand apart from—their peer group. As such, their musical pursuits are often initially tame. Their willingness to pursue artistic risks is hard won.

Novice Composers

Upper middle school composers are able to think critically about their compositional intentions. Product intentions are often guided by an immense need to be accepted by peers. This leads many young adolescents to seek out the music that fits with their immediate peer culture. Music such as country, hip-hop, and pop are often cited among their favorites. However, when individual students are asked, apart from their peers, to identify preferred styles, a wider range of music is likely to emerge. Any and all of these may appear within their compositional work.

Intermediate Composers

Intermediate composers in the upper middle school develop their intentional capacity through a consistent refining of a narrow range of products. They often gravitate to one or two styles of music and invest considerable time exploring and refining their approach to those styles. Other composers may limit their work by focusing on a specific set of instruments across several compositions. In many ways, these actions represent

Table 10.2 Compositional Capacities in Older Middle-School Students

Compositional Capacities	Novice	Intermediate	Advanced
Intention	Popular music continues to attract the attention of young adolescents. The desire to conform to peer norms and be accepted narrows the overall range of product intention.	Young adolescents are becoming increasingly self-aware and are able to consider a range of intentions that extend beyond those acceptable to the peer group.	Young adolescents are actively seeking to create pieces that expand peer group norms. Novel ideas may be interspersed into peer-accepted styles.
Expressivity	Young adolescents often use a more limited expressive vocabulary in their efforts to conform to peer-accepted norms.	The expressive choices made by young adolescents become increasingly deliberate. They may purposefully focus on a narrow range of expressive gestures.	Young adolescents are often torn between making expressive choices reflective of personal affect and that of their intended audience. Expressive gestures may continue to be narrow in scope or may expand rapidly as young composers seek their individual voice.
Artistic craftsmanship	Young adolescents are often musically conservative as they experiment with the elements and principles of sound. Students may begin to adopt favorite musical gestures as "signatures."	Young adolescents focus attention on a narrower range of musical material. They often choose to develop a single principle either within one piece or across multiple pieces.	Young adolescents use conventional tools and forms in creative ways. They can imagine how principle relationships shape expressive outcomes.

a form of self-imposed compositional constraint. As such, intermediate composers often unknowingly lead themselves into experimentation.

The feelingful capacities found in the work of intermediate composers are still somewhat experimental, but testing becomes increasingly focused. Rather than exploring happy or sad, intermediate composers are seeking to define the range of a particular feeling or set of feelings. They are trying to identify the boundaries of feeling in their work.

Advanced Composers

Young adolescents who are advanced composers actively seek to create pieces that expand and even exceed peer group expectations. Their initial intentions may simply flirt with novel ideas, but eventually these new ideas garner more and more of their attention. Eventually their compositions become novel in and of themselves. Familiar styles and forms often provide a safety zone for experimental work. When success is found, even previously accepted styles and forms become too confining. At this point, composers begin to significantly expand the parameters of their work.

Attention to the feelingful aspects of compositional work may lead or follow refinement in product intention. As students develop increasingly complex product intentions, they may simplify or amplify feelingful intentions as attempts to balance the challenges they face in bringing their musical thoughts to sound. Complex feeling-based intentions can inspire either simple or complicated music, just as technically difficult constructions can boost or hinder affect. In either case, the composer is increasingly aware of the relationship between product and feeling.

Encouraging Expressivity in Upper Middle School Composers

Middle school is an emotionally loaded time in the lives of many students. While emotions often appear to be at the very surface of interactions between students, there are also deeper-seated feelings underpinning every situation. Students who are made aware of the surface and depth of their emotional lives are able to draw upon their feelingful experiences as a body of knowledge germane to their artistic work. The degree to which they access this knowledge defines their continuing development.

Novice Composers

Young adolescents often use a limited musical vocabulary in the area of expressivity. Their choices are heavily influenced by efforts to conform to peer-accepted norms. Because they are hesitant to try new means of expression, representation, or meaning making, novice composers work within familiar contexts that allow them to become increasingly adept at creating pieces that fit culturally defined sound norms. Many of their musical products can be broadly described with mood words. These initial pieces are very important as they serve to help novice composers define the norms that they eventually adopt or challenge as they develop their own compositional voices.

Intermediate Composers

As intermediate composers continue to explore the relationship between sound and feeling, their expressive choices become increasingly deliberate. They may purposefully focus on a narrow range of expressive gestures and use them in a variety of settings, or, conversely, they may use a single ensemble or genre to frame experimentation with a wide range of expressive techniques. In either case, intermediate composers in the upper grades of middle school tend to impose constraints in one area so that they may explore freedoms in others.

Advanced Composers

Young adolescents are often torn between making expressive choices reflective of personal affect and that of their intended audience. Expressive gestures may continue to be narrow in scope or may expand rapidly as young composers seek their individual voice. The works created by advanced composers during their middle-school years often reflect this personal conflict. Sketchbooks are predictable overall, but with a few pieces that do not quite fit in. These pieces are the experiments that highlight musical risk taking.

As advanced composers become increasingly confident in their compositional choices, a greater range of expressivity emerges. Purposeful connections between sound choices and feelingful intentions are evident in their work. This transition may be apparent in the early planning stages of composition. It is in this phase of the process that composers first begin to define the parameters of their work and draw relationships between expressive needs and product intentions.

Developing Artistic Craftsmanship in the Upper Middle School Composer

Many upper middle school composers are particularly interested in learning how to use compositional devices commonly and prominently featured within the music that they select for recreational listening. Another area that draws nearly equal attention is that of idiomatic devices found within the literature that students are studying as performers. These two forms of interaction—listening and performance—are deeply personal. They require serious commitments of personal time and are uniquely reflective of the tastes and preferences of the individual composer. Consequently, the musical works crafted by upper middle school musicians gravitate toward these two categories.

Novice Composers

Novice composers favor crafting patterns, ostinati, and other forms of repetitive musical gestures. These devices are memorable, predictable, and comfortable, which makes them a perfect match for the conservative nature of middle school composers. Although hesitant to explore the extremes of musical principles, novice composers experiment within a range that they find comfortable. Through this experimentation, favorite musical gestures begin to emerge and may even become signatures of their work.

Intermediate Composers

Young adolescents often choose to develop a single principle either within one piece or across multiple pieces. This focus relates more to comfort than ability. Once a gesture or series of gestures is easily executed, it functions as a safety net. The composer turns to this device again and again because it has proven successful in earlier work. However, with time, familiar gestures become too mundane, and intermediate composers begin to subtly expand these previously employed ideas. They may even abandon signature ideas outright in a search for techniques that allow for greater expressivity or that are necessary to fulfill product intentions.

Advanced Composers

While young adolescents use conventional tools and forms, advanced composers soon begin to use them in creative ways. They can imagine how principle relationships shape expressive outcomes and are eager to acquire the technical skills that allow them to achieve their musical intentions. At this point in their development, advanced composers are increasingly able to identify their own learning needs. They can actively seek models of the techniques they wish to employ and can manipulate the materials of music to discover how sounds can be structured to achieve desired effects.

COMPOSITION IN MIDDLE SCHOOL CONTEXTS

Middle school music programs typically comprise three types of offerings: classroom music, ensemble music, and special activities that are scheduled outside of the formal school day. As mentioned in chapter 9, classroom music courses at this level of schooling are often referred to as "exploratories." Rather than providing a sampling of a wide array of musical practices and activities over a year, exploratory music courses are often structured in nine-, twelve-, or eighteen-week periods and focus on a particular topic or skill.

Composing in Exploratory Music Courses

Guitar, keyboard, and historically or culturally oriented music offerings are commonly offered for students in grades seven and eight. Songwriting is a particularly appealing activity for upper middle school students who identify with popular music and who are eager to create their music. It can easily fit within any of the exploratory courses. More importantly, well-planned songwriting tasks can be accessible to novice, intermediate, and advanced composers.

Experiences with songwriting work best when students have some ability to sing and play an accompanying instrument or when they are familiar with software programs that can be used to generate an accompaniment. A unit within one of the courses listed above or an entire exploratory can easily be devoted to studying the musical, lyrical, and stylistic aspects of songwriting. Musical aspects of songwriting include developing aural skills and theoretical knowledge of song form—intro, verse, chorus, prebridge, bridge, outro, and so on. Discovering how rhyme, alliteration, metaphor, storytelling, description, and messaging relate to the lyrical aspects of songwriting provides opportunities for interdisciplinary connections to language arts studies. Through these activities, young songwriters can learn how to invite people to think about issues through the use of song.

Songwriting, however, is about more than just writing songs. Although they may eventually seek a professional singer, most songwriters perform their own songs as part of the process of writing. Songwriters also need to give careful consideration to the lyrical and musical content of songs they write. The skills required to objectively assess personal songs can be developed through the critical analysis of models or of songs created by peers. Moreover, in order for songwriters to gauge the effectiveness of their products, it is important that songwriters have access to audiences beyond their classmates.

Songwriting circles can provide budding songwriters with a forum for collecting feedback and reading audience reactions to their work. Songwriting circles can be used when songs are in process or in final form. Songwriters preparing to share their pieces can either introduce their works and perform them or can pose questions to the circle members. Introductions might include telling the circle what they might listen for or asking for other songwriters to suggest solutions to particular challenges or problems.

The main component of the circle experience is that the songwriting effort receives immediate feedback. Informal feedback is gathered as the songwriter observes audience reaction to his or her piece. Formal feedback in sharing circles needs to be guided carefully because songwriting is such an intensely personal experience. Since novice songwriters can be very nervous, it is important that initial feedback simply describe what has been heard and acknowledge points where the songwriter has indicated satisfaction with the work (Kratus, 2008). When greater levels of confidence have been achieved, more constructive criticism or suggestions can be offered. Above all, it is important to support the work of the songwriter as he or she attempts to fulfill musical intentions.

Composing in Performance Ensembles

Composition plays an important role in developing both independent musicianship and ensemble cohesion when incorporated into choral and instrumental settings. Experiences in composing music can increase young performers' awareness of the composer intentions that may lead to enhanced interpretations and performances (Kaschub, 1997). Students sometimes are eager to create music similar to that which they have been studying as performers. The works they create uniquely represent their developing musicianship.

Composing in ensemble settings requires careful planning. Ensembles tend to have large numbers of students. They usually comprise students of varied experiential and musical backgrounds. These students hold a multitude of expectations that may or may not include composition.

Project Introductions

It is important to invite student participation in the early stages of planning a project so that group ownership is established. Students may contribute ideas related to the character of the work, the formal organization, the mood scheme, or perhaps the intended audience. Involve the entire ensemble in brainstorming as many facets of the project as possible, since this contributes to sustaining interest and motivation when the project becomes more challenging.

Inspirations

The members of the ensemble should have a voice in selecting the inspiration for their piece. Texts, pictures, film excerpts, stories, and feelings can all be used to organize sound events. It may be helpful for the ensemble to generate a list of possible inspirations to discover whether any themes of interest emerge from within the group. The common experiences of middle-school students can lead to pieces that are inspired by everything from friendship to gym shoes stuck in lockers. Inspiration has many origins.

Planning Work

Teachers need to consider how much time will be devoted to working on the composition project within rehearsals. Designating a specific number of minutes per rehearsal or a rehearsal each week for composition establishes a routine that fosters anticipation and engagement. A timetable helps to focus the work and to keep track of progress. Having a deadline can both assist and impede the work, so care should be taken when planning first ensemble composition projects to allow plenty of time longitudinally to accomplish the work. It may or may not be possible to create and perform the piece all in the same year.

One common concern of teachers is the rehearsal time that is lost when composing with ensembles. Teachers are often charged with presenting concerts and need a particular number of pieces to form a concert of appropriate length. Often the time invested in creating an original composition means omitting one piece from the immediately impending concert roster. However, the attention that students give to score construction develops skills that they begin to apply to other pieces (Kaschub, 1997). This usually means that pieces prepared for future concerts come together much more quickly.

Creating a Shared Vision

As Wiggins (1999/2000) has noted, successful group composition rests in the ability of the members to form a shared vision of their product intention. In large ensemble settings, the teacher needs to facilitate this process. Asking questions that guide students in outlining formal sections, identifying characteristics of the sound in those sections, and suggesting what instruments or voices might be featured are all helpful starting points. As these and other musical considerations are discussed within the ensemble, unity in the ensemble's definition of the compositional challenge usually emerges.

Collecting and Preserving Ideas

Since ensembles tend to be made up of many students, it is important to develop a system for efficiently collecting and processing ideas. Students may be able to sing or play their ideas. Recordings can be made of these models. Students may also be able to notate their ideas. It is helpful to appoint one or two students with strong dictation skills to enter ideas into a computer notation program. If this is not possible, then rehearsal must be recorded so that the teacher can notate ideas before the next working session.

Choral Considerations

In choral settings, text often serves as the focus of composition activities. The process begins by finding a text. Chorus members can collectively write a poem, or individual members can author and submit poems for review. Inviting a panel of other subject area teachers to review submissions and select the top three or four poems frees the music teacher from accusations of favoritism. The three or four top poems are then presented to the ensemble, and their relative musical merits are discussed.

Selecting song lyrics requires careful consideration of both poetic meanings and the actual words used in the poem. It is best is if the author remain anonymous while the poem is in process. This removes personal biases from the discussion.

Composers should consider what words in the text imply sounds. How does the poem come to have meaning? Are there interesting juxtapositions of words or sounds? What sounds can be imagined to match the overall mood of the poem? What might happen if the music were used to contrast with the mood of the poem?

As each poem is reviewed, it is important to note the musical advantages that each presents. Sometimes a clear winner emerges, but in the case of close contestants, it is often best to allow the ensemble to vote for a favorite. Each poem title can be listed on a ballot and students can indicate their preferences using a one (low potential) to five (high potential) scale. With scores tallied, the text for the project can be announced.

Once a text has been chosen and an overall plan of the piece created, it is time for specific ideas to be developed. This process can begin with students reading the text with slightly exaggerated inflection, or it may begin with one or more ensemble members singing an idea. The entire ensemble should be invited to echo either inflections or sung ideas. This allows every member of the group to experience each idea as it is suggested. After several ideas are offered, it is time to compare them. This can be done using a process similar to that used in selecting the text. The relative merits of each idea should be discussed and the strongest idea carried forward. Since many wonderful ideas emerge in this process, it is quite important that ideas not selected be saved and kept at hand. They may prove useful as the piece unfolds.

Instrumental Considerations

Although the inspirational items for composing in instrumental settings perhaps will not include text, many aspects of the process are very similar to those used in choral ensembles. Once a sequence of musical events has been outlined, even one as simple as beginning-middle-end, students can begin to suggest ideas to place in each formal section of the work. Just as in the choral setting, it is important that each member of an instrumental ensemble play and experience the ideas being suggested whenever the idea can be created on every instrument. It is at this point that the process needs special attention.

In order for instrumental ensembles to share ideas effectively, the teacher needs to present strategies for overcoming the challenges of transposition. It is possible for the teacher to collect ideas, notate and transpose ideas outside of the rehearsal, and bring the transposed parts back for everyone to play, but this takes considerable time. A faster way to work involves the use of solfège syllables. The ensemble is taught to sing *do–re–mi–fa–sol–la–ti–do* and chromatic alterations as needed. A simple chart can be placed on the rehearsal room wall that shows the solfège syllables in each instrument key. For example, working in the key of C major, flutes use C for *do*, trumpets and B♭ clarinets use D for *do*, and so forth. When a student plays a musical idea, the ensemble should echo sing it, perhaps first on "loo" but then on the syllables. The teacher can model this first if necessary, but gradually the students should be able to sing the syllables for themselves. Corrections may be needed to the solfège syllables, but then they play the idea on their instruments while working in their own key. Notated versions of the ideas still are needed, but the use of solfège eliminates waiting time and creates an immediacy that helps students maintain focus and energy in the process of composing. It also improves their music dictation skills.

Developing Pieces

Since many people contribute to the process of composition within an ensemble, it is easy for idea after idea to spill out in a linear and horizontal fashion. Developing this long line of ideas into vertical, perhaps harmonic, structures often requires teacher guidance. Once an idea has been presented, tested, and selected for use, it should be played with. Composers should consider what may be done to develop the idea. This often begins with a search for composition techniques used in other pieces that the ensemble has recently performed or is currently preparing for performance.

The use of canons, imitation, chordal underpinning, ictus orchestration, timbral shifts, and other techniques used to vary sound are all worthy of exploration. Some techniques may seem more appropriate than others when considered in relation to the overall product intention or goals of a particular formal section. The key aspect of the ensemble process at this point is that each idea is tested and its merits and potential considered. Through this process of idea generation, testing, and selection, the piece begins to emerge.

Editing

Ensemble-composed works tend to exist in various stages of rough draft throughout the process. When the ensemble seems content with the product, it generally falls to the teacher to produce a clean score for editing and end-stage refinements. The ensemble should be given opportunity to sing or play through the entire work while marking edits for expressive indicators, note changes, phrase marking, and other performance instructions. The final version can then be produced and distributed for performance preparation.

Performance

The premiere of an ensemble-composed piece deserves considerable fanfare. The ensemble may wish to create program notes or have the piece introduced by one or more of the ensemble members. Whenever possible, students should fill all performance roles—singers, instrumentalists, accompanist, and conductor. This allows for complete ownership in the process. Audiences usually appreciate the work put into the creation and performance of original pieces. It is important to feature student work in a significant way within the overall concert program.

Reflection

Young composers often begin the process of reflection with how they felt as their piece was performed. These impressions then are often substantiated with observations made of the audience. The teacher can guide these reflections back to the process of creating the music to draw attention to the ways in which the composers made artistic decisions. Once students make the connection between their compositional capacities and audience reactions, they will have achieved a sphericity of knowing in which intentions (intended outcomes) and musical products (physical outcomes) are encompassed. This is often the time when young composers ask, "What are we going to compose for the next concert?"

TOUCHPOINTS FOR TEACHING

1. Recognize and honor student autonomy.

Upper middle-school students need opportunities to define and test who they are within the processes of their daily lives. Musically, they want to and need to create music that is uniquely reflective of their personal interests and development.

2. Offer opportunities for social interaction, even during single-composer projects.

Social learning is a key component of human development during the middle-school years. Young composers benefit from opportunities to work with friends, musical peers, compositional peers, and performance-skilled peers. Each of these interactions builds their compositional knowledge in different ways. Similarly, young composers need opportunities to work alone, but with access to peers who can provide feedback and encouragement.

3. Encourage diversity in collaboration with peers.

Composers of all ages benefit from working with composers who are interested in creating material that differs from what others are doing. Exposure to multiple perspectives on products and processes provides young composers with models to assimilate or dismiss as their compositional voices develop.

4. Invite musical risk taking.

Because much of middle school is devoted to attempts to conform and fit in, upper middle-school composers sometimes benefit from gentle nudges toward new musical ideas, forms, and sounds. Composers who use the same basic musical gestures in numerous pieces may be budding minimalists, but more likely they need exposure to a wider range of music and a safe environment in which to conduct their own experiments.

5. Foster discovery. Learning to compose is not linear.

It is very easy to outline a composition process that leads from idea formation to performance. However, that is but one approach. Composers may find it helpful to be able to jump from idea to idea or to refine one idea while another section of the work sits in draft form. Composition is a creative process, not a race. Interaction with materials and the subsequent growth of the creator make possible processes that are rarely predictable or linear.

6. Welcome and encourage a wide range of processes and products.

Since upper middle school is a peak point in the development of self-definition, as a group young composers tend to create widely varying products. These products stem from an equally broad representation of personal processes. Asking questions allows the teacher to explore the composer's intentions and provides students the freedom they need to develop who they are as young composers.

7. Teach by being a mentor, guide, and resource.

The ever-present need for autonomy coupled with young adolescents' desire to work with their peers seems to leave little room for a traditional conception or practice of teaching. However, young composers work best when they feel safe, and their safety often lies in knowing that an expert is nearby to help them should they run into problems. Teachers who initiate projects and then serve as sounding boards for compositional thinking find great success.

8. Be collaborative. Listening to students allows you to learn with them.

Just as the process of learning to compose is full of unique challenges, so, too, is the process of learning to teach composition ripe with potential pitfalls. Listening to young composers' descriptions of their intentions, problems, and challenges may offer insight to the teachable moments that lead to good teaching practice. By following the students' lead, teachers can develop a manner of guiding composition that synergistically weaves education, music, teaching, and learning.

A TEACHING SCENARIO

Teaching Scenario (Excerpts from Days One and Four)

Day One

Mr. Razmuth enters the band rehearsal room and spreads out thirty single-color paint chips on the table behind his podium. He sets stacks of staff paper, plain white paper, and a large can of markers beside the chips. As the students enter the room, Mr. Razmuth instructs them to look at the list of five things that they will rehearse today. In slot number five is "Personify Color." Several students ask whether it's a new piece, but Mr. Razmuth doesn't offer a strongly committed answer.

Once the students have settled in and run through their opening warm-ups and the familiar pieces on today's rehearsal plan, Mr. Razmuth points to "Personify Color." He tells the group that they will be creating some short compositions over the next few rehearsals. For today, he helps them get organized into groups and describes the project. Over the next several minutes, Mr. Razmuth reads off students' names, and students move to sit with their soon-to-be co-composers. When everyone is settled in, Mr. Razmuth begins to describe the project.

"Class, we are going to compose some pieces inspired by color chips. Yes, I know it sounds odd. But I just got a recording of some pieces that were created this way and I thought we might try the same project. The man who created the music on my CD, Ken Nordine, was asked to write short pieces representing different colors for a paint company. He liked the project so much that he created more pieces than the company needed. Mike, what's your question?"

"Are we going to listen to the CD?"

"Absolutely, we will, Mike. But . . ." Mr. Razmuth stretches this out to tease the group a bit, "not until after we make up our own." Groans follow.

PERSONIFYING COLORS

Unit: Interdisciplinary Arts Project: Personifying Colors Level: Intermediate	
Planning Elements	*Thinking Guides*

Composer Characteristics	Grade: Seventh or eighth
	Skill level: Intermediate composers, intermediate
	    instrumental performers
	Setting: Instrumental lesson group
	Time: Three components: ten to fifteen minutes for poem
	    (could be done outside of school), ten to fifteen minutes
	    for crafting composition, enough time for each group to
	    perform for full band or orchestra

Focus and Supporting
    Principles
	Unity and variety is the focus; others support as related to
	    poem

Compositional Capacities	Intention: Feeling associated with particular colors (be
	    aware of cultural influences)
	Expressivity: Discuss precomposition. How do people feel
	    about this color?
	Artistic craftsmanship: Student determined

Compositional Context	Small group
Tools	Instruments: Band and orchestra
Prerequisites	Concepts: Awareness of associations between color and meaning Musical skills: Ability to perform on instrument Intuitive understandings: Ensemble

Co-compositional
    Activities (When?)
	Listening: Postcomposition listen to works by Ken Nordine
	    and look at book *Colors*

Task Guidelines	Product: Word jazz about color chip; picture Length: +/– one minute Other: Draw picture of personified color Specs: Use expressive gestures to enhance personification; one narrator and everyone else plays instrument Time: 10–15 minutes to compose; 10–15 minutes to share Preservation: Recordings, scores as needed Performance: For full class
Assessments	What: One-page reflection describing what compositional devices were used to match poem and music How: Completed before performance Why: To determine success in executing product intention
Connections	Ties to visual arts and ELA

Mr. Razmuth draws the students' attention to a handout that he has distributed while providing the background for this project. The sheet of project guidelines specifies that the students collaborate within the groups assigned by Mr. Razmuth. The students are to select a color chip, write a poem that personifies the color, and create a drawing that represents the color as personified. They are given ten minutes in today's rehearsal to draft their poem and create a rough sketch. As they read through the project, Mr. Razmuth notes how important it is for the group members to talk over what they imagine their finished piece will be like.

The students discover that they have six ten-minute work sessions over the next two weeks of rehearsals to create the music that underscores a dramatic reading of their poem. Finished drawings will be scanned into presentation software and partnered with a recording of each group's performance of its piece. Mr. Razmuth explains that each group will have the opportunity to share its piece in next week's rehearsal and will have additional time to polish its work before making the final recording.

"Are there any questions?" invites Mr. Razmuth.

"Yes," Michael raises his hand. "Are we going to write this down?" Mr. Razmuth moves to the head table and holds up a piece of staff paper and a piece of plain paper. "I suggest that you write down whatever your group needs to write down in order to remember how to perform your piece. You can use staff paper or plain paper. Do whatever works for your group. However, I want to caution you that this project is going to take about two weeks. Making some sort of notes is probably helpful."

Mr. Razmuth then gives the students one minute to discuss what general color they would like before inviting one member of each group to come to the table to select a color chip. Lively discussion breaks out around the room. A few students play music on their instruments while others draw and write lines of poetry. When ten minutes have passed, Mr. Razmuth tells the group to collect instruments and folders and pack up before the bell.

Day Four

Now that the students have had a few days to work on their projects, Mr. Razmuth notes that most poems and drawings are complete. Midway through the rehearsal, he instructs the students to shift the room setup to a large circle and to sit in their color groups.

"Let's hear some projects. I know that a few groups are done and others are still in the process of completing one or more parts of the project, but we are going to use the remainder of today's rehearsal to do a progress check. Is there a group that would like to share its piece? For today, let's introduce our pieces, name the color, show the drawing if you wish, and then maybe tell us about what you are trying to do or ask us a question if you'd like some feedback. Who's first? Ah, orange bursts, you're up!"

After a little stand shuffling, three clarinets sit together, and Susan stands before the group. "Our piece is based on the color orange burst. We imagined orange as high energy, sunny, fierce, and sassy. We've got the beginning of our piece, but we're kind of stuck as to how to finish it. So any suggestions would be great." The three clarinets play as Susan narrates, but the final line of text lingers alone.

Mr. Razmuth begins the feedback, "Can anyone tell the Orange Bursts a couple of things that are working well in their piece?" Several hands go up, and comments include that the piece is bouncy and energetic. "Does anyone have any suggestions for the end—where the group is stuck?" Again, the ensemble is quick to respond. Students suggest a loud, high ending, a busy burst of activity, and a declarative final staccato chord. Mr. Razmuth asks the group whether they have enough ideas or have any other questions and then moves onto the next group. This process continues for about twenty minutes, and then the class ends.

SUGGESTED LESSONS

Unit: Marketing and Music
Project: Radio Jingles
Level: Novice
Overview: The Radio Jingles étude appeals to upper middle-school students with little to no compositional experience. Usually very familiar with marketing jingles, students can often sing or parody a number of songs or musical motifs used in product promotion. The creation of original jingles allows young composers to exercise their knowledge of music in marketing and can be a powerful introductory exercise for a unit focusing on how marketing companies use music to influence consumers.

Planning Elements	*Thinking Guides*
Composer Characteristics	Grade level: Seventh to eighth Skill level: Novice composers Setting: General music class Time: One class period
Focus and Supporting Principles	Students should pick one to emphasize as it relates to their product
Compositional Capacities	Intention: Discuss precomposition—what is the feeling the product manufacturer wants associated with the product? Expressivity: What does this feeling sound like? Artistic craftsmanship: Dependent on the first two categories
Compositional Context	Small group or partnered
Tools	Instruments: Computer with software featuring samples, loops, and the ability to record and edit tracks Preservations: Computer-generated score and recording
Prerequisites	Concepts: Radio jingle Musical skills: Familiarity with computers and software programs Intuitive understandings: General characteristics of radio jingles

Planning Elements	Thinking Guides
Prerequisites	Concepts: Radio jingle Musical skills: Familiarity with computers and software programs Intuitive understandings: General characteristics of radio jingles
Co-compositional Activities	Listening: Precompositional modeling of radio jingles
Task Guidelines	Product: Radio jingle promoting a product (have an array of products available; students select one) Length: Twenty-five to thirty seconds Specs: Students identify focus principle in relation to intention and expressivity Time: Thirty minutes—ten to work and twenty to share and discuss. Preservation: Recording—save your work Performance: Computer performs for the class
Assessments	Verbal explanation of product intention, satisfaction; what worked and what did not Within-group process reporting (multifold)
Connections	Relationships to other ways music is used in marketing

CHAMBER MUSIC QUINTET

Unit: Chamber Music
Project: Quintet
Level: Advanced
Overview: Upper middle-school composers are often eager to create music for ensembles. Chamber music groups, being small in number of voices or parts, provide a perfect match for this type of work. Additionally, composers who are also performers may wish to compose for chamber ensembles that feature the instrument that they play. Within this project, students will learn about transposition, consider vertical voicings, explore the timbral qualities of instruments, and learn to interact with performers both in the formative composing stages (learning what instruments and performers are capable of doing) and in preparation for performance. Although the planning grid below suggests individual composition work, it is important that young composers be given access to an ensemble that can play through the work periodically in the process. This will allow the composer to reconcile imagined or computer-generated performances with the reality of human performers.

Planning Elements	Thinking Guides
Composer Characteristics	Grade level: Seventh to eighth Skill level: Advanced Setting: Independent study or composition class Time: Composer determined

Planning Elements	Thinking Guides
Focus and Supporting Principles	Determined by the composer; emphasis identified in initial plan (proposal to be shared with the teacher), but may change as piece evolves
Compositional Capacities	Intention: Composer determined Expressivity: Composer determined Artistic craftsmanship: Idiomatic writing for selected quintet
Compositional Context	Individual
Tools	Instruments: Choice of woodwind quintet, string quartet and piano, brass quintet, SSATB, percussion ensemble Preservations: Traditional notation
Prerequisites	Concepts: Relationships between voices/instruments Musical skills: Familiarity with ranges and transpositions Intuitive understandings: Aural frame for quintet sound
Co-compositional Activities	Listening: before and during process as needed to complement aural frame for particular quintet sound
Task Guidelines	Composer proposed in consultation with teacher
Assessments	Self- and teacher assessment in relation to guidelines established by composer
Connections	Relationships to other pieces for quintet

ETUDES

1. What aspects of human development are unfolding with upper middle-school students? How do these developmental points influence work in music composition?

2. Observe a seventh or eighth grade general music class. What types of peer interactions are evident? How might these interactions impact small group work?

3. Consider how tools impact learning. What tools are likely to appeal to upper middle school students, and what tools might seem too young? Can you envision a composition project that matches these interests for novice composers? Intermediate composers? Advanced composers?

4. Using the planning template, write a lesson that features vocal sound and body percussion as sound-making tools. How will you balance freedoms and constraints so that you and the students collaboratively define this project?

5. Many upper middle school students feel compelled to limit their compositional efforts in ways that lead to peer acceptance. What activities might you use to encourage students to try new things and experiment with intention, expressivity, and artistic craftsmanship?

6. Explain why access to computer music workstations is important for this age group.

7. Select a piece of music currently found on a top-forty chart. Describe how you would use this piece as the basis for a composition lesson with class of eighth grade students of varying compositional ability.

8. Improvisation is a musical activity of immediacy. Students have no time to evaluate how their peers might judge their improvisations. Given the highly social nature of this age group, is improvisation an appropriate teaching tool? Why or why not?

9. Observe an upper middle school classroom in any subject area. Describe how the lesson flows from activity to activity. Are the students working individually or in groups? What keeps them focused on learning? What is distracting? How might these observations inform your lesson planning?

11

Composing in High School

Students interested in creating their own musical works should find ample opportunity within the music offerings at the high school level. Whether novice, intermediate, or advanced in skill level, high school composers can use composition to further their understanding of music's role in history and culture in music appreciation, theory, ensembles, and other settings. Because high school is a time of increasingly specialized study, courses directed toward a focused study of compositional skills and techniques are especially appropriate and appealing.

HIGH SCHOOL COMPOSERS AND COMPOSITION ACTIVITIES

Composer Characteristics

As a group, high school composers span a larger range of compositional abilities and musical knowledge than any other age group. Their aural libraries, constructed over fifteen to eighteen years of listening experiences, allow them to imagine music far more complex than what they may be able to produce. Some students have composed throughout their school years, while others may have invented their last original creations at some point in early childhood. These broad spans present instructional challenges. This may also be frustrating to novice composers whose musical imaginations greatly exceed their technical capacities.

The additional maturity that high school students bring to the study of composition results in feelingful intentions that are purposefully chosen. The emotional and social turmoil of middle school may linger for some, but it eventually gives way to a more settled and centered sense of self. The strong listening backgrounds that many students bring to the experience of composing contribute to their ability to envision highly defined product intentions. High school composers often know exactly what they want to create and are eager to pursue their own processes as they create their pieces. Their engagements with music allow them to portray an image of themselves as well as fulfill their emotional needs (North et al., 2000).

As young composers progress toward adulthood, their compositional choices and preferences vary widely. While novice composers are generally interested in writing in styles akin to what they choose for listening, more advanced composers and composers with performance training are likely to compose for their own instrument as well as ensembles that feature that instrument. Regardless of the product frame, high school composers of all abilities are capable of producing music that is expressive, artistic, and highly original.

Understanding and Use of Compositional Principles

The ability to think abstractly allows high school composers to consider the impact of the balances they construct within and between pairs of expressive musical principles. Rather than needing to physically enact each principle, these composers are increasingly able to imagine, even at the novice level, how shifting emphases along the continuum of any principle pair impacts their musical products. Developing the artistic craftsmanship to fully realize these conceptions is particularly challenging to novice composers. However, it is also the main thrust of the work of more advanced composers. Each composer seeks to develop his or her own way of interacting with musical sounds.

High school students who enjoy using motion and stasis are used to controlling the time parameters of their work. Composers are intrigued by the notion of creating time frames that are unique and apart from those experienced in daily life. More conservative composers working in familiar genres may simply parallel stylistic norms, but some composers purposefully seek new ways of controlling time. Exploring the far boundaries of motion and stasis in the creation of pieces that are full of rapid motion or seemingly devoid of any motion are initial extremes that eventually find balance as compositional capacities develop.

While novice composers are drawn to patterning across multiple elements, intermediate and advanced composers often seek additional means for creating unity and variety within their compositions. These composers are curious about mixing styles, introducing unexpected or odd instrumentations, and exploring a wide range of harmonic languages. Experimentation across every possible conception of unity and variety can be expected from most advanced composers.

Unity and variety is also observable across the pieces created by single composers. High school students frequently adopt signature musical gestures that represent their compositional voices. These gestures reveal themselves within each piece regardless of style and genre. Some composers consider it a game to hide their signatures within pieces and challenge their peers to find them. High school composers may limit their work to a particular area of composition (e.g., songwriting, piano pieces, brass quintet) and often hold one of these types of pieces in the works while exploring other forms and styles for their self-defined compositions.

Although sound and silence have been found interesting and even featured in the work of younger composers, high school students realize and actively seek to employ the power of sound/silence balances and effects within their work. Composers use this relationship subtly or in strikingly obvious and provocative ways. Sound and silence figure prominently in the development of expressive capacities. Their use often constitutes the most memorable aspect of works pivotal in the development of young composers.

Just as sound and silence are more appreciated for their expressive potentials, tension and release are increasingly woven into the work of high school composers. As representatives of the implied energy of music, tension and release are applied either lightly or at full throttle before high school composers find a balance that is effective. Developing the ability to judiciously apply tension and release is one of the major challenges within the area of artistic craftsmanship. The composer's ability to use tension and release discriminately in ways that maintain a delicate balance constitutes a measure of compositional sophistication within particular styles and genres.

Composers of all ages can understand and employ craftsmanship techniques related to stability and instability, but older students possessing a broader range of general musical knowledge are best able to grasp its importance. The ability to define and characterize a multitude of styles and genres allows composers to seek innovations in making music that are not only new to them but genuinely original in music. Though rarely fully met, this challenge is one that high school composers find extremely appealing. The quest for new sounds used in new ways is highly motivating.

Compositional Context

Within ensemble settings, students are increasingly able to collaborate in the creation of full-ensemble works. Novices can be introduced to composition through teacher-facilitated projects, while more advanced composers find themselves ready to self-direct larger and more complex independent projects within the ensemble setting. These more advanced composers are often ready to create compositions or arrangements for chamber ensembles and thrive on the opportunity to both create and perform original works.

Partnered and small group work is appropriate in music courses intensely focused on the development of particular performance skills or musicological topic areas. Guitar and keyboard classes offer students opportunities to apply their developing performance skills in compositional activities. Students studying music appreciation benefit from opportunities to create music within particular historical or cultural definitions. These types of activities allow students to explore how music was part of a larger milieu or how particular technical or expressive aspects of music were developed.

Composition and music theory courses may provide opportunities for individual composers to develop their own compositional styles or to more fully explore the styles and techniques developed by previous generations of composers. Similarly, music courses exploring particular genres or constructed in interdisciplinary partnerships provide students opportunities for collaborations such as composer-to-cinematographer, composer-lyricist, and other pairings.

Tools of Creation and Preservation

Novice composers at the high school level need exposure to many tools so that they can develop a range of compositional thinking, as well as find the tool that works best within their personal process. These composers may gravitate toward a particular tool but may gain valuable insight through engaging with materials of music in different ways. It is particularly important that novice composers experience making and performing their own music so that they develop "within-performance" knowledge. Then they can better appreciate and evaluate the performance challenges they create for others within their own compositions.

More advanced composers also benefit from experiences that allow them to access tools closely related to the products they intend to produce. When composing for a particular instrument, composers need access to the instrument and someone who can play it sufficiently to perform the piece currently being created. Interaction with the musical tools that will be used in performance, whether they are living performers or computers, is paramount to composer success. This is especially true for composers who create pieces intended for living performers through the use of computer tools. It is important that students realize that the computer's ability to facilitate musical thinking and performance may not be directly matched to the realities of human performance. Only direct interaction with a variety of tools can create the experiences vital to the development of this type of knowledge and understanding.

Considering Prerequisites

Each composition project or activity designed for high school students must be considered in light of what they currently know and are able to do. Individual students are likely to vary significantly in previous experiences and musical exposures, but as a group, all students are likely to benefit from experiences that provide the group with a common experiential base and set of core understandings.

Two key questions to consider in planning activities that prepare students to compose are (1) What have the students heard that is like the product they will create? and (2) What have the students composed that uses a similar skill set? Exposure to the work of other composers expands the students' internal ear and awakens knowledge of new possibilities. Similarly, direct experiences that have required the use of particular techniques to control sounds and gain the desired effect prepare students to undertake new challenges. Guided listening and compositional études are often pre-compositional experiences that serve to enhance student learning within a particular compositional activity.

Co-compositional Activities

While the musical activities of singing, playing, and improvising continue to inform the development of young composers, the most influential co-compositional experience is listening. Through listening, composers' feelings and intellect can travel far and wide. Exposure to a multitude of styles, genres, and historical and cultural influences directly shapes their development as well as the products that they are likely to create. High school composers need experiences in singing, playing, and improvising that include ample time to be creative with their new discoveries. Unstructured time supports and invites exploration and experimentation that may lead to compositional breakthroughs. The inclusion of this type of working time often reduces the pressures that leave young composers frustrated and unable to produce.

Of greatest importance is that the co-compositional activities presented to high school composers foster developing creativity. Each engagement must take place in a space that is psychologically safe and inviting. Many high school students who have elected to avoid participation in ensembles are hesitant to sing or play publicly. While singing may improve their compositional understanding, singing activities require careful planning and presentation in order to constitute a safe experience for these students. Playing and improvisation offer similar challenges as playing tasks typically require some form of performance instruction and improvisation requires some form of either singing or playing. As is always true, careful planning, presentation, and implementation of co-compositional activities is required in order to create positive learning experiences.

Task Guidelines

The task guidelines created for high school composers must carefully account for their previous experiences and skills. Novice composers are routinely intermediate to advanced listeners. They are capable of self-defining compositional products, but they may need a substantial degree of guidance in formulating compositional projects that allow them to make best use of their newly emerging technical skills. Teacher guidance in project development is necessary to minimize the frustrations that may appear when envisioned projects greatly outpace skill development. As students engage in composition projects, they gain a better sense of their compositional skills and begin to understand how to envision projects that are appealing and manageable.

The task guidelines created for études continue to require significant teacher input as particular skills and knowledge are sought. However, as teachers increase technical requirements for high-school composers, they may also leave ample space for students to make creative choices. Demonstrating an understanding of common tone modulation, for example, can be achieved in pieces constructed for any pitched instruments, in any meter, and in many styles. The careful blending of teacher-imposed constraints with student-defined freedoms provides a needed balance as high school composers continue to grow and develop.

When students are defining their own compositional projects, it is important that the teacher facilitate the process of setting parameters for creative work. Young composers need to develop the ability to define their own work realistically so that they are able to imagine, undertake, and complete projects in reasonable time frames. High school students come to composition with varying degrees of time management skills. While some students are able to draw up a project outline with little trouble, other students benefit from studying models and discussing their intentions with more experienced peers and teachers.

Assessment

As compositional skills continue to develop, assessment plays a critical role in providing students with objective and reliable information about their growth as composers. At the high school level, teachers are almost always charged with carrying out highly detailed summative assessments for internal and external reporting. While summative assessment is important in gathering information about student and program outcomes, baseline and formative assessments are equally important as part of the educational process. Baseline assessments allow teachers to formulate a starting point for instruction and to tailor starting points to the unique needs of each student. Formative assessment, however, is the tool most important for gauging and pacing instruction. Assessments carried out at regular intervals allow teachers and students to determine progress and establish goals for future study.

High school students are also adept at reading criteria and using rubrics to monitor and assess their own work. As students gain compositional skill and the ability to self-define projects, they also need to develop the skills that allow them to objectively evaluate their own work. As students develop composition projects and describe their product intentions, expressive outcomes, and crafting techniques, they should also be able to list and describe in detail how they will determine the success of their products. Assessment can take many forms, but the ability of each composer to determine and use criteria for assessment is an important part of his or her individual growth and development.

DEVELOPING COMPOSITIONAL CAPACITIES IN GRADES NINE THROUGH TWELVE

Extending from absolute novices to students who have created hundreds of compositions, high school students span a capacities range wider than that found at any other grade level (see table 11.1). Their individual development is greatly influenced by the breadth of their previous experiences, and their future growth is potentially boundless. Yet within each young composer lies a unique voice, a musical knowing that is either tentatively or eagerly expressed, and a person who is capable of more than she might believe until she is provided with a space that invites her artistry to reveal itself.

The Growth of Compositional Intention

Growth in compositional intention is marked by the ability to identify the feelingful overtones that shape and influence desired products. As high school composers develop this capacity, their products shift from works that simply parallel their daily listening to pieces that explore human feeling in deep and meaningful ways.

Novice Composers

Highly influenced by the music that pervades their daily listening, novice composers are eager to create music that represents their musical identity.

Table 11.1. Compositional Capacities in High School Students

Compositional Capacities	Novice	Intermediate	Advanced
Intention	Adolescents' product intentions are highly influenced by the music with which they personally identify. Style and genre choices may vary widely among students.	Personal identification with a particular genre may lead adolescents to an in-depth pursuit of specific styles. Feelingful intentions are often therapeutic.	Deep engagement with a particular genre may continue, but adolescents also are able to consider the range of genres available and may choose to expand their creative intentions.
Expressivity	Adolescents are able to recognize a broad range of expressive gestures but often exhibit a narrower range in their own compositions.	Each adolescent composer begins to reveal an idiosyncratic voice through the use of expressive gestures.	Adolescents are able to recognize a broad range of expressive gestures but often exhibit a narrower range in their own compositions.
Artistic Craftsmanship	Adolescents search for sounds that are personally satisfying, pushing the boundaries of individual principles to their full expressive potential.	Adolescents give increasing attention to how the elements are combined to create principle relationships that lead to specific desired expressive outcomes.	Adolescents make deliberate choices as they pursue artistic expression. They are able to imaginatively manipulate principle relationships in both conventional and innovative ways.

Style and genre choices may vary widely among students, but students are typically eager to create their own music. Novice high school composers are heavily product oriented. They are able to describe their product intentions in great detail but may need to be guided to consider the feelingful aspects of intention. Once they consider how mood and affect relate to the success of their products, they are able to weave these ideas into their initial planning stages and overall compositional process.

Novice composers are sometimes hesitant to begin projects. They tend to worry about whether or not their products will be successful. Teachers can assuage these fears by providing models and scaffolding for initial projects to ensure success. Because immediacy is often paramount in maintaining interest, providing students access to tools that yield quick rewards is helpful. Guitar and computer-based tools are particularly appealing to this age group and are often well matched to the products they wish to create. Once students become comfortable in composing, they can be challenged to greater autonomy.

Intermediate Composers

Having discovered the power of feelingful intention, intermediate composers are eager to explore the range of feelings that can be expressed within a particular genre. Still somewhat conservative in their overall practices, intermediate composers often compose multiple pieces for a single ensemble or within a single style. This focus of attention allows them to use a particular type of product as a frame (or self-imposed constraint) for explorations of varied effects.

While some composers purposefully set out on such explorations, other composers discover a range of compositional actions as they employ feelingful intentions in a therapeutic manner related to their present mood. This approach certainly introduces a range of intentions, but composers usually discover that it is difficult to carry these intentions across multiple composing episodes unless they have predetermined a particular mood or feeling as an anchor for their work.

Advanced Composers

Knowledge of a wide array of possible products and a correspondingly vast assortment of feelingful intentions allow advanced composers to expand their creative intention exponentially throughout their high school years. Some composers delve deeply into creating works for a single ensemble or focus on a particular style of writing, but others use their knowledge to travel far and wide compositionally.

It is at this point that composers often turn to intensive listening in search of new products and new ways of presenting feeling within their own works. Rather than investing time in full-blown compositions, advanced composers may turn to creating a multitude of sketches. These works in miniature are self-defined études allowing composers to explore and sort through new discoveries without committing to longer time investments. Composers are often rewarded for these studies as their new works take on dimensions previously not found in their compositions.

Encouraging Expressivity in High School Composers

The range of expressivity found in the works of high school composers spans from a complete lack of consciousness to an equally intense preoccupation. Novice composers, who may be aware of the expressive nuances of music through their listening practices, benefit from guided exposure. More advanced composers often seek to discover new expressive gestures and eventually move toward a point of carefully controlling how each and every aspect of a musical feeling unfolds. Progressive development in expressivity can be rapid across the high school years. Composers themselves are often surprised at the changes in their work over even just a few pieces.

Novice Composers

The products created by novice composers typically exhibit a narrow range of expressive gestures. This, however, is not for a lack of understanding. High school students are able to recognize, identify, and describe a broad arrange of expressive qualities. Lack of expressive gesture is often attributable to two factors: (1) the music that students choose to listen to represents a particular set of expressive gestures, and (2) students may lack the technical skills to deliver their expressive ideas in their work. Identifying student listening preferences is the first step in guiding young composers to expand their expressive palettes. While students may listen to music that is full of expressive gestures, listening dominated by one type of music is likely to present a narrow range of the musical gestures found across the world of music. Students may begin their study of expressivity by identifying and listing the gestures and influences found within their preferred listening. They can then study other music and further develop the list of options available to them for their own work.

Intermediate Composers

As composers become increasingly comfortable with the options available to them, they begin to develop a set of preferences for gestures that will form their compositional voice. Guided listening that explores a range of expressive intentions remains important and introduces students to the many approaches that composers have used to link feeling and sound.

Intermediate composers may initially seek external references to guide their thinking processes. The use of texts, pictures, films, and even other pieces of music may help them shape the expressive qualities of their work. Over time, composers grow increasingly confident in their own decisions and may find models distracting. A progression from pieces that focus on composer feelings to pieces that show an increasing awareness of possible audience responses is usually observable as composers transition from novice to advanced.

Advanced Composers

Advanced composers often give very thoughtful consideration to the expressive content of their pieces in the initial stages of artistic conception. While these initial intentions may change as the piece evolves, advanced composers are able to make deliberate choices to synergistically unite personal expression and audience response. They are highly aware of the emotional potentials of their work and seek to highlight and feature those aspects.

Since they devote significant attention to the expressivity of their work, advanced composers may adopt new approaches to sharing their work. Some composers desire to keep their pieces very private and wish to reveal them only when they are complete. Other composers seek frequent presentation opportunities so that they can gauge the effectiveness of their efforts. In both cases, increased attention to expressivity shapes and alters the composer, the process, and the resulting products.

Developing Artistic Craftsmanship in High-School Composers

Artistic craftsmanship is often understood theoretically long before it is employed artistically. High school students are wonderful sleuths and find example after example of techniques that they wish to use. This skill is very useful but must be met with careful and supportive teacher guidance to balance overall musicianship with budding compositional skills. As composers gain experience, they are increasingly able to identify what they believe they need to learn and eventually are able to figure out how other composers have achieved particular structures and effects. Because high school students often come to composition with extensive listening backgrounds, their ability to find models and their desire to emulate pieces that they enjoy often motivate a rapid learning pace.

Novice Composers

Cultivating artistic craftsmanship at the high school level is especially challenging at the novice level. Composers are able to envision products that easily exceed their production skills. Composers need to be engaged in projects that are musically challenging and satisfying to prevent early frustration. While novice composers are open to études that encourage the development of technical skills, it is important to balance études with self-designed composition projects to maintain personal motivation.

Artistic craftsmanship études designed for novice composers should explore the extremes of each principle pair to allow students to discover opposite ends of each spectrum. Novice composers are drawn to sounds that are personally satisfying and that push the boundaries of the principles to their fullest expressive potential. Once novices have defined the possible parameters of the principles, they adjust their vision and work within their own perceptions of stylistic norms. These experiments, however, are critical in the development of the composer's palette of sound possibilities, and the understandings developed through these engagements will inform future work.

Intermediate Composers

High school composers working at the intermediate level are perhaps at the nexus of skill development and a personally recognized need to know. They are able to offer detailed descriptions of the pieces they wish to create. In many cases, they can also identify the skills that they need to develop to reach their musical goals.

Intermediate composers learn best when they are engaged in self-defined composition projects that are supported by teacher-created études. When composers find a compositional challenge that they are unable to resolve, they often ask for assistance. At the intermediate level, the assistance required is often in the area of technical skill development. The teacher, acting as a guide, sets forth compositional études that allow the composer to briefly step away from her main project and develop a particular skill set. These newly developed skills can then be applied to the work in progress.

Throughout the process of composing, intermediate composers focus diligent attention on the ways that the elements of music can be combined to create expressive relationships between the principles of music. Intermediate composers are secure in the knowledge that they can create pieces, so they turn their attention to producing pieces that are highly effective. Reaching beyond finding personal satisfaction in their compositions, intermediate composers are mindful of audience reactions and seek to control the expressive capacities of their work.

Advanced Composers

High school composers working at the advanced level are particularly conscious of the choices they pursue. They approach large works purposefully and attend to the greater and lesser details of each piece with heightened attention. Because they have developed a large repertoire of techniques to manipulate elements and principles, they are able to achieve the expressive outcomes they desire. The major challenge for advanced composers is not to rest on the skill set that they already possess, but to continue to seek new and imaginative ways of structuring and presenting sounds.

Portfolios developed by advanced composers include works that range from conventional to highly innovative. Students intending to study composition beyond their high school years need to give careful consideration to the pieces that they create. While many schools and colleges reviewing compositional portfolios wish to see a wide range of pieces, it is also good for students to write several pieces within the same genre to refine their artistry and skills in a single area. The creation of multiple string quartets, for example, allows students to experiment and develop ways of weaving and featuring individual voices or of using extended techniques effectively. Students should also consider developing a few pieces that are innovative and that they believe represent their own unique interests and perspective on the world of music composition.

COMPOSITION IN HIGH SCHOOL CONTEXTS

The range of courses offered in high school music programs provides ample opportunity for students to explore composition from a multitude of perspectives. Courses addressing music's historical evolution, cultural variations, theoretical constructs, and performance practices are all appropriate places for compositional activities to contribute to student learning. Additionally, it is often at the high school level where courses specifically addressing composition as an area of study are likely to be offered. Regardless of specific instructional focus, music composition is an important component of every student's musical development.

Composing in Music Appreciation Classes

Music appreciation is a common high school course offering for students who wish to explore their interests in music and perhaps fulfill fine arts requirements for graduation. Reading about music's evolution and listening to exemplars is one way of developing understanding, but the addition of composition to music study allows students to experience music from another perspective—that of the creator. By inviting them to grapple with the same types of musical challenges faced by composers of other times, they develop a more thorough understanding of the twists and turns of music's growth. In presenting the essential qualities of music from varied sources and practices, students reveal the connections that they are making between their own relationship with music and the musical experiences of others.

Students in music appreciation courses are most likely compositional novices. They benefit from engagement in compositional projects that are teacher directed at the outset, but over time they likely will desire to control more of the compositional process. It is very important that these young composers be comfortable in early compositional experiences. Projects that are whole class and teacher facilitated or teacher modeled and then enacted by small groups are likely to be the most successful.

Composing in Music Theory Classes

Music theory courses present a historical examination of the practices commonly employed by composers throughout one or more cultural practices. As these common practices, or rules, of theory are learned, it is important for students to emulate the work of earlier composers to gain a direct understanding of the techniques they developed and applied. It is equally important, however, that students learn to incorporate these techniques into their own musicianship.

Most prevalent within theory instruction, études can be used to introduce and explore specific compositional techniques. While études initially offer an effective instructional strategy, students benefit from self-defining projects that allow them the freedom to select those historical practices that are most relevant to their personal interests and preferences. Balancing études with self-defined compositions helps students realize how the historical evolution of compositional techniques has contributed to their own expressive language.

Composing in Guitar and Keyboard Classes

The ability to apply newly emerging performance skills in the creation of music is appealing to young musicians. Using their voices to carry a tune, guitarists who have mastered just one or two chords can compose folk and popular songs. Similarly, keyboardists with just a few minutes' worth of guidance can produce simple melodies with limited chordal accompaniment that are well within their personal performance capabilities. These creations can also help students remain interested in instrumental study when skill development lags behind musical imagination.

Each newly acquired performance skill can lead to the creation of a new piece. Students can create pieces that parallel those found in their performance literature or may create completely original work. Students who use an early composition as a theme can then create variations that include or feature newly developed skills. Theme and variations pieces of this type may constitute a formative assessment in which students can readily see, hear, and feel (through performance) their developing compositional and performance skills.

Whether creating one long piece or several smaller works, the pieces created in these types of classes represent newly emerging musical thinking. As they are personally produced, they are highly valued. Students are also challenged to develop their notation skills as they are eager to exchange pieces with their peers. Classes enjoy creating and publishing their own songbooks.

Music and Media Courses

Composition projects that focus on scoring films, cartoons, electronic games, advertisements, and cell phone ringtones logically follow the addition of sounds to children's books (described in chapter 8) and the creation of soundscapes underpinning oral interpretations of poetry (described in chapter 9). Wingstedt and others (2008) have noted that adolescents are highly conversant in and able to produce musical expressions within the context of media work. While these media are attractive to young composers, benefits can still be derived from a guided study of how these types of music function across multiples uses and contexts.

Students interested in adding music to film and other art forms need to expand their artistic vision to consider how music may support, complement, or contrast the visual information it partners. Aspiring film composers need to expand their compositional ears and palettes to include the sounds and expectations of film scoring. Most students are familiar with a number of movies that have earned awards for their outstanding film scores. However, they may not have paid any particular attention to the music as they watched the film. Effective film scoring often results in music that is present but that does not overpower the visual aspect of the movie. Fortunately, most popular movies are easy to access, and post-theater DVD releases often feature interviews that provide some access to the processes used by the composer in creating the score.

Beyond artistic sensitivity, young composers need to develop an incredible array of technical skills. As creators of film scores, young composers need to generate musical ideas, orchestrate this material effectively, and interact with performers as conductors or perhaps use computers or synthesizers to generate music. Further, throughout this process composers need to be aware of the issues of synchronizing musical gestures and dramatic actions. Within this context, musical principles are manipulated to reveal relationships between drama, music, and feeling in ways that are shaped by the movements of time.

An important co-compositional activity within the realm of film scoring is film score analysis. Just as students are guided to develop critical and analytical listening skills for music, they need to develop similar and complementary skills for listening to music in partnership with visual imagery. Film music should be analyzed in relation to the film it accompanies and not apart from it. Consideration of film music includes appropriateness, impact, message, and technique. Key questions for each category include the following:

1. Appropriateness—Does the music fulfill the needs of the film?
2. Impact—Does the music tell the story, focus the audience on critical dramatic events, or reveal a perspective different from that of the narration or drama?
3. Message—Does the composer seek to convey a message complementary or contrary to that of the film?
4. Technique—How does the composer accomplish the above?

As young composers consider scoring films, these same questions can help them plan their work. Determining what a film needs and creating that music in a manner that achieves the highest degree of artistic expression is the primary job of the composer within this medium.

Composing in Performance Ensembles

As discussed in the previous chapter, young performing musicians are often eager to create pieces that can be performed within their own ensembles. While much of the ensemble-based composition of middle school and work by novice high school composers requires teacher facilitation, students who have participated in the creation of ensemble compositions may be ready to pursue similar projects within new structures.

Group composition works particularly well within chamber music ensembles. Pieces created by the ensemble membership can be tested frequently and tailored to the specific needs of the group. Within choral settings, musicians may divide into smaller groups to create multiple verses within a single work or movements within a collection. Singer-composers also enjoy creating themes and variations on existing folk songs. These types of activities can be accomplished in relatively little time, result in performable pieces, and engage students in thinking about music from the dual perspectives of performer and composer.

Within instrumental settings, performers can create amazing works for duos, trios, quartets, and larger ensembles. Novice composers are often able to work very successfully in like-instrument groupings. Working with instruments that share notational requirements and tunings allows for attention to be given to the generation of creative ideas. Intermediate and advanced composers are ready for the challenges of transposition and a wider range of timbral choices. Familiarity with notation is highly desirable, but the creation of new notational symbols to achieve extended techniques or unexpected sounds can also add additional challenges for experienced composers.

Composition Courses

High school is often the first place that students encounter courses entirely devoted to the development of compositional skills and artistry. Composition courses can be created for novice through advanced-level composers. In preparing a curricular sequence, many music teachers position composition study after theory study. This structure suggests that the formal practices of music theory are prerequisite to the study of composition. While the skills developed in music theory courses may assist composers of certain types of music, not all composition requires this background.

Composition courses designed for high school composers may focus on computers as facilitators of musical thinking. In such courses, students work with software that features loops and tracks and that may allow for new sounds or performances to be recorded. Some software programs are designed to allow traditional notations to be derived, but others are designed to deliver performances via computer. Although such courses are appropriate for students of all skill levels, it is important for teachers to consider the pros and cons of working predominantly with one compositional tool.

For students planning continued music study, composition courses can foster the development of independent musical thinking. Students who are involved in self-defining projects, implementing compositional plans, and arranging for performances of their work encounter a multitude of musical roles. Interactions with performing musicians allow them to consider the role of the performer as an interpreter of a composer's intention, while observation of audience members allows them to evaluate their musical products in new ways.

Courses focused on composition are also ideal settings for the creation of very active composing communities. Drawing on the resources of the school music program and the community-based arts organizations, young composers are often able to work with professional performers, composers, and songwriters, as well as musicians who work in radio, television, and film. These alliances introduce highly motivated students to occupations that they may find appealing as they consider long-range career goals.

TOUCHPOINTS FOR TEACHING

1. Students can identify their individual "need to know" moments.

As students become increasingly aware of the problems that arise within composition, they are able to ask for specific assistance. Rather than providing answers and assuming ownership of the process, teachers can model problem-solving skills. Designing études, suggesting listening examples, or referring students to the scores created by other composers can set them on a pathway where they can discover their own solutions.

2. Teacher-directed projects are good for initiating composition at the high school level, but ultimately, students learn more by adopting a more active stance.

Novice composers of all ages benefit from engaging in processes that are teacher led so that they can develop models for their own work. However, high-school composers have been working independently or with peers in other learning situations for a considerable length of time. They may require less teacher modeling than younger students and are eager to define their own processes and products.

3. Be mindful of individual student portfolios.

Encourage students to develop a variety of pieces but also to compose several pieces within the same style or genre to master specific techniques. High school students are often tempted to find one successful product and repeat it over and over. Portfolios can function as a tool for monitoring student work. Students who create a table of contents for their collections should include title, date of completion, instruments, and a few words about style or genre. Creating this list allows students to know at a glance whether they are falling into a compositional rut or challenging themselves to explore the many options that exist within composition.

4. Tool choice influences composer development.

Computers are incredible tools for achieving fast results, but students need to explore a range of thinking tools to learn which ones best fit their individual processes. Musicological concerns should also be considered. While it is possible to compose pieces for djembe, udu, and djun djunn at a computer workstation, authentic practice probably involves creating music directly on the drum. Composers should consider how tools positively and negatively shape the processes of composition.

5. Compositional growth is fostered through listening that expands sonic and personal horizons.

No matter how many études and composition projects a student might undertake, the development of compositional thinking and its companion understanding of music are best grown through broad exposure to as many types of music as can be accessed. Young composers need to hear recordings and live performances, they need opportunities to ask question of composers and performers, and they need to see that there is a world awaiting their contributions to the evolution of music.

6. Compositional autonomy is the ultimate objective.

Students should be taught to self-define projects, identify solutions, test ideas, determine assessment criteria, and evaluate the products of their work. Composers who can successfully execute these operations are ready to make music independently and can continue their composing activities beyond their high-school years.

A TEACHING SCENARIO

Project: Art Song
Level: Intermediate
Overview: The art song project is ideal for a general high-school chorus comprising singers of various skill levels with some compositional experiences. Prior compositional work may include writing choral warm-ups related to literature under study or creating variations on thematic material. This project involves the creation of a fully original work intended for choral performance. The project requires thirty minutes of weekly work time in rehearsals throughout the fall semester. The final product can easily be prepared for spring concert performance and will occupy one rehearsal slot on the spring concert program.

Planning Elements	Thinking Guides
Composer Characteristics	High-school general chorus Intermediate composers Setting: Classroom, rehearsal hall, computer lab, lesson, home Time allocation estimate: One semester of once-weekly work, one semester to prepare for performance
Focus and Supporting Principles	Students identify in relation to text choice
Compositional Capacities	Intention: Student determined Expressivity: Student determined Artistic craftsmanship: Text setting
Compositional Context	Teacher-facilitated ensemble; interspersion of small group, partnered, and individual (idea development and testing)
Tools	Instruments: Voices (piano/computer as support; others as needed) Preservations: Traditional notation and recording

Planning Elements	Thinking Guides
Prerequisites	Concepts: Relationships between text and music Musical skills: Ability to imagine and share musical ideas through singing Intuitive understandings: Phrase structures, relationship between parts
Co-compositional Activities	Bring in as needed to support process
Task Guidelines	Product: Collaboratively planned by composers Length: Collaboratively planned by composers Specs: Collaboratively planned by composers Time: Twenty minutes/once a week Preservation: Traditional notation, recording as needed Performance: In concert
Assessments	Formative as related to process
Connections	Project as strand across multiple rehearsals

Day 1—Introducing the Project

"Singers, those of you who have been in chorus for the past couple of years know that we've sung many wonderful pieces, but I think we need to find some new music. Actually, I think, given our experience and our new members, that we can write our own song. What do you think?" Miss Patterson surveyed her sixty-five-voice choir of returning and new students. They had just completed their warm-ups on the first morning of the second week of school. Ami-Lyn's hand shot up.

"What do you mean, exactly, Miss Patterson? I mean, how can all of us write a song?"

"Good question. I bet you're all wondering that," Miss Patterson acknowledged as she watched the nervous whispering ripple across the rehearsal room. "Well, I have a plan that I think will allow us all to work together, if you are up to the challenge. Are you?"

Met with timid nods, Miss Patterson continued. "The first thing we need to do is find a good set of song lyrics. Does anyone have any suggestions for how we might do that? Yes, Michael?"

"We could look at some poetry books and see if there are any poems that we might like. Lots of the pieces that we've sung have used poems."

"Or," said Leisa, "we could write our own poems."

"But how would that work?" Robert asked. "I mean, that would be like seventy poems, right?"

Miss Patterson was overjoyed that a conversation leading into planning had begun with so little prompting on her part. She asked, "What if we had a poetry, well really a song lyrics, writing contest? Everyone who is interested could write a poem and we could invite some of the teachers to act as judges to help us select the best poems. What do we think?"

After some excited discussion it was decided that poems would be due in two weeks and would be reviewed by a panel of teachers. The students eagerly nominated their favorite teachers to the panel, and Miss Patterson promised to invite each teacher to read and rate poems. She also promised that student names would be removed from the poems before they were given to the panel. The poems with the top three ratings would be brought back to the chorus for consideration and final selection. Miss Patterson was pleased with the process and, while acknowledging that she steered the conversation at times, found that the students seemed quite eager to begin.

Day 3—Defining Intentions

Now that the students had reviewed the final three poems indicated as "strongest candidates" by the panel of teachers, the final text had been selected. While each poem had been considered in terms of what it might hold for song potential, the winner, *Lasting Impressions*, was ready for more detailed musical analysis. Miss Patterson planned to spend roughly half of today's rehearsal working on the composition project. She projected the text of *Lasting Impressions* onto the sidewall of the rehearsal hall and outlined today's work.

"Class, when we selected this text we decided that it offered us the most musical options of the three poems we reviewed. Today, we need to think about how this poem will become a piece of music. Let's begin by considering how we can organize this piece into sections. Does anyone have any ideas?" After a few moments of quiet discussion, several hands were raised. "Tomika?"

"I think we should have an introduction to set the tone for the piece." Miss Patterson drew a box and wrote "intro" in it above the first line of the text. She made marks on the computer screen for each suggestion as it was made so that the students would be able to keep track of each idea.

"Cynthia, what do you think?" invited Miss Patterson.

"I don't know about the introduction idea, I kind of hear the piece just starting," said Cynthia rather hesitantly as she caught Tomika's eye. She continued, ". . . Uh, in any case, there are clearly three verses and then the line between each verse could be the refrain."

"I like that," responded Tomika. Miss Patterson paused for a moment and then said, "Class, let's just throw out as many ideas as we can come up with and we can sort them out later. All ideas are worthy of consideration and we don't have to make decisions now."

The students continued to offer ideas until a clear form for the work had emerged. Through class discussion, it was determined that the piece would begin with an introduction followed by verse/refrain/verse/refrain/verse/refrain, extended refrain, and a repetition of the opening line. The students seemed pleased with their work. Noting a positive energy in the room, Miss Patterson invited the students to pull out their most challenging piece from the fall lineup and played the opening pitches.

Day 8—Still a Work in Progress

After leading five composition work sessions to generate musical material, Miss Patterson stood at the photocopier printing three-page rough drafts of the score. Today's work session would focus on refining the verse and developing additional musical material for the refrain. The piece was really coming together and was now recognizable as a choral work, although further refinement was definitely still needed.

In rehearsal, Miss Patterson distributed the score and sat at the piano prepared to play starting pitches. Suddenly, Miguel called out, "Wait, wait. I've got a great idea. You know how last time we came up with this quiet entrance from the basses at the beginning? Well, what if we flipped that upside down and had the tenors sing it, like, three beats later? Listen. Tom, sing the bass part." Miss Patterson reached for the low D as the other choristers turned their attention to Miguel and Tom.

Tom glanced around and noting the expectant faces quickly said, "I'm not singing alone!" After a few chuckles from around the room acknowledging Tom's role as a good-natured comedian, Miss Patterson called for all the basses to sing the beginning of the piece. When they reached the point at which Miguel thought his idea would work, he sang out. The class responded enthusiastically to what they had heard. Miss Patterson asked Miguel to sing his idea again and invited everyone to sing it a few times. Once the idea seemed to have solidified, Miss Patterson asked the basses and tenors to sing the introduction one more time while the sopranos and altos listened carefully to determine whether the idea really worked for the piece.

After hearing the idea performed a few times, the choir discussed what made this idea work in the introduction. They decided that overlapping tenor and bass voices set up the first verse nicely and that, for contrast, the sopranos and altos would join in at the beginning of the first verse. The thirty-minute work session was soon over, but the students were eager to continue working on the piece. "Flexibility is key, right?" Miss Patterson reminded herself before allowing an additional ten minutes to finish up the work on the first verse. The class concluded with a brief rehearsal and run-through of a piece scheduled for the January concert.

Day 12—Compositional End Stage

As Miss Patterson stood at the photocopier watching the pages collate with methodical rhythm, she recalled how hard she had worked to appear confident when introducing this project so that the chorus members, nervous as she had predicted they would be, would believe in their ability to create their own song. She quickly grabbed the last copy and headed for the rehearsal room. The students had worked very hard to piece together their ideas, and *Lasting Impressions* would indeed leave a strong lasting impression on the chorus and the audience after the April concert. For today, though, the goal was to take a final run-through, edit as necessary, polish minimally, and then return to the computer to produce the final version of the score to be inserted in the January rehearsal folders.

Miss Patterson handed the scores to the three choral librarians for dissemination and walked to the podium. "Class, the librarians are distributing the final draft of *Lasting Impressions*. We will sing through the work and then talk it through measure by measure to complete final edits, polish up any rough spots, and just generally check it all out before I make the finished scores for your January folders. Are there any spots that we should focus on as we sing it through?" Several hands went up, and Miss Patterson made a list of each suggestion on the board before returning to the podium.

"Nathaniel, are you able to play the accompaniment today?" Miss Patterson inquired of one of the student accompanists. After a few moments of settling in, the chorus sang through the entire work. When they had finished singing, spontaneous applause rang through the hall. The students were so excited with the piece that they had created. Miss Patterson allowed a few moments for the students to congratulate themselves and then asked, "Well, what do we need to fix?"

For the next twenty minutes the chorus discussed and sang through brief excerpts of the piece. They sang single passages two or three ways and compared various interpretations, sometimes immediately agreeing and other times debating the merits of one interpretation over another. When they had finally exhausted their list of spots to fix, they sang through the piece one more time and then turned in all the scores. Miss Patterson promised "real copies" by January 3 and then dismissed the class for their winter break.

SUGGESTED LESSONS

TONIC AND DOMINANT SONGS

Project: Tonic and Dominant Songs
Level: Novice
Overview: The creation of songs with simple harmonic motion fits perfectly into guitar classes designed to teach students basic guitar performance skills. Examples of songs using simple chordal structures can easily be found within most popular musical styles. Students, many of whom will be familiar with such models, will be eager to exercise their new performance skills in the creation of music that matches their listening tastes.

Planning Elements	Thinking Guides
Composer Characteristics	High school guitar class Beginning composer, beginning guitar Classroom Two to three class periods
Focus and Supporting Principles	Unity/variety: Verse and refrain Stability/instability: Working within established form
Compositional Capacities	Intention: Student determined Expressivity: Student determined Artistic craftsmanship: I and V chords
Compositional Context	Partnered
Tools	Instruments: Guitars Preservations: Lyric sheet with chords
Prerequisites	Concepts: Tonic and dominant relationships Musical skills: Ability to play I and V in some key Intuitive understandings: Popular song form
Co-compositional Activities	Listening: Models of songs using only I and V chords
Task Guidelines	Product: Song using I and V chords Length: One to two minutes Specs (suggested): Intro, v1, v2, transitional 8, v3, and outro) Time: Two class periods Preservation: Lyrics with chord changes, forms sections identified Performance: In class for peers
Assessments	N/A
Connections	Song forms, performance skills

FILM SCORING

Project: Film Scoring
Level: Advanced
Overview: Film scoring challenges students to work within a dramatic context that is predetermined. Composers must analyze the intent of the dramatic action and then decide how music might be used to complement, contrast, or enhance the unfolding of the film. Composers are further challenged to work within tightly controlled time frames as dramatic highs and lows must be synchronized. Engaging in this process in an ensemble setting provides opportunities for students to experience music making in settings similar to those experienced by studio musicians.

Planning Elements	*Thinking Guides*
Composer Characteristics	High school orchestra Advanced composers Rehearsal Fifteen to twenty minutes
Focus and Supporting Principles	Focus arises from student discussion of the film clip (limit clip to about one minute)
Compositional Capacities (When?)	Intention: To support implied feelingful nature of film excerpt Expression: What sounds sound like the implied feeling Artistic craftsmanship: Techniques related to focus principle
Compositional Context	Teacher-facilitated large group
Tools	Instruments: String orchestra Preservations: Recording, notations if needed
Prerequisites	Concepts: Ensemble; improvisation Musical skills: Range of performance skills (various bowing techniques) Intuitive understandings: What sounds match, contrast, or serve to heighten dramatic elements of film
Co-compositional Activities (When?)	Listening and watching film excerpts before or after composing activities Watch excerpts that feature pianists or organists accompanying silent films
Task Guidelines	Product: Film score Length: One minute in length Specs: Everyone has to play! Time: Fifteen to twenty minutes Preservation: Recording; other if needed Performance: In class for ourselves
Assessments	N/A
Connections	Film scoring techniques

ETUDES

1. Select a concept from a music theory text and design an étude that will allow the students to explore the concept while defining some parameters of the assignment for themselves.
2. Identify three movie excerpts that could be used as exemplars of varied approaches to the same feelingful capacity. Scary, joyous, surprised, anxious, adventuresome, and fear are good starting places.
3. Observe a small-group instrumental music lesson. Identify the performance skills the students are studying. Create a ten-minute compositional activity that the students could use to enhance their performance skills and develop an understanding of one compositional capacity.
4. Select a poem and write a sound description of the text. Identify words that are appealing for their inherent sounds (slam, tinkle, spray, etc.). How would these words sound if played on an instrument? If sung?
5. Serve as the facilitator of a group of three to five high school students as they create a piece that uses body percussion and vocal sounds to imitate a common machine or household appliance. Observe how students invent ideas, make decisions, test their ideas, and formulate the final version of their pieces.
6. Develop an equipment list and budget for a multimedia music lab. Identify hardware, software, and auxiliary equipment needs. Describe how you would present this budget to the department head for instructional technology or to the high school principal.
7. Explain how the study of music theory can benefit the practices of the composer and why composition can enhance the study of music theory. What is the relationship between theory and composition?
8. How would you engage a student who is reluctant to share his or her compositional work? Conversely, how would you focus a student who is overeager to share (perhaps a students who shares and shares while making little progress between sessions)?

IV

THE FUTURE OF COMPOSITION EDUCATION

12

The Composition Program

At present, very few schools offer a regular program of instruction in music composition. In much of music education, what is taught in schools depends highly on the interests and skills of the music educator. The inclusion of composition in the National Standards for Arts Education (1994) has led to more interest in composition pedagogy. However, since very few music education degree programs in the past required composition classes, many current music educators lack the skills and confidence to teach composition even when they realize that they should be. When composition is included in a school's curriculum, it is often because the music educator in that school has a background in composition and an interest in teaching it.

One way of altering this situation is to require courses in composition at the undergraduate level and to teach composition pedagogy during methods classes. However, that curriculum change is beyond the scope of this book. What this chapter provides is a plan for a composition program that could be taught. This can happen whenever music educators take it upon themselves to study composition and implement a composition curriculum in schools.

WHY OFFER A COMPOSITION PROGRAM?

The reasons for offering all students the chance to compose are tied to the rationale stated in chapter 1 of this book: children should be taught to compose because it is something humans can do. Bennett Reimer (2003) suggests that one reason humans create music is so that they can explore deeper aspects of ineffable feelings. Composition should be taught because it is a human way of constructing feelingful meaning.

Children should have the opportunity to compose because composing can change the ways they understand their world. Composing draws on all the other ways of musical knowing that the student has experienced and, in turn, influences all the other ways of being musical. Children listen to music differently when they have created their own pieces. They perform music with greater intentionality when they have created works that others perform. Composing draws attention to the ways sounds exist in their world and to the meanings those sounds convey. It heightens the students' awareness of all the ways sounds are used to influence people's feelings in advertising and other fields of endeavor. It also allows them to use music to intentionally express their own feelings and to attempt to alter the feelings of other people.

Children should also compose because it allows them to create—to exercise their abilities to generate unique expressions of their understandings and feelings. The process of composing allows children to grow artistically, to discover meanings, and to create aspects of themselves. All this can be accomplished by acting on and with sounds in expressive ways. The purpose of composing in schools is not to find the next great composer, but rather to better understand the human experience; in particular, to better understand human *musical* experience.

Composition in Schools

Composition should be taught in schools because, at least for now, that is where education takes place in this society. This parallels other forms of human expression such as literature, poetry, and the multitude of visual arts. Students have culturally dependent concepts of how music works. It makes sense, then, that they be taught in the culturally accepted location for learning. In an ideal world, a teacher notices the child's need to know and then facilitates learning. This can happen in private studio lessons as well, but for many students, exposure to music instruction comes primarily through schooling. This exposure should include experience with composing.

Schools also provide a social milieu for experiencing the results of composing. Students not only hear their own creations but are exposed to the ideas of others both in group composition experiences and in composers' workshop settings. This can become a recursive process for influencing a young composer's own compositional thinking. Ideas shared in class can be reshaped, modified, and recreated to become one's own. Cooperation and collaboration take their places alongside individual inspiration.

COMPOSITION AS A UNIQUE THREAD IN MUSIC STUDY

If composition is to become an important part of music education, there needs to be a sequence of learning experienced over time. This includes the skills, concepts, and activities of a music program. However, it is similar to a well-planned program of instruction designed to teach children to write expressively for various purposes: the music composition program needs to be a student-driven one. There has been an emphasis throughout this book on the idea of "the teachable moment" in instruction. Composition, when well taught, follows the needs of the child and uses those needs to build skill and understanding. So how does the teacher decide what experiences to offer and when to offer them?

Over time, a composition curriculum should offer access to traditional compositional styles as well as computer-based composing. Many children gravitate to one means of sound production as their preferred sounds source for periods of time. Then new sounds may cause a shift in their preferences. There should be multiple opportunities for experiencing different approaches to composing as a student progresses through formal schooling.

The Composition Program in the Elementary School

At the youngest ages, composition should be included in general music classes. Opportunities for creating with sound should begin in tandem with formal music instruction. This may take the form of many improvisatory activities, some of which become more formalized when the teacher preserves the results and helps the children remember what was created. Individual children may show a definite proclivity and interest in composing even at this age. Their efforts should be affirmed and encouraged.

Composing in general music should take many forms over the course of the elementary school years. It should include individual, paired, and group experiences and experiences with acoustic as well as electronic sounds sources. Perhaps the most important aspect of elementary school composition experiences should be the construction of a repertoire of sound sources for the young composer to use. The more sounds the students have experienced repeatedly, the more sounds they have to use in their creations.

Composition as a unique track of music study should begin along with choral and instrumental programs. These programs often begin between fourth and sixth grade, and so should a separate composition track. Experiences with composition continue to be a part of general music classes at this level. Composition should also be included as a part of well-taught choral and instrumental experiences. However, there should also be specialized opportunities for students specifically interested in composition.

At the elementary school level, composition should not be considered exclusively a "gifted/talented" program, although this is certainly one way composition instruction could be offered to children showing exceptional abilities. Composition should be made available in ways that can include many children. This type of opportunity is appropriate for all students with an interest. Children with exceptionalities and those who are learning English as an additional language can be included, since the primary skills of composing have little to do with spoken language and because of the focus on individual expression.

There are several ways that composition as a separate thread of instruction can be organized. One way is the familiar "pull-out" program that is often used for instrumental lessons. The students would meet on a regular basis at a specific time during the school day. They meet in small groups to share their work and receive guidance from the teacher and their peers. While this might be the ideal way to organize a program, there are many political issues that have to be resolved before principals, teachers, and parents value composition highly enough to permit composition to become a regular part of school in this manner. Nonetheless, it is probably the most effective way to teach composition as a separate thread of music instruction, except possibly for private composition lessons.

Another way of offering this type of instruction is to form an elementary composers club that meets at times abutting the school day or at lunch time. Teachers would need to find the time to be available, and the students would have to be able to give up some of their free time to work on their pieces. This can also supplement a pull-out program. It usually works best for students who are quite motivated to work on their own and bring their work to the club for feedback and encouragement. It can also work as a way to give a few private composing lessons to interested students. The teacher sets an appointment with an interested student, who comes before or after school and works with the teacher for a specific time period.

Composing can also be a part of group and private instrumental lessons. The purpose of these classes is to master the technical and expressive qualities of a specific instrument. However, composing can often aid in that process. Children who compose for the instrument that they are studying often learn some of the technical aspects of playing that instrument more quickly. If they are also learning to use standard notation, they more rapidly increase their ability to read that notation as they attempt to use it to preserve their compositions. By creating, notating, and playing their own pieces, they become much more aware of the notational aspects of other people's music. They follow other composer's notational instructions much more closely when they understand the meaning and importance of what has been written.

Finally, when teachers encounter a truly gifted young composer, there should be the opportunity for that student to study composition privately. Once the aptitude and interest of the child has been noticed, a private teacher willing to work with a young person should be sought. Sometimes this should be a person with formal training in composition who likes and enjoys working with children. Sometimes it may be a person with much compositional experience, possibly without formal study, but who understands the styles to which the child is attracted. Like all areas of musical study, there often comes a point when switching teachers is beneficial to artistic growth.

The Composition Program in Middle and Secondary Schools

As students approach adolescence, composing often becomes a more personal activity. Their compositions become more expressive of their own lives, and they may be less willing to share their works partly out of fear of peer responses. Nonetheless, composing in middle schools and high schools should offer access to a wide variety of composing ensembles, including school-based groups, student-organized formal and informal groups, and composer groups. These should offer a range of traditional compositional styles, computer-based styles, and pop music ensemble styles. Teachers should still be able to track the growth of individual composers over time, but the scope and sequence of the program must be even more student focused and student driven in order to be successful.

There should be the opportunity for students to begin compositional study at any time during their formal schooling and not, for example, just in fifth grade or whenever the teacher begins a separate track for composition. A truly student-centered composition program allows access at many times across an academic career. (Even adults may wish there were a community-based songwriting or composing program to turn to with their creations.) Schools can provide beginning as well as more advanced instruction throughout middle and secondary schools.

Composition can continue to be a part of general music classes at the secondary level. In middle schools these can often be offered in the form of "exploratories." Exploratories offer students who have never participated in some activity an opportunity to "explore" it by taking a short-term course in the subject. While this can offer some initial exposure to composition, some students will want to continue their previous studies, and others will want to continue beyond the exploratory experience. Consequently, there should also be composition classes offered for more experienced composers that build on their skills and understandings. Again, these should be offered during the school day. Composition might be offered as a track of general music or opposite other music offerings.

Here is one model for how a middle-level composition sequence might be structured in a grades-six-through-eight middle school. Teachers need to adapt this to their own situations. Much depends on the skills, willingness, and availability of the faculty to implement a composition program. This is just one possible model, but it does offer a wide variety of composing opportunities for middle-level students.

A composing exploratory is offered in sixth grade that provides a basic introduction to composing, some group work, and perhaps the basics of setting a text. A more advanced exploratory for composers that have taken the first level or that already have composing experience—perhaps documented in a portfolio—is also offered and would include the basics of film scoring. In seventh grade, the composition exploratory would have a prerequisite of a guitar exploratory, which would give students fluency with a basic set of chords. The seventh grade exploratory would focus on song-writing. It would not be necessary to have had the sixth-grade exploratory to participate in the seventh-grade ones.

In the eighth grade composing class, there is a prerequisite of a keyboard-ing exploratory. This is followed by a broad-based and somewhat individu-alized composition class. Some of the students would have been involved in three years of composing classes at this point. Others might be taking it for the first time. Projects would be designed around common interests and might include group composing projects using keyboards, guitars, and percussion, traditional classical groups such as string quartets or wind trios, and individual projects of various styles. Electronic sounds and acoustic ones would both be available. An exploratory on beginning sound engi-neering and recording might also be included at the middle school level.

Additionally, at least one composition per year would be created and performed as part of the large ensemble experiences in middle school. If small group lessons are included at this level, compositions should be cre-ated in those settings as well. These might include solos, duets, and other small ensembles. These pieces would lend themselves well to a recital per-formance near the end of the year. They might also be published in some format such as a collection of scores with a CD or on the school's website with scores and sound files.

Beyond this, students with a continuing interest in composition may want to compose for school-based ensembles. They will begin to work individually on pieces that are more challenging. Access to computer soft-ware for notation and creating more complex scores should be available. Software of the highest-quality sampled sound for playing back their ideas will assist these students' development. When possible, they should have the opportunity for adult professionals to perform completed works that are written for musicians beyond the level of their classmates. Sometimes an area string quartet or brass ensemble can be recruited and students can be encouraged to write specifically for those musicians.

Students should be encouraged to enter their pieces in regional and statewide composition contests and festivals such as those sponsored by MENC, the PTA, and state music associations. These are most helpful when the composers receive comments and feedback on their pieces from other composers regardless of whether or not their pieces are selected for performances or prizes. Similarly, developing a working relationship with a professional composer can be very helpful when that person can encourage and respond to a student's efforts. This is often possible via Internet connections. These types of relationships can be facilitated by the student's school music teacher.

High school electives would begin similarly to the middle-school exploratories but last longer and include more offerings. Students should be able to continue their compositional studies throughout their high-school careers with ever-increasing levels of conceptual understanding and skill. There can still be basic classes with prerequisites of guitar or keyboarding before expanding into songwriting. There should be electronic composition opportunities, small ensembles of pop musicians working in and out of school to create pieces in those genres, and more traditional composition classes for students drawn to those styles. Large ensemble classes should continue to create one piece per year that they subsequently perform. Smaller ensembles may also create works or be pressed into service to perform works created specifically for them by young composers.

Popular music ensembles may have been formed in middle school and continue into high school. However, they are often more successful when formed by high school students who are able to get together outside of school to create and rehearse on their own. Students who begin playing guitars and keyboard in middle school are usually looking for band members. After copying a fair number of pieces they know, they often begin to create their own pieces. Sometimes they benefit from some assistance in organizing themselves or their pieces, but often they can proceed on their own with appropriate peer feedback.

High school electives should also expose young composers to the various ways composers earn a living. This should include more work with advertising and film scoring as well as more formal compositions done for personal satisfaction. There should also be an entry-level songwriting class as well as an opportunity to create works for musical theater. These possibly could be created and performed in collaboration with peers in a theater class. Many other opportunities will be created by teachers who understand the workings of their own schools, the interests of their students, and the opportunities for composing inherent in their musical worlds.

IMPLEMENTING A COMPOSITION PROGRAM

Like any area of instruction, composition programs need facilities, resources, and faculty for student learning to occur. At the beginning levels
of younger students, ordinary music classrooms easily serve these needs. As
students increase in expertise and age, there are increasing space and equipment needs. Composition programs should also include opportunities and
venues to perform or share the musical products that have been created.

Facilities for Composition Programs

Facilities for composing are often already in place in school settings.
However, it is often useful to have several adjoining smaller workspaces for
group work. This would work best if there were available several oversized
practice rooms that were acoustically isolated from one another, but this
is rarely the case. Other areas can sometimes be pressed into service. These
include stages, office spaces, music library rooms, hallways, and simply the
various corners of a single room.

Teachers may need to be very resourceful in their use of space when they are
building composition programs in their schools. One of the authors of this
text used the adjoining playground in good weather as a practice space. When
the physical education teacher took the students outdoors, the gym was also
used as a composing space. Auditoriums can be used if they are available. Creative teachers can find unoccupied spaces that can be used for composing.

Spaces such as these are not ideal because of the sound levels and the
problems the students have trying to hear one another. Designers of music
suites in middle schools and high schools can be made aware of the needs
for such spaces when composition programs become more common in
schools. This may lead to more appropriate spaces for them.

Similarly, music computer labs are becoming more common in well-
equipped schools. These can easily include all the materials electronic
composers require, but they should also include the materials for video
production and editing to allow young composers access to this creative
outlet. Composition rooms also need access to the Internet for young composers to share their works if they choose. Even for the youngest composers,
a website can be a valuable way for parents and others to see what has been
accomplished. In the not-too-distant future, the Internet will be the most
common way of sharing one's music.

Equipping the Composition Program

Probably the single most important piece of equipment needed for most
composition programs is a recording device to preserve the works the stu-

dents are creating. This can be as simple as a small digital recorder or a laptop computer for younger grades or as complicated as a recording studio for advanced secondary students. As composition programs grow and develop, the sophistication of the means of sound preservation also should increase. For even the youngest students there should be a recording device that they can operate without teacher assistance.

Similarly, children need a way to listen to recordings, and a high-quality sound reproduction system should be available for this purpose. Video cameras and the means for viewing videos of the students' work are also very useful. This is particularly true for elementary-school intermediate-level composers and other levels of students who are creating group compositions.

Composition requires sounds that can be manipulated. While there are always vocal sounds, found sounds, and homemade instruments, a well-equipped composition program has a wide variety of musical instruments and other sound sources available for young composers to explore. In an elementary school, these would include a wide variety of pitched and nonpitched percussion, keyboards, fretted instruments, string and wind instruments, and instruments from a variety of non-Western cultures. There should particularly be instruments from non-Western cultures represented by the ethnicity of the students in that school.

Faculty for Composition Programs

Any competent music educator can guide novice composers, but ultimately, composition should be taught by teachers who enthusiastically pursue composition themselves. Teachers can take it upon themselves to learn the skills of composition through additional classes, summer workshops, or private study with a composer. It is likely that more opportunities to study composing and how to teach composition to young people will become available as more schools implement composition programs. Until then, teachers have to find ways to enhance their own skills in order to best serve the needs of their students. This book is one step in that direction, but one cannot learn any skill simply by reading about it. It takes continuing commitment and effort to develop those skills. Like all areas of music, artistry in composing and in teaching composition develops over time and with practice.

Opportunities for Sharing Compositions

Throughout this book there have been many references to allowing young composers to share their works with audiences. All young composers should be encouraged to share finished works—and to finish works so that they might be shared. Most are quite willing to do this if it is done in nonthreatening and noncompetitive ways. Recitals where many students present their works for parents and friends are one way of public sharing. Posting a completed work on a website is another. Some compositions lend themselves well to creating a book of student works. Group compositions can be presented at assemblies or other public concerts. Recordings and DVDs of performances are other ways of sharing. Whatever the means chosen, there should be public recognition of the work that has been done and of resulting compositions. Not all students want to share their works and—especially at the beginning levels—this need not be a requirement. However, many students are eager to share works with which they are satisfied and willingly participate in public venues.

Entering local, state, and national composition competitions appeals to some young composers. Sharing the results from previous competitions with current students can be one way of encouraging students to participate. When the students see what their peers have accomplished, they can become inspired and encouraged in their own work. Participants often return to their composition classes with renewed enthusiasm and fresh ideas that can be shared with classmates. If no such opportunities exist in a particular geographic region, music educators can work with local composers and others to create them.

EVALUATION OF COMPOSING PROGRAMS

Ultimately it is the value placed on a composition program by the community where it exists that serves as the evaluation of the program. However, it can take several years of work to attain that type of recognition and esteem. It is necessary to build student, parent, colleague, and community expectations for the composition program over time. Thoughtful educators need to reflect on the composition program's successes and determine for themselves whether the program is working well, how it might be improved, and what next steps might be taken.

Indicators of Success

While successful participation in composition competitions could be one measure of a composition program's achievements, it is a rather limited view based on a few examples. A factor worth considering is the opinions of the students themselves. Are they enthusiastic about composing? Do they seek more opportunities for creating their own music? Do they compose on their own outside of school? Do they mention composing in their other musical activities? When asked to reflect on composition activities and projects, what do they say about their experiences? Asking students how they feel about composing can be a very revealing experience.

Similarly, how do the parents of the young composers feel about the program? Do they attend performances and listen to or view their student's work on websites? Do they talk to other parents about the value of the program? Do they value the abilities of their children to communicate in sound?

Many times it is the parents of young musicians who most vocally support the inclusion of music study in schools because they see the value it has for their children. This may need to be especially true for new composition programs. Teachers have to be highly proactive in reaching out to parents and enthusiastically keeping them informed about the progress of their children and the value composition has in the children's lives. They should help parents understand what the children are learning and how it can contribute to their musical growth and expressive potential. Parents then will be in a better position to evaluate the benefits of the composition program in their children's lives. They also will be better advocates for this type of instruction in schools.

Do colleagues at school value the composition program? If it is being truly well taught, then other music teachers, administrators, and other school personnel value composition for the ways it enhances the growth of individual children and for the positive recognition it brings to the music program and to the school community as a whole.

Performance ensemble teachers may initially worry about a composition program's impact on their ensembles. They usually come to see the benefits of composition programs in terms of the listening and reading skills that the composers in their ensembles display. Some of the children in composition programs are not part of ensembles. They may be encouraged to join as a result of their composition studies. Others compose in media not typically included in school programs and have little or no impact on performance ensembles.

Principals are often very interested in the public relations aspects of composition programs because of the positive recognition that they can bring to a school. Composition recitals and performances invite community visibility in the same manner as science fairs, art exhibits, concerts, and open house events do. Principals also like to boast about programs that are on the vanguard of educational practice.

When composition creates a positive visible presence in the community, everyone benefits. Communities with well-established composition programs support the programs financially and by attendance at public performances. In evaluating a composition program's successes after several years, it is worth asking whether there is support for the program from beyond the school's doors. The best programs are able to point to indicators of that support within the larger community.

A LOOK FORWARD: COMPOSITION'S ROLE
IN MUSIC EDUCATION

Designing a music curriculum is one of the most exciting aspects of teaching. It is the opportunity to imagine new ways of guiding what children understand and what they can learn to do. When given the opportunity and support needed to compose, it is difficult to imagine what the limitations on the growth of young composers might be. As part of a balanced education, all children learn to invent prose for various purposes. Why could it not be that they all learn to compose? They write stories, poems, letters, essays, and much more. Why should they not also write solos, duets, songs, and a wide array of pieces? Over time, they develop skills in cursive writing and in using a computer. All students could learn to write music notation and then to use notation software on computers.

Student composers are often limited by the offerings of their schools and the knowledge of their teachers. This book envisions a successful composition program taught by well-trained teachers that would be naturally appealing to many students. What is needed is the willingness to start including composition at all levels of schooling.

At first the results vary widely in quality. However, with guidance and practice, teachers and their students develop skill and artistry, and exceptional products emerge. Students can learn the skills of critical listening and receiving community-based critique. They can consistently enhance their abilities to use creative thinking as they compose and as they respond to the compositions of others.

Eventually it is possible to create composition programs of the magnitude and quality of the performance programs that are commonly found in American schools. These composition programs will appeal to many students not currently involved in school music programs as well as a few who choose to both perform and compose. Notions of musical talent will expand to include much more than exceptional performance skills.

Composition programs allow teachers and students to capture their feelings, experiences, and understandings in ways that are intellectually satisfying, emotionally engaging, and deeply human. The impact of their work can only be suggested within the pages of this text. When actively promoted in classrooms, rehearsal halls, and studios, children's artistic engagements with sound will create a sonically exciting musical world that allows everyone involved to participate in what it is to be musical—and musically human.

References

Abrahams, F. (2005). *Reconceptualizing multiculturalism in music education: A Freirian perspective*. V Colóquio Internacional Paulo Freire—Recife. www.paulofreire.org. Retrieved June 3, 2008.

Adachi, M., & Trehub, S. (1998). Children's expression and emotion in song. *Psychology of Music, 6*(2), 133–153.

Ainsworth, J. (1970). Research project in creativity in music education. *Bulletin of the Council for Research in Music Education, 22,* 43–48.

Airy, S., & Parr, J. (2001). MIDI, music and me: Students' perspectives on composing with MIDI. *Music Education Research, 3*(1), 41–49.

Allsup, R. E. (2002). *Crossing over: Mutual learning and democratic action in instrumental music education*. Unpublished doctoral dissertation, Teachers College, Columbia University, NY.

Atlas, G. D., Taggart, T., & Goodell, D. J. (2004). The effects of sensitivity to criticism on motivation and performance in music students. *British Journal of Music Education, 21,* 81–87.

Auh, M., & Walker, R. (1999). Compositional strategies and musical creativity when composing with staff notation versus graphic notation in Korean students. *Bulletin of the Council for Research in Music Education, 141,* 2–9.

Bakhtin, M. M. (1981). *The dialogic imagination*. (C. Emerson and M. Holquist, Trans.). Austin: University of Texas Press.

Bamberger, J. (1991). *The mind behind the musical ear*. Cambridge, MA: Harvard University Press.

Bamberger, J. (1994). Coming to hear in a new way. In R. Aiello and J. Sloboda (Eds.), *Musical Perceptions* (pp 131–151). NY: Oxford University Press.

Barrett, M. (1996). Children's aesthetic decision-making: An analysis of children's musical discourse as composers. *International Journal of Music Education, 28,* 37–62.

Barrett, M. (1997). Invented notations: A view of young children's musical thinking. *Research Studies in Music Education, 8,* 2–14.

Barrett, M. (2000). Windows, mirrors and reflections: A case study of adult constructions of children's musical thinking. *Bulletin of the Council for Research in Music Education, 145,* 43–61.

Barrett, M. (2001). Constructing a view of children's meaning-making as notators: A case-study of a five-year-old's descriptions and explanations of invented notations. *Research Studies in Music Education, 16,* 33–45.

Barrett, M. (2003). Freedoms and constraints. In M. Hickey (Ed.), *Why and how to teach music composition* (pp. 3–27). Reston, VA: MENC.

Barrett, M. (2006). "Creative collaboration": An "eminence" study of teaching and learning in music composition. *Psychology of Music, 34*(2), 195–218.

Barrett, M. (April 2006). *Keynote VI.* Keynote speech presented at the Narrative Soundings Conference, Phoenix, AZ.

Beals, D. E. (1998). Reappropriating schema: Conceptions of development from Bartlett to Bakhtin. *Mind, Culture, and Activity: An International Journal, 5*(1), 3–24.

Berkley, R. (2001). Why is teaching composing so challenging? *British Journal of Music Education, 18*(2), 119–38.

Blacking, J. (1967). *Venda children's songs.* Chicago: University of Chicago Press.

Blacking, J. (1973). *How musical is man?* Seattle: University of Washington Press.

Bruner, J. (1990). *Acts of Meaning.* Cambridge, MA: Harvard University Press.

Bunting, R. (1987). Composing music: Case studies in the teaching and learning process. *British Journal of Music Education, 4*(1), 25–52.

Burland, K., & Davidson, J. W. (2001). Investigating social processes in group musical composition. *Research Studies in Music Education, 16,* 46–56.

Burnard, P. (1995). Task design and experience in composition. *Research Studies in Music Education, 5,* 159–174.

Burnard, P. (1999). *Into different worlds: Children's experience of musical improvisation and composition.* Unpublished doctoral dissertation, School of Education, University of Reading.

Burnard, P., & Younker, B. A. (2004). Problem-solving and creativity. *International Journal of Music Education, 22*(1), 59–76.

Burton, S. (2002). An exploration of preschool children's spontaneous songs and chants. *Visions of Research in Music Education, 2.* wwwusr.rider.edu/~vrme/articles2/explor/index.htm. Retrieved April 21, 2008.

Campbell, P. (1995). Of garage bands and song-getting: The musical development of young rock musicians. *Research Studies in Music Education, 4,* 12–20.

Campbell, P. S. (2005). Deep listening. *Music Educators Journal, 92*(1), 30–36.

Carlin, J. (1997). Musical preferences for compositions by selected students aged 9–15 years. *Bulletin of the Council for Research in Music Education, 133,* 9–133.

Carroll-Phelan, B., & Hampson, P. J. (1996). Multiple components of the perception of musical sequences: A cognitive neuroscience analysis and some implications for auditory imagery. *Music Perception, 13*(4), 517–561.

Christensen, C. (1995). Musical composition, invented notation and reflection: tools for music learning and assessment. Unpublished doctoral dissertation, Rutgers, The State University of New Jersey.

Cohen, V. W. (1980). *The emergence of musical gestures in kindergarten children.* Unpublished doctoral dissertation, University of Illinois, Urbana-Champaign.

Consortium of National Arts Education Associations (1994). National Standards for Arts Education: Reston, VA.

Cooper, C. R., Marquis, A., & Edward, D. (1986). Four perspectives on peer learning among elementary school children. In E. C. Mueller & C. R. Cooper (Eds.), *Process and outcome in peer relationships* (pp. 269–298). New York: Academic Press.

Cutietta, R. A. (2004). When we question popular music in education, what is the question? In C. Rodriguez (Ed.), *Bridging the gap: Popular music and education* (pp. 242–247). Reston, VA: MENC.

Daignault, L. (1996). *Children's creative musical thinking within the context of a computer-supported improvisational approach to composition.* Unpublished doctoral dissertation, Northwestern University, Evanston, IL.

Damasio, A. (1999). *The feeling of what happens: Body and emotion in the making of consciousness.* New York: Harcourt.

Davidson, L. (1990). Tools and environments for musical creativity. *Music Educators Journal, 76*(9), 47–51.

Davidson, L., & Scripp, L. (1988). Young children's musical representations: Windows on cognition. In J. A. Sloboda (Ed.), *Generative processes in music: The psychology of performance, improvisation, and composition* (pp. 195–230). Oxford: Clarendon Press.

Davies, C. (1992). Listen to my song: A study of songs invented by children aged 5 to 7 years. *British Journal of Music Education, 9,* 19–48.

Davis, S. G. (2005). That thing you do: Compositional processes of a rock band. *International Journal of Education in the Arts, 6*(16). http://ijea.asu.edu/v6n16/. Retrieved January 2, 2008.

DeLorenzo, L. (1989). A field study of sixth-grade students' creative music problem-solving processes. *Journal of Research in Music Education, 37*(3), 188–200.

Dewey, J. (1925). *Experience and nature.* La Salle, IL: Open Court.

Dissanayake, E. (1988). *What is art for?* Seattle: University of Washington Press.

Eisner, E. W. (2002). What can education learn from the arts about the practice of education? In *The encyclopedia of informal education.* www.infed.org/biblio/eisner_art_and_the_practice_of_education.htm. Retrieved June 2, 2008.

Emmons, S. E. (1998). *Analysis of musical creativity in middle school students through composition using computer-assisted instruction: A multiple case study.* Unpublished doctoral dissertation, University of Rochester, Eastman School of Music, Rochester, NY.

Erkunt, H. (1998). Computers as cognitive tools in music composition. Unpublished doctoral dissertation, Boston University, Boston, MA.

Espeland, M. (2003). The African drum: The compositional process as discourse and interaction in a school context. In M. Hickey (Ed.), *Why and how to teach music composition* (pp. 167–192). Reston, VA: MENC.

Fautley, M. (2003). *A new model of group composing process of lower secondary students.* Paper presented at Research in Music Education: The Third International Research in Music Education Conference, Exeter, UK. www.tandf.co.uk/journals/titles/rime_conf/Papers/Fautley.pdf. Retrieved May 24, 2008.

Folkestad, G. (1996). *Computer based creative music making.* Guteborg, Sweden: Acta Universitatis Gothoburgensis.

Folkestad, G. (2004). A meta-analytic approach to qualitative studies in music education: A new model applied to creativity and composition. Bulletin of the Council for Research in Music Education, 161/162, 83–90.

Folkestad, G., Hargreaves, D. J., & Lindstrom, B. (1998). Compositional strategies in computer-based music-making. *British Journal of Music Education, 15*(1), 83–97.

Freed-Carlin, J. (1998). *Can you think a little louder? A classroom-based enthnography of eight- and nine-year-olds composing with music and language.* Unpublished doctoral dissertation, University of British Columbia.

Freed-Garrod, J. (1999). Assessment in the arts. *Bulletin of the Council for Research in Music Education, 139,* 50–63.

Friedman, S. L., & Scholnick, E. K. (1997). *The developmental psychology of planning.* Hillsdale, NJ: Lawrence Erlbaum Associates.

Gibson, J. J. (1979). *The ecological approach to visual perception.* Boston: Houghton Mifflin.

Glaser, B. G. (1992). *Basics of grounded theory analysis: Emergence vs forcing.* Mill Valley, CA: Sociology Press.

Glover, J. (2000). *Children composing: 4–14.* London: Routledge.

Glykeria (1999). *Tik tik tak.* On *World playground: A musical adventure for kids* [CD]. New York: Putumayo World Music.

Green, L. (2000). Music as a media art: Evaluation and assessment in the contemporary classroom. In J. Sefton-Green & R. Sinker (Eds.), *Evaluating creativity: Making and learning by young people* (pp. 88–105). London: Routledge.

Gromko, J. E. (1994). Children's invented notations as measures of musical understanding. *Psychology of Music, 22*(2), 136–147.

Hall, M. M. (2007). *Composing in a second grade music class: Crossing a watershed as children begin to understand song as structure.* Unpublished doctoral dissertation, University of Maryland, College Park.

Hamilton, H. J. (1999). *Music learning through composition, improvisation, and peer interaction in the context of three sixth grade music classes.* Unpublished doctoral dissertation, University of Minnesota, Minneapolis.

Henry, W. (1995). *The effects of pattern instruction, repeated composing opportunities, and musical aptitudes on the compositional processes and products of fourth-grade students.* Unpublished doctoral dissertation, Michigan State University, East Lansing.

Hickey, M. (1995). *Qualitative and quantitative relationships between children's creative musical thinking processes and products.* Unpublished doctoral dissertation, Northwestern University, Evanston, IL.

Hickey, M. (1997). The computer as a tool in creative music. *Research Studies in Music Education, 8,* 56–70.

Hickey, M., & Reese, S. (2002). *Teaching composition—Ideas for projects and assessments.* Presentation at the MENC Biennial In-Service Conference, Nashville, TN.

Hollenberg, J. (2004). See the big picture: Create a word wall. *Teaching Music, 12*(1), 50–54.

Huron, D. (2006). *Sweet anticipation: Music and the psychology of expectation.* Cambridge, MA: MIT Press.

Jaffurs, S. E. (2004). The impact of informal music learning practices in the classroom, or how I learned how to teach from a garage band. *International Journal of Music Education, 22,* 189–200.

Jung, Carl G. (1971). *The collected works, vol. 6, Bollingen series XX*. Princeton: Princeton University Press, p. 495.

Kagan, S. (1992). *Cooperative learning*. San Juan Capistrano, CA: Resources for Teachers.

Kaschub, M. (1997). A comparison of two composer-guided large group composition projects. *Research Studies in Music Education, 8*, 15–22.

Kaschub, M. (1999). *Student's descriptions of their individual and collaborative music composition processes and products initiating from prompted and unprompted task structures in grade six*. Unpublished doctoral dissertation, Northwestern University, Evanston, IL.

Kaschub, M. (2007). Concurrent, collaborative and executive working styles in small group composition: Research to practical application. Paper presented at the 5th International Conference for Research in Music Education. Exeter, UK.

Kaschub, M., & Smith, J. (2007). Principled praxis: A re-visioned approach to teaching composition to children. Paper presented at the Fifth Annual Suncoast Music Education Research Symposium, Tampa, Florida.

Kerr, N. L., & Bruun, S. E. (1983). Dispensability of member effort and group motivation losses: Free-rider effects. *Journal of Personality and Social Psychology, 44*, 78–94.

Kratus, J. K. (1985). *Rhythm, melody, motive, and phrase characteristics of original songs by children aged five to thirteen*. Unpublished doctoral dissertation, Northwestern University, Evanston, IL.

Kratus, J. K. (1989). A time analysis of the compositional processes used by children ages 7 to 11. *Journal of Research in Music Education, 37*(1), 5–20.

Kratus, J. K. (1994). Relationships among children's music audiation and their compositional process and products. *Journal of Research in Music Education, 42*, 115–130.

Kratus, J. (2001). Effect of available tonality and pitch options on children's compositional processes and products. *Journal of Research in Music Education, 49*(4), 294–306.

Kratus, J. (2008). *Songwriting at the secondary level*. Paper presented at the MENC National Biennial In-Service Conference, Milwaukee, WI.

Kronman, U., & Sundberg, J. (1987). Is the musical ritard an allusion to physical motion? In Alf Gabrielsson (Ed.), *Action and perception in rhythm and music* (pp. 57–68). Stockholm: Royal Swedish Academy of Music.

Kruger, A. C. (1993). Peer collaboration: Conflict, co-operation or both? *Social Development, 2*(3), 165–182.

Landányi, K. S. (1995). *Processes of musical composition facilitated by digital music equipment*. Unpublished doctoral dissertation, University of Illinois at Urbana-Champaign.

Lapidaki, E. (2007). Learning from masters of music creativity: Shaping compositional experiences in music education. *Philosophy of Music Education Review, 15*(2), 93–117.

Lebler, D. (2007). Student-as-master? Reflections on a learning innovation in popular music pedagogy. *International Journal of Music Education, 25*(3), 205–221.

Lehrer, J. (2007). *Proust was a neuroscientist*. Boston: Houghton Mifflin.

Levi, R. (1991). Investigating the creative process: The role of regular music composition experiences for the elementary child. *Journal of Creative Behavior, 25*(2), 123–136.

MacDonald, R. A. R., Miell, D., & Mitchell, L. (2002). An investigaton of chidren's musical collaborations: The effect of friendship and age. *Psychology of Music, 30*(2), 148–163.

Marsh, K. (1995). Children's singing games: Composing in the playground? *Research Studies in Music Education, 4*, 2–11.

McCoy, P. (1999). *Effects of variable task structuring and guided self-reflection on compositional quality, self-assessments, and attitudes of novice student composers.* Unpublished doctoral dissertation, Northwestern University, Evanston, IL.

McGillen, C., & McMillan, R. (2005). Engaging with adolescent musicians: Lessons in song writing, cooperation and the power of original music. *Research Studies in Music Education, 25*(1), 1–20.

Meyer, L. B. (1956). *Emotion and meaning in music.* Chicago: Chicago University Press.

Miell, D., & MacDonald, R. (2000). Children's creative collaborations: The importance of friendship when working together on a musical composition. *Social Development, 9*(3), 348–369.

Moore, B. (1994). Technology in middle school: A powerful potential. In J. Hinckley (Ed.), *Music at the middle level* (p. 91–94). Reston, VA: MENC.

Morgan, L. A., Hargreaves, D. J., & Joiner, R. W. (1997). How do children make music? Compositions in small groups. *Early Childhood Connections, 4*(1), 15–21.

Nawrot, E. (2003). The perception of emotional expression in music: Evidence from infants, children and adults. *Psychology of Music, 31*(1), 75–92.

Nordine, K. (1967/2000). *Ken Nordine Colors.* Asphodel Records.

Nordine, K. (2000). *Colors.* Orlando: Harcourt.

North, A. C., Hargreaves, D. J., & O'Neill, S. A. (2000). The importance of music to adolescents. *British Journal of Educational Psychology, 70*(2), 255–272.

Papert, S. (1993). *Teaching children thinking.* Artificial Intelligence Memo No. 247. Massachusetts Institute of Technology. Cambridge, MA: Artificial Intelligence Lab.

Paynter, J. (1992). *Sound and structure.* Cambridge: Cambridge University Press.

Piaget, J. (1976). *The grasp of consciousness: Action and concept in the young child.* Cambridge, MA: Harvard University Press.

Polyani, M. (1967). *The tacit dimension.* London: Routledge and Kegan Paul.

Reber, A. S. (1993). *Implicit learning and tacit knowledge: An essay on the cognitive unconscious.* New York: Oxford University Press.

Regelski, T. (1981). *Teaching General Music: Action Learning for Middle and Secondary Schools.* NY: Schirmer Books.

Reimer, B. (1989). *A philosophy of music eduction* (2nd ed.). Englewood Cliffs, NJ: Prentice-Hall.

Reimer, B. (2003). *A philosophy of music education: Advancing the vision* (3rd ed.). Englewood Cliffs, NJ: Prentice-Hall.

Reybrouck, M. (2006). Music cognition and the bodily approach: Musical instruments as tools for musical semantics. *Contemporary Music Review, 25*(1–2), 59–68.

Rogoff, B. (1990). *Apprenticeship in thinking: Cognitive development in a social context.* New York: Oxford University Press.

Ruthmann, S. A. (2005). *Inside the composers' workshop.* Paper presented at New Directions in Music Education, Michigan State University, East Lansing.

Ruthmann, S. A. (2008). Whose agency matters? Negotiating pedagogical and creative intent during composing experiences. *Research Studies in Music Education*, *30*(1), 43–58.

Savage, J. (2003). Informal approaches to the development of young people's composition skills. *Music Education Research* 5(1), 81–85.

Schafer, R. M. (1967). *Ear cleaning: Notes for an experimental music course.* Don Mills, Ontario: BMI Canada.

Schenker, H. (1979). *New musical theories and fantasies, vol. III.* (E. Oster, Trans.). New York: Longman. (Original work published posthumously 1935 as *Der freie Satz?*)

Seddon, F. A., & O'Neill, S. A. (2003). Creative thinking processes in adolescent computer-based composition: An analysis of strategies adopted and the influence of instrumental music training. *Music Education Research, 5*(2), 125–137.

Shove, P., & Repp, B. (1995). Musical motion and performance: Theoretical and empirical perspectives. In J. Rink (Ed.), *The practice of performance* (pp. 55–83). Cambridge: Cambridge University Press.

Sierra, J., & Hildebrand, W. (1998). *The house that Drac built.* New York: Voyager Books.

Sloboda, J. A. (1991). Music structure and emotional response: Some empirical findings. *Psychology of Music, 19*(2), 110–120.

Smith, J. P. (2004). *Music compositions of upper elementary students created under various conditions of structure.* Unpublished doctoral dissertation, Northwestern University, Evanston, IL.

Smith, J. P. (2007). *Encouraging young composers to revise: Two techniques and twelve children.* Paper presented at the Research in Music Education Conference, Exeter, UK.

Smith, J. P. (2008). *Nurturing young composers in elementary school: A case study of an exemplary music composition program.* Unpublished manuscript.

Stake, R., Migotsky, C., Chaves, C., Cisneros, E., Dacis, R., DePaul, G., Feltovich, J., Dunbar, C., Farmer, R., Johnson, E., Williams, B., & Zurita, M. (1999). *The evolving synthesis.* University of Illinois, Champaign-Urbana. www.ed.uiuc.edu/CIRCE/Publications/Synthesis.pdf. Retrieved September 1, 2008.

Stauffer, S. L. (1998). *Children as composers: Changes over time.* Paper presented at the Creativity Special Research Interest Group, MENC National Biennial In-Service Conference, Phoenix, AZ.

Stauffer, S. L. (2001). Composing with computers: Meg makes music. *Bulletin of the Council for Research in Music Education, 150*, 1–20.

Stauffer, S. L. (2002). Connections between the musical and life experiences of young composers and their compositions. *Journal of Research in Music Education, 50*(4), 301–322.

Stauffer, S. L. (2003). Identity and voice in young composers. In M. Hickey (Ed.), *Why and how to teach music composition* (pp. 91–111). Reston, VA: MENC.

Steinbeis, N., Koelsch, S., & Sloboda, J. A. (2006). The role of harmonic expectancy violations in musical emotions: Evidence from subjective, physiological, and neural responses. *Journal of Cognitive Neuroscience, 18*(8), 1380–1393.

Stravinsky, I. (1947). *The poetics of music: In the form of six lessons.* (A. Knodell & I. Dahl, Trans.). New York: Vintage Books.

Swanwick, K., & Franca, C. (1999). Composing, performing, and audience-listening as indicators of music understanding. *British Journal of Music Education, 16,* 5–19.

Swanwick, K., & Tillman, J. (1986). The sequence of musical development: A study of children's composition. *British Journal of Music Education, 3,* 305–339.

Todd, N. (1992). The dynamics of dynamics: A model of musical expression. *The Journal of Acoustical Society of America, 91*(6), 3540–3550.

Trowbridge, D., & Durnin, R. (1984). *Research from an investigation of groups working together at the computer.* Unpublished manuscript, University of California, Irvine.

Upitis, R. (1989). The craft of composition: Helping children create music with computer tools. *Psychomusicology, 8*(2), 151–162.

Upitis, R. (1990). *This too is music.* Portsmouth, NH: Heinemann.

Upitis, R. (1992). *Can I play you my song? The compositions and invented notations of children.* Portsmouth, NH: Heinemann Educational Books.

Van Ernst, B. (1993). A study of the learning and teaching processes of non-native music students engaged in composition. *Research Studies in Music Education, 1,* 22–39.

Vygotsky, L. (1978). *Mind in society: The development of high psychological process.* (M. Cole, V. John-Steiner, S. Scribner, & E. Souberman, Trans.). Cambridge, MA: Harvard University Press.

Webster, P. W. (2003). "What do you mean, make my music different"? Encouraging revision and extensions in children's music composition. In M. Hickey (Ed.), *Why and how to teach music composition* (pp. 233–242). Reston, VA: MENC.

Wertsch, J. V. (1991). *Voices of the mind.* Cambridge, MA: Harvard University Press.

Wiggins, J. H. (1992). *The nature of children's musical learning in the context of a music classroom.* Unpublished doctoral dissertation, University of Illinois at Urbana-Champaign.

Wiggins, J. H. (1994). Children's strategies for solving compositional problems with peers. *Journal of Research in Music Education, 42,* 232–252.

Wiggins, J. H. (1995). Building structural understanding: Sam's story. *The Quarterly Journal of Music Teaching and Learning, 6*(3), 57–73.

Wiggins, J. H. (1998). *Recurring themes: Same compositional strategies—different settings.* Paper presented at the Southeastern Music Education Symposium, Athens, GA.

Wiggins, J. H. (1999) Teacher control and creativity. *Music Educators Journal, 85*(5), 30–35, 44.

Wiggins J. H. (1999/2000). The nature of shared musical understanding and its role in empowering independent musical thinking. *Bulletin of the Council for Research in Music Education, 143,* 65–90.

Wilson, S. J., & Wales, R. J. (1995). An exploration of children's musical compositions. *Journal of Research in Music Education, 43,* 94–111.

Wingstedt, J., Brändström, S., & Berg, J. (2008). Young adolescents' usage of narrative functions of media music by manipulation of musical expressions. *Psychology of Music, 36*(2), 193–214.

Younker, B. A. (2000). Thought processes and strategies of students engaged in music composition. *Research Studies in Music Education, 14,* 24–39.

Younker, B. A. (2003). The nature of feedback in a community of composing. In M. Hickey (Ed.), *Why and how to teach music composition* (pp. 233–242). Reston, VA: MENC.

Zur, S. (2007). *Cultural perspectives of experienced time: An investigation of children's music making as manifested in schools and communities in three countries.* Unpublished doctoral dissertation, Teachers College, Columbia University, New York.

Zeki, S. (1999). *Inner vision: An exploration of art and the brain.* Oxford: Oxford University Press.

Zeki, S. (2001). Artistic creativity and the brain. *Science, 293*(5527), 51. Available from MAS Ultra—School Edition, Ipswich, MA. Accessed December 7, 2006.

About the Authors

Michele Kaschub is an associate professor of music and the coordinator of music teacher education and graduate studies for the University of Southern Maine School of Music. She teaches both undergraduate and graduate courses in music education, philosophy, research, and curriculum, as well as general and choral methods. Her writings have appeared in numerous music and arts journals. An active presenter, Dr. Kaschub has offered sessions for national and eastern division MENC conferences, the inaugural conference of the Center for Applied Research in Music Understanding, the New Directions in Music Education Conferences on the Teaching of Music Composition and Improvisation, the Society for Music Teacher Education, and the Symposium for Research in Music Education. Her current research interests include teacher education and critical pedagogy in music education.

Janice Smith is an assistant professor of music education at the Aaron Copland School of Music, Queens College, City University of New York. She teaches graduate and undergraduate courses in general music, foundations of music education, and music methods for elementary teachers. Prior to coming to the Aaron Copland School of Music, Dr. Smith had a thirty-year career as a general music specialist in the public schools of Maine. She is also an active presenter and presented sessions at the Research in Music Education Conference in Exeter, United Kingdom, divisional and national MENC conferences, the Suncoast Music Education Research Symposium, the College Music Society National Conference, the Mountain Lake Colloquium, the International Narrative Inquiry in Music Education conference, and state conferences in Maine and New York. Her current research interests include teaching music in urban settings and encouraging revision processes in child composers.